Dear Paul (handwritten)

C000230624

Foresight

The Association for the Promotion of
Pre-Conceptual Care
(Registered Charity No. 279160)

Foresight believes in looking to the future.
Care for both parents before conception
means that the problems of birth defects and child
ill-health are tackled before they start.
Join Foresight and help extend this vital work.

Write to:
Foresight, The Old Vicarage, Witley,
Godalming, Surrey GU8 5PN

Part of the proceeds from the sale of this book are being
donated to the Foresight Research Fund.

The Authors with their family

© 1984   Norman and Ruth Jervis
Published by
Roberts Publications Ltd.,
225 Putney Bridge Road,
London SW15 2PY,
England.

ISBN 0 906185 20 3

"The Foresight Wholefoods Cookbook – for Building Healthy Families"

by
Norman and Ruth Jervis
Founder family members of Enton Hall Health Hydro, Surrey, U.K.

Contents

FOREWORD

In the Book of Judges, chapter 13, one reads, "An angel of God appeared to the wife of Manoah and said, 'You are barren and have no child. But from now on take great care. Take no wine or strong drink, and eat nothing unclean. For you will conceive and bear a son'." The child subsequently born was Samson, renowned for his strength and stamina. Pre-conception care, therefore, is as old as the hills even though we tend today to speak of it as something new, almost revolutionary. This state of affairs was recently impressed on me by my being invited to address an audience of doctors, nurses and health visitors in a modern post-graduate centre of a large district hospital on the subject, "What is pre-conception care?" Most present had never heard of the idea although two or three afterwards admitted that it was "common sense". Yes, of course, it IS common sense.

Perhaps part of the price we are paying for over-emphasising the importance of modern science and technology is the risk of losing our common sense – certainly in matters affecting health. How absurd it is when detailed scientific research, often at great cost, 'proves' that "we reap what we sow"; if we eat live foods we live, if we eat dead foods we die.

Anyone familiar with animal husbandry or breeding will know of the importance of pre-conception health in the breeding stock – in the male as well as in the female of the species. Many rural societies in our present world have long known and practiced such health cultivation before conception. We in Great Britain are particularly plagued by a rising tide of degenerative diseases, poor reproductive efficiency amongst them. No doubt the mass migration of people from the land into towns and cities as a consequence of the Industrial Revolution, with its subsequent reliance on convenience foods, has some part to play in this degeneration.

Sufficient is known already to confidently state that much of present day failure in reproduction – inability to conceive, inability to hold on to a pregnancy, difficulties during childbirth, and less than perfect offspring – is directly related to malnutrition and other forms of pollution. We do indeed reap what we sow. It is heartening, therefore, to see a re-awakening of interest in this all important aspect of human health. The courage, dedication and tenacity of those who are cultivating "Foresight" ideas in our society deserves full recognition and credit. Pre-conception care will one day play its part as ante-natal care does today and physical nutrition is the cornerstone of such care.

Having personally worked with couples preparing themselves for conception, for more than ten years now, I have long felt the need for a book such as this written with the interests of such couples in mind. I have no hesitation in recommending this present carefully produced wholefoods cookbook to all those who, in varying ways, are associated with preparation for pregnancy. This book will be particularly helpful to couples planning their pregnancy, whether their first or their sixth. If they use this book as their guide to nutrition, not only before, but during and after pregnancy, then they will be well on their way to having a "bespoke" baby – healthy in every way – the greatest joy of any parents.

Dr. James Witchalls, M.B., B.S.(Lond), L.R.C.P., M.R.C.S., D.Obst.R.C.O.G.
26th September 1983.

Preface

The authors gratefully acknowledge the influence, teaching and help of many – my parents (the founders) colleagues and patients at Enton Hall Health Hydro, our health-seeking family and friends, fellow nutritionists, Foresight, the McCarrison Society, A.N.A.C. and Guild of Health lecturers and friends.

Fortunately I started life with wise parents devoted to attaining optimum health of body, mind and spirit through natural methods. These included wholefoods, a disciplined healthy life-style, and the peace of mind which comes from being right with God, with neighbour, with self and with the soil. Following these principles in our lives and work, our children's health was similarly our concern before their conception – and now we have two beautiful Foresight grandchildren!

To my darling husband and co-author, my most grateful thanks for contributing recipes intended for his long-planned Enton Hall recipe book. Particular thanks to my dear friend, Nim Barnes, indefatigable founder and chairman of Foresight, who inspired me to write this book, and kindly contributed chapter 22.

To Louise Templeton, S.R.D., I owe a tremendous debt of gratitude for her painstaking assistance and constructive criticism throughout. Especial thanks also to our daughter, Juliana Burden, and to Helen Thaxter for careful typing, and to Professor John Dickerson for vetting my nutritional chapters to earn his approval as Nutrition Adviser to Foresight. Many thanks to Rita Greer for her kindness in donating the illustrations.

May God bless all who read this book and inspire us all to attain better health, vitality, serenity and happiness, for ourselves, our children and our nation.

Good cooking, good eating, good health!

Ruth Jervis, M.R.S.H.

CHAPTER 1

The Case for *Foresight*

The highest rates of spina bifida in the world occur in South Wales, Scotland and Northern Ireland.

True good health is becoming increasingly rare in our Western society. Since 1945 degenerative diseases have markedly increased, and more people suffer from allergy and impaired health. Infant mortality figures for Britain compare poorly with other European countries, and show that our unborn babies are at risk now. 1981 figures showed 4,207 were stillborn, 7,021 died during the first year and 13,450 had congenital malformations which are not reversible. Add to this the cleft palates, club feet, hyperactivity, learning difficulties and allergic syndromes (e.g. eczema, asthma, hay-fever and headaches) and there is an even greater total of heartbreak and suffering. Many of these latter problems follow premature birth, low birth weight or early feeding problems leading to failure in breast-feeding.

One in six babies born to-day in Britain is likely to be disadvantaged by physical or mental handicap or a learning disability (e.g. dyslexia, autism, hyperactivity) which will show later. One pregnancy in four ends in miscarriage. Foresight Association believes that much could be done with nutrition and education of both prospective parents to prevent the onset of these disabling conditions.

Where a family has already suffered a tragedy, parents often ask themselves "why?" – "what could we have done to prevent this?" The opportunity to discover how to strive for better health for future children will be welcomed with open arms by them. Sadly they have had to learn the hard way.

Those of us who feel reasonably healthy and cannot believe that our life-style can possibly harm our unborn children may do well to look around us at our family and friends and their children. Are they all perfectly healthy? Look back into the family tree and trace out the patterns of health and allergy. Is there room for improvement?

We who have learnt from Foresight carry an urgent message of hope to so many anxious parents.

What is Foresight?

Foresight Association for the Promotion of Pre-conceptual Care is a charity formed to give every baby the opportunity of starting life in perfect health. Foresight aims to ensure that each baby enters this world free from congenital abnormality or mental damage. Foresight believes that with proper care for both parents **before** conception, the problems of birth defects and child ill-health can be tackled before they start.

Foresight works with prospective parents through enlightened health professionals, both in the expanding network of Foresight Pre-conceptual Clinics and Foresight Counselling Centres. Sympathetic doctors who appreciate the Foresight approach lead these Clinics, while other suitably trained health professionals will give guidance and help at the Counselling Centres.

The work of Foresight is educational as well as practical. Three conferences have been held in London:

1980 "Environmental Factors and Foetal Health – the case for pre-coneptual care"

1981 "Running a Foresight Clinic"

1982 "The Next Generation – avoiding damage before birth"

Besides its own publications covering these conferences, Foresight has two other helpful booklets, "Guidelines for Future Parents" and "Supplementary Chapters" which fully explain how its aims can be achieved by caring parents who choose to assume responsibility for their own and their family's good health.

1983 has seen the start of regional "Teach Ins" for interested health professionals. Teaching cards are being prepared to spread the message among schoolchildren.

Foresight members are helped in their quest for better health for all the family, kept informed of training programmes, research work and progress, and do invaluable public relations work.

How does Foresight help parents?

The Foresight approach covers four major areas, which are:

1. Improved nutrition – the reason for this book!
2. Protection from pollution.
3. Combatting allergy.
4. Discouraging the use of common social poisons (e.g. alcohol, smoking, the Pill, Tranquillisers, sleeping pills, etc.).

Many authorities have recently drawn attention to the part played by lead in the environment, in causing stillbirth, congenital damage to the brain and central nervous system, and mental retardation. Various methods of assessment in the U.S.A. have shown correlation between lead levels in children, and hyperactivity and learning difficulties. Foresight believes that the detection and cleansing from the system of toxic metals (lead, mercury, cadmium and aluminium) prior to conception is vital to the health of the baby.

Where allergies exist, malabsorption syndromes are often found – i.e. all the nutrients in the foods eaten may not be assimilated and used by the body: malnutrition is often the result. This is thought to be due to the lack of the necessary digestive enzymes. So Foresight advocates the detection and treatment of allergies, and the adoption of a balanced wholefood diet which avoids the individual's known allergens. Sometimes it may be advisable to rebalance the nutritional status with vitamin and mineral supplements to help normalise the metabolism. Hair analysis is very helpful in revealing the unique nutritional status of minerals in the individual and the presense of toxic metals from pollution. (See Chapter 23)

All the principles upon which Foresight's work is based have been thoroughly researched, mostly in the U.S.A., and are summarised in Foresight literature. Widest acceptance and application of this life-saving knowledge will only be won by British verification. So Foresight is raising funds for two major projects.

Foresight's Research Programme:
This is a five-year project monitoring and analysing all the data from our Foresight Clinics. We are confident that these results will command support for extending these pre-conceptual clinic facilities across the nation, and thus prevent much needless tragedy.

Foresight is also helping to fund the research project "Trace Elements in Abnormal Foetal Development" under Professor D. Bryce-Smith at the University of Reading, which is well under way. This detailed study, involving large numbers of both normal and abnormal births in high and low risk areas, will help unravel the relationship of toxic and essential non-toxic minerals in different geographical areas. This research could provide a vital key to the riddle why thousands of babies are stillborn, die within a year, or survive with permanent physical or mental handicaps – a solution to untold anguish which could also save the nation millions of pounds.

Of necessity, Foresight Clinics are privately run. Since there are many parents at risk who are unable to take advantage of the present Foresight Clinics, it is a matter of urgency that preconceptual clinics are established throughout the country, under the auspices of the National Health Service – hence our need to demonstrate the efficacy of Foresight Clinics through these research projects. Help with fund-raising is urgently needed to speed this vital work – you have already helped by buying this book! Thank you.

Happiness is a Foresight Family
Colin and Judy are intelligent but impecunious Foresight parents who became members when they were engaged. They both worked at a day centre for the mentally and physically handicapped, so they were extra aware of the problems of birth handicap. Seeking help from Foresight before many Foresight Clinics were in operation, they shopped around for a sympathetic N.H.S. doctor and maternity hospital, and sent their hair for analysis.

Judy's hair analysis chart revealed a toxic level of copper (from using the contraceptive pill) and a little cadmium (from smoking) and some deficient trace minerals, including manganese. Colin was also a smoker, and his hair chart showed some toxic cadmium and deficient manganese. Both claimed to be wholefood enthusiasts, and their good zinc levels bore this out.

Faithfully they carried out the recommended individual supplementation programmes for eight months, and studied all the Foresight literature. Judy had stopped smoking two years before, and Colin cut down his cigarettes. Shortly before conceiving, Judy had her last alcoholic drink, and then enjoyed a pregnancy in extremely good health, free from morning sickness (and without any drugs).

Baby Joy was born on the expected day, with only a whiff of gas and air to ease her arrival, with tired but delighted parents together welcoming and sharing her first two hours of newborn life. Joy was a perfect 6 lb 13 oz at birth, and is now contentedly thriving as her serenely competent and loving mother breast feeds her on demand.

Despite cramped housing conditions, with no possibility of a washing machine to help her, Judy has suffered no post-natal depression, and is thoroughly enjoying motherhood. Colin is justifyably proud of them both, and is quick to express his gratitude to Foresight.

Pre-conceptual care for fertility.

Among farmers, there is a practice to feed sheep on rich pasture for two weeks before conception, as this considerably increases the health of the lambs. The importance of a healthy sire as well as dam has long been recognised in stock breeding.

A healthy plant starts from a healthy seed. The ovum and sperm will be less healthy from parents whose eating patterns and life-style deplete their nutritional resourses and good health. Smoking, alcohol and drugs all multiply the effects of poor nutrition, and thus increase susceptibility to infections which could also endanger foetal development.

Where many adverse factors coincide, usually Nature over-rules to produce infertility. But between infertility and truly healthy reproduction is a shadowy phase where conception may occur, but maximum health be unlikely. This is another reason for consolidating a good diet and healthier life-style for several months before conception.

Usually, by the time a woman knows she is pregnant, the first five to six weeks growth of the foetus has already taken place. This is the most vital period for the laying down of the major organs. The raw materials needed for this crucial stage will have been drawn from the mother's body stores. Improved feeding during pregnancy, though commendable, is too late to make up the deficiencies occurring at the time of conception.

This is the case for pre-conceptual care. Prevention of handicap is better than cure.

CHAPTER 2

Improving Nutrition
with Wholefoods

The Relationship of food to health.

Sir Robert McCarrison, pioneer nutritionist, said "I know nothing so potent in maintaining good health in laboratory animals as perfectly constituted food; I know of nothing so potent in producing ill-health as improperly constituted food." This too is the experience of stock-breeders. Is man an exception to a rule so universally applicable to the higher animals?

McCarrison's work was unique in that it showed how human health is related to the wholeness of food. In recent years research has shown that healthy people of any ethnic group who change from their natural traditional wholefood diet to a Western-style diet develop the degenerative, non-infectious diseases now common in Europe and North America. These diseases include dental decay, obesity, arthritis, allergic syndromes, gastro-intestinal disorders (appendicitis, peptic ulcer, diverticulosis, constipation, cancer of the colon), coronary heart disease, haemorrhoids, varicose veins, mental illness, birth defects and lactation failure.

Good nutrition helps every area of our lives.

Good nutrition helps build not only a healthy body, but also a resilient healthy mind and good emotional balance, which can cope better with the stresses of everyday life. For the brain and endocrine glands are nourished by the same food, water and air as the rest of the cells in the body. In addition our diet affects our physical appearance, our energy levels, our intellectual and creative abilities, our mental health and general feeling of well-being. It even affects our ability to enjoy love and sexuality.

Health is also affected by our thoughts – our emotions, our hopes and fears, our loves and hates; whether we think positively or negatively; whether we have faith or fear. Stress is a component of life. Our bodies need six to seven times as much zinc and vitamin B6 and more vitamin C in times of stress – which to-day's "normal" diets cannot provide. The natural protective immune response will be depressed, and we will become more susceptible to infections, allergies, mental problems and to more serious illness if our nutritional stores are too low to allow God's natural self-defence mechanisms to be implemented.

Why a "normal good diet" can be deficient.
There are a variety of reasons to-day why our daily food is lacking many
vital nutrients. Modern farming methods may prevent the plants from
taking up manganese because of liming. The minerals may be depleted
from the soil because artificial fertilisers do not supply the complete
range of minerals taken out by previous cropping (e.g. zinc and
selenium). Nutrients may be removed during processing (e.g. the
refining of whole wheat to white flour results in considerable losses of
many trace minerals and vitamins (see page 199). Commercially frozen
green vegetables lose zinc, manganese and calcium (but home freezing
does not). Crop spraying with insecticides prevents manganese
absorption from food. Food additives affect the balance of vital nutrient
uptake. The heat of cooking affects the B complex and vitamin C. Many
water-soluble minerals and vitamins are thrown away with the cooking
water.

Furthermore, common social poisons (caffeine, nicotine, alcohol,
etc.) and the Pill increase the requirement of some minerals and
vitamins. Exposure to pollutants increases the need for protecting
nutrients.

The nutrients in foods relate to the soil.
Health-building begins with the living soil, for the full nutritional value
of wholefoods depends on the availability of the trace minerals as well
as basic nutrients in the soil from which they originate. So believed my
father, Robert Atkinson Reddell, founder of Enton Hall Health Hydro,
where the bio-dynamic composted vegetable garden was the essential
source of the fresh vital salads and vegetables served daily there. These
were complemented by eggs and milk organically produced on the
home farm.

Traditionally over the centuries, food crops were always grown this
way, returning to the soil all the waste left over from its production,
adding the farmyard manure – "The Law of Return". Fresh locally
grown vegetables and fruit were enjoyed in their seasons; home-baked
bread was made from stone-ground local wholewheat flour; poultry and
live-stock were reared naturally; chemical fertilisers, pesticide sprays
and dusts were unknown. The hard labour of man working with the laws
of Nature produced healthy herds and crops on fertile soils; natural
predators controlled the pests. Man had no need to study nutrition for
healthy eating.

"Progress" has brought us far beyond this Utopian self-sufficiency.
Farming and marketing methods have changed, and the Law of Return
is rarely obeyed. In listing rich food sources of nutrients at the end of
this book, we acknowledge past research to help guide food selection.
But the precise nutrient value of any specific food sample will depend
upon many factors – the geographical location, the soil, the fertilisers
and pesticides used, the production methods employed.

The value of organically grown food.
Organic produce really is preferrable, when we can obtain it. The Gerson Diet for cancer relies on it. We who enjoy good health may cope well without it, but some reach the point in ill-health or allergy where they need bio-dynamic food i.e. organically grown (on compost-fed soil, without chemical fertilisers) and unsprayed by any chemicals (insecticides, pesticides, herbicides, fungicides, sprouting inhibitors). If you have a garden and grow your own vegetables, this is the best way. Tracking down organic produce can be difficult. Foresight members can obtain information on local sources of supply from their branch secretaries.

Where organic produce is unobtainable, ask your greengrocer for unsprayed produce. Some aware farmers use biological control (natural predators) and companion planting instead of chemicals, and more will follow when we increase the demand for it.

The use of chemical sprays on fruit, vegetables and salads is a cause for great concern, as is cereal crop aerial spraying. Some apples and lettuces, particularly, may have been sprayed many times during growth – and most chemical residues are toxic and cumulative. Brassicas and soft fruits are commonly sprayed too – the consumer's distaste for greenfly and caterpillars is to blame, rather than the grower.

To remove chemical sprays from the surface of salads, brassicas, vegetables and fruit (but not soft fruits), wash them in cider vinegar solution (1 tablespoon vinegar to 2 pints water).

There is an organic lotion concentrate available, especially made for washing off chemical sprays, which is useful for soft fruits as well. Apples can be scrubbed with hot water. Otherwise peel your fruit and avoid lettuce unless grown without sprays.

Happily, a good wholefood diet does help protect us from these poisons (see chapter 23).

The need for fibre.
While peeling apples may be a necessary expediency, eating wholefoods will provide the right balance of nutrients and fibre. The bran is still there in 100% wholemeal flour and bread, crushed and whole grains; fibre is naturally present in potato, tomato and apple skins, pulses, vegetables and salads. It makes better sense to eat the whole food the way God provides it rather than separate the parts and then eat added bran.

Healthy food need not be expensive.
Wholegrains, sea vegetables, dried peas and beans (pulses) are really cheap nourishing foods. Soups and stocks can use up bones and outer vegetable leaves, saving waste. Most people spend more than they need to on meat (see Proteins page 195) – by economising here the budget

should stretch to buy more vegetables and wholemeal bread. Cutting down on bought cakes, pies, biscuits and sweets helps finance the free-range eggs, nuts, fresh and dried fruits and salads. Buy fruit, vegetables and salads in season, when they are less expensive, and save on tinned goods. Water is cheaper than bought squashes and colas. Baking our own wholefood pies, biscuits, cakes and sweet nibbles can save money too.

Home baking takes time, but our wholefood way of eating can save preparation time too. Salads are quickly prepared and need no cooking. Potatoes are better left unpeeled. Soups can be quickly made from left-overs. Fresh and stewed fruit or yoghurt are quicker to prepare than puddings or pies. What could be quicker than a bowl of wholefood muesli and some raw fruit? Nuts are Nature's convenience food – instant quick nourishment. Slow cookers and vacuum jars can simplify long cooking and time spent on duty in the kitchen. Check your health food store for packeted foods made from wholefoods.

Avoiding the usual instant packeted or tinned convenience foods will eventually save time nursing sick children. "Fast food = quick sick" is a graffiti with a ring of truth!

The next chapter gives more practical help.

How we can build healthy families from wholefoods.
The health of all the family depends on the food we eat. How we look, how we feel, how long we retain our youthful vitality despite the passing years, largely relates to our diet. Every part of our bodies – eyes, brain, bones, teeth, glands, heart, muscles, blood, skin, hair – is built from the food and water we consume and the air we breathe. What we choose to eat is important. So is the life-style and eating habits we adopt and then pass on to our children. Family health and happiness is in the homemakers' hands as they plan and shop, prepare and cook, serve and eat with their family.

Healthy meals, intelligently chosen and prepared with loving care, will taste different from the devitalised foods made from white flour and the processed foodstuffs which are liberally seasoned with salt or sweetened with sugar (and perhaps have chemical "enhancers") to disguise their lack of flavour. Make the change-over from traditional to wholefood cooking gradually to win the approval of the sceptical members of the family.

Man has evolved from a wholefood diet which supplies both known and presently unrecognised nutrients. The use of supplements should never be a substitute for a balanced wholefood diet. A lifetime of better nutrition can prevent the development of many diseases. The choice is ours.

Cooking is caring! Enjoy participating in your family's good health.

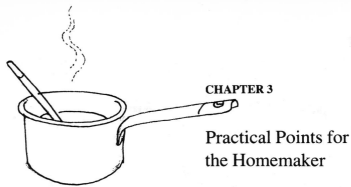

CHAPTER 3

Practical Points for the Homemaker

The enjoyment of a good meal starts with the eyes and the nose! To enhance the appetite and aid digestion the food should be attractive to look at, with a good contrast of colour and texture, and have an appealing aroma. Simple meals made from wholefoods are both satisfying and nourishing and can be delicious.

Every person is an individual and will vary in his dietary requirements, and from day to day. Only you know your exact needs and circumstances, likes and dislikes. Where you do not have the co-operation of your family, think out your plan of action carefully and make improvements where you can. Increasing vegetable and fresh fruit consumption, cutting back on frying, and using more wholegrains are all worthwhile changes to introduce gradually. Choose foods free from chemical additives, colourings, flavourings, anti-oxidants, flavour-enhancers, etc.

Savour the satisfation of knowing that your careful food preparation and menu planning are making a positive contribution to the health of all the family.

Keeping the goodness in our foods.

Vitamins are vital nutrients which can readily be lost en route to the table. The water-soluble Vitamins C and B complex are most vulnerable, being also sensitive to heat. Here are some guidelines to help you:

1. *Avoid storage of perishable vegetables (greens especially).* When necessary, store them in a cool, ventilated place. Wilted vegetables have lost much of their Vitamin C.

2. *Avoid preparing in advance.* Cut surfaces cause greater destruction of vitamins, and soaking leeches them out too. When prior preparation is necessary, leave in a closed container, in as large pieces as possible, in a cool place, out of the light, with just sufficient water to cover. Then use this water for cooking, and retain and use it for gravy, soup, as sauce or stock.

3. *Use the minimum amount of water* when boiling vegetables and keep pot covered with a tightly fitting lid. Minerals as well as some vitamins are water soluble and should not be poured down the sink. In some homes, the sink is the best fed mouth in the family! Nearly all stock is useable.

4. *Do not overcook.* Most foods have a better colour and flavour when cooked to "slightly rare", and food with a texture which encourages chewing will be better digested and more satisfying. Heat destroys most of the B complex vitamins and Vitamin C as well as enzymes.

5. *Do not add bicarbonate of soda* to greens. It destroys vitamins B_1 and C. For this reason, home-made bread made from yeast is more nutritious than quick breads made with sodium bicarbonate.

6. *Boil the water first* before adding the prepared vegetables to minimise oxidation and losses of vitamin C.

7. *Serve all hot foods promptly.* Keeping foods hot destroys further the vitamin C.

8. *Use stainless steel, enamelled or pyrex cookware* – copper and iron accelerate the destruction of vitamin C. Aluminium is a toxic mineral which reacts with foods and gradually accumulates in the body.

Comparison of Cooking Methods

Grilling is superior to *frying* from a nutritional point of view. The larger the proportion of cut surface, the greater the nutrient loss. Grilling also aids in extracting some of the animal fat present in most meats, whereas frying adds more fat. *Deep frying* seals in more nutrients, so is better than shallow frying.

Steaming is better than boiling in a lot of water, though it may take a little longer in cooking vegetables. Fewer nutrients are dissolved into the steam than would be dissolved into surroundings water. When *boiling* vegetables till just tender in the minimum amount of water in a closed pan, most of them will be well above the water level, and virtually steamed. This is what we mean by **conservative cooking.**

Baking in the skin is the best way of retaining all the nutrients in potatoes. With baking and roasting, excess time or heat is destructive of thiamine (B_1).

Long slow heating, boiling dry, boiling in a lot of water, fast boiling with no lid (i.e. exposed to the air), and discarding of the cooking water are all causes of unnecessary nutrient loss from vegetables.

Long slow cooking is an effective way of tenderising tough cuts of meat. *Electric slow cookers* are the modern equivalent of the old-fashioned "hay-box" for producing the same effect.

When camping, we have brought stews or soups to the boil and then transferred them quickly to a well-heated *wide-necked vacuum jar*, so that they would cook slowly in our absence. When using a thermos jar, it is wisest to transfer the hot food to a saucepan and simmer it for five minutes before serving. Food left in a thermos flask or jar for more than 18 hours would be suspect for producing food poisoning. Pulses need to be cooked at a fast boil for ten minutes before transferring to a slow cooker.

Microwave cooking sounds appealing when you read the list of advantages claimed. But this cooking method shatters the life force of the food and so cannot be recommended here.

Pressure cooking is another way to save time, and, done in a stainless steel pressure cooker*, can also save valuable nutrients by:
1. Cutting down on cooking time.
2. Cooking in the absence of air.
3. Using a steamer basket, fewer nutrients are dissolved out of the foods.
4. The higher speed in reaching the cooking temperature again lessens the loss of vitamin C.

Other advantages are the savings in being able to use cheaper cuts of meat to produce good meals, lower fuel costs with shorter cooking times. Another economy note is that even old woody root vegetables become tender and retain their flavour well.

The disadvantages are minimal. Most necessary is the need to adhere to the cooking times exactly, or the food could be spoiled.

Alternatives

While it is better to use wholefoods rather than the refined foods to which we may be accustomed, it is useful to know which alternatives are practical, hence the following suggestions:

Instead of:

Cornflour used for thickening, use half the quantity of arrowroot.

White flour for thickening gravy, use 100% wholemeal flour, 85% wheatmeal flour, barley flour, fine oatmeal, yellow cornmeal, chick pea flour or brown rice flour. Or avoid using flour altogether by liquidising together a few potatoes, onions (or any other available suitable vegetable) together with the meat juices and vegetable stock to make a gluten-free gravy.

White flour for baking, use 100% wholemeal flour. Or start by trying 85% brown flour until you are confident to change over to the 100% wholemeal. When substituting wholemeal for white flour in a recipe, be prepared to use about 20% more liquid, as the wheatgerm and bran in the wholemeal flour make it more absorptive, so the finished produce will be more moist as well as more full of flavour. Rye flour, barley flour, buckwheat flour, cornmeal, oatmeal, gram (chick pea) flour, potato flour, brown rice flour, soya flour.

White sugar, substitute with genuine Demarara sugar (check its country of origin – Guyana – some apparent Demarara is white beet sugar, coloured!) light soft brown sugar, dark soft brown sugar, raw

---

*As with all cooking saucepans, stainless steel is recommended because it does not react with the food cooked, as does aluminium. Aluminium is a toxic metal and the tiny amount absorbed into the food is cumulative in the body, so do not use it for saucepans, frying pans, kettles, teapots or pressure cookers.

Muscovado sugar, molasses sugar, honey, malt and apple juice concentrate. The last five are the best of them all. Honey is sweeter than white sugar, so about 20% less is needed. Molasses and molasses sugar have a distinctive flavour which goes well with gingerbread and on porridge.

Golden syrup, substitute honey or a little black treacle, or honey and molasses mixed. Apple juice concentrate and malt are possibilities.

Cow's milk, try goat's milk, which is often tolerated where cow's milk is not – in cases of eczema for example. Otherwise soyabean milk, Plamil, nut milks (e.g. coconut milk, sesame milk, almond milk, etc) (see Drinks chapter).

Fruit squash, use pure fruit juices (check the labels to ensure that no sugar, colourings, flavourings, or sugar substitutes are present) home-made lemon drink, water, apple drink made from apple juice concentrate etc.

Coffee: Decaffeinated coffee (if it is just the caffeine that is to be avoided), otherwise roasted dandelion root coffee, Pioneer, Bambu (contains wheat) or Barleycup – the last four actually being good for you, as well as tasting reasonably like coffee.

Tea: Japanese twig tea, 11 o'clock Rooibosch tea (a red tea from South Africa which has scarcely any tannin and no caffeine, but does taste like tea!) herb teas, mint tea, weak China tea, green buckwheat tea.

Salt: Seasalt, Biosalt, Lane's Herb Salt, onion, garlic and celery salt: in cases of potassium deficiency, Ruthmol and Trufree (salt replacers). All these **salty seasonings** should be used sparingly. Vegit, Spike, garlic powder and kelp powder are other alternative seasonings.

Vinegar: Lemon juice, natural yoghurt, whey.

Meat: Fish, eggs, cheese, cottage cheese, beans and pulses, soya beans, whole grain cereals, beansprouts, nuts and seeds – see chapter on proteins.

Bread: Corn on the cob, potatoes, parsnips, beetroot, brown rice, tapioca, lentils, peas and beans, sprouted wheat, kasha and kruska.

Gelatine: Gelozone and Agar Agar (both made from seaweed) are good jelling agents. Agar Agar is tasteless – use 2 teaspoons to set one pint of liquid by sprinkling over the boiling liquid and stirring until dissolved. Gelozone has a stronger flavour and needs to be mixed with cold water first, then the hot liquid poured over, stirring, and the mixture simmered, stirring, for three minutes – in the same quantities as for Agar Agar.

Pasta: In place of the usual pastas made with white flour, wholewheat and buckwheat macaroni, spaghetti, etc., are available and have a good flavour.

Tinned fruits in syrup: Look for the fruits tinned in either their own or another natural fruit juice; better still, use fresh fruits, home stewed fruit sweetened with honey, raw brown sugar or dried fruits. (Choose tins with covered seams).

Conversion Tables for Quantities

25 gm	1 oz	275 gm	10 oz
50 gm	2 oz	300 gm	11 oz
75 gm	3 oz	350 gm	12 oz
100–125 gm	4 oz	375 gm	13 oz
150 gm	5 oz	400 gm	14 oz
175 gm	6 oz	425 gm	15 oz
200 gm	7 oz	450 gm	16 oz (1 lb)
225 gm	8 oz	900 gm	2 lb
250 gm	9 oz	1000 gm (1 Kgm)	2 lb 4 oz

Liquid Measurements

25 ml	1 fluid oz
50 ml	2 fluid oz
100-125 ml	4 fluid oz
150 ml	5 fluid oz (¼ pint)
300 ml	10 fluid oz (½ pint)
450 ml	15 fluid oz (¾ pint)
600 ml	20 fluid oz (1 pint)
1000 ml (1 litre)	35 fl oz (1¾ pint)

Spoon Measurements

1 tablespoon	15 ml approx
2 teaspoons	10 ml approx
1 dessertspoon	10 ml approx
1 teaspoon	5 ml approx
½ teaspoon	2.5 ml approx
Pinch = less than ⅛ teaspoon	
1 cup =	7 fl oz = 200 ml

All spoon and cup measurements, whether for wet or dry ingredients, are for **level** spoons or cups in this book, unless otherwise indicated.

Equivalent Oven Temperatures

Very, very cool			
150° – 175°F	70° – 80°C		
Very cool			
200° – 275°F	100° – 140°C		¼ – 1 Gas
Cool			
300°F		150°C	2 Gas
Warm			
325°F		160°C	3 Gas
Moderate			
350°F		180°C	4 Gas
Fairly hot			
375° – 400°F	190° – 200°C		5 – 6 Gas
Hot			
425° – 450°F	220° – 230°C		7 – 8 Gas
Very hot			
475° – 500°F	240° – 260°C		9 Gas

Stock cubes: There are several stock cubes available in good health food shops which contain no monosodium glutamate, artificial flavourings, colourings or anti-oxidants – e.g. Morga's Vegetable Bouillon Cubes (unsalted) and Hugli's Clear Vegetable Stock Cubes (with small salt content). Other quick flavour enhancers are: Lea and Perrins Worcestershire Sauce, Tamari/Shoyu, Tabasco, Miso soya purée, and of course herbs and spices and good home-made stock, (see chapter on flavour).

Cocoa: Use carob powder, (see page 159).

Chocolate: Use carob confectionery bar made with raw sugar.

CHAPTER 4

Planning Balanced Meals

The exact proportions of foods in a balanced diet will depend on our metabolism, digestion and physical workload, as well as the climate. As a guide, our daily diet should include:

10-20% protein foods (see list on page 196)

45-65% vegetables, fruits and salads

20-40% natural wholegrains (in bread, baking, muesli, etc. – see chapter 12)

5-7% natural sugars (sweet fresh and dried fruits, honey and molasses)

25-30% total dietary fat* including 3-5% natural polyunsaturates for vitamin F

These proportions are for a diet including protein of animal origin.

Additionally, each day's meals should include all the water soluble nutrients which cannot be stored by the body – vitamins C, P and the B complex, and trace minerals. Each week's menus should include the oil soluble vitamins A, D, E and F, and a good source of iron – by the inclusion of organ meats, fish, nuts, seeds and cold-pressed vegetable oils. The wholegrains, vegetables and salads will also provide vital fibre to ensure efficient peristaltic action throughout the digestive tract and prevent constipation.

Plan your meals to contrast colours, flavours and textures. To complement a smooth food, serve one that is crisp and chewy (e.g. scrambled egg on wholemeal toast). Every meal should include something which needs thorough chewing – teeth and jaws need to be exercised in mastication as well as talking! Chewing mixes the food with the first digestive juices and triggers the preparation of later stages of digestion, as well as helping develop healthy well spaced teeth in our youngsters.

Try to include something raw at each meal and to finish with a food which will leave the teeth clean, such as raw fruit or celery.

The basic daily plan for an ideal balanced diet is as follows:

---

*This diet is likely to include at least 20% total dietary fat before the addition of any butter, margarine or oil. Meat, oily fish, cheese, eggs, nuts, seeds, avocados and olives all contain a high proportion of dietary fat. Natural wholegrains, shellfish, white fish and pulses contain a smaller amount of hidden fat. Fried foods, the generous use of butter, margarine and oil, and the inclusion of rich foods (e.g. pastries, cakes, gravy, mayonnaise) quickly exceed the ideal of 30%. See chapter 25.

On Waking:
Natural fruit juice, unsugared and diluted with water (orange, lemon, grapefruit, tomato, pineapple, grape or apple). Or drink of hot water with a slice of fresh lemon, or herb or Rooibosch tea (unsugared) with a vitamin C tablet (100-250g).

Breakfast:
A fresh fruit meal with non-flesh protein. Generous helping of fresh fruit muesli which includes mixed raw soaked cereal grains and sunflower seeds, nuts and lots of fruit. Or 4 tablespoons raw wheatgerm with milk, apples, and boiled, poached, scrambled or coddled free range egg with wholemeal toast.
(Growing children and those doing hard manual work can double up!)

Mid Morning:
Drink of pure water, or fresh fruit, or fruit or vegetable juice, herb tea, Rooibosch tea or Barleycup or Pioneer. For hungry ones, a wholemeal sandwich.

Lunch or Supper:
Principally a starch and vegetable meal, with a little protein. Ideally (digestion and climate allowing), this will consist of a large fresh salad of mostly raw ingredients, with cheese, nuts, egg (if not eaten for breakfast!) or little cold meat or vegetarian savoury. Wholemeal bread or baked jacket potatoes. Hot soup on cold days. Natural yoghurt with wheatgerm and honey as dessert if needed.

Mid Afternoon:
As mid morning.

Main Meal:
Principally a meal of protein and conservatively cooked vegetables. Include a green leafy vegetable and a root vegetable – or a raw green garnish of parsley, watercress, mustard and cress or beansprouts (to be eaten!). Raw fresh fruit for dessert, or cheese and apples or celery.

On Retiring:
Bedtime drink (see chapter 20).

Drinks:
Remember that the body needs pure water as well as good foods, and that fluid intake is best taken ½ hour before or 2 hours after a meal – not with it. Milk is the exception as it is a food requiring digestion.

Menu Planning

In planning a week's menu, try to include fish once or twice, organ meat once, muscle meat or poultry 3-4 times and a vegetarian meal once or twice for the main meals. Try to avoid serving meat more than once a day.

It is even a good idea to have one day free from all animal produce, using pulses with wholegrains or nuts for protein (see 'Proteins' page 195). This serves to boost our lecithin intake and give the body a rest from high cholesterol foods.

In the following suggested menus, desserts are included for those not yet accustomed to making a meal from a large salad or a one course main meal where fresh vegetables predominate. Where puddings are part of your life-style, try these wholefood desserts, but feel no qualms about omitting them whenever practical!

See 'Muesli and Grain Dishes' (page 103), breakfast suggestions (page 25), 'Drinks' (page 166) and 'Packed Lunch' (page 174) chapters for other possibilities.

Menu Suggestions

Week 1 – Spring

Monday
Chicken Fricasse
Wholemeal Toast
Spring Greens
Leeks
Fruit Fluff
–
Soup
Hard-boiled egg and salad
Yoghurt

Tuesday
Moussaka
Baked Potatoes
Brussel Sprouts
Leeks
Apple Sponge
–
Meal in a glass

Wednesday
Fricandelles
Artichokes
Carrots
Spring Greens
Orange Ice-cream

Quick Hazelnut Roast
Watercress
Fresh Fruit

Thursday
Vegetable Soup
Grilled Plaice, Lemon and Parsley
Crunchy Mashed Potato
Apple and Orange Foam
–
Waldorf Salad
Apple Crumble in a Hurry

Friday
Cassoulet
Baked Potatoes
Green Salad
Rhubarb Snow
–
Sardine Special
Baked Potato
Toasted Betty

Saturday
Braised Lamb's Hearts
Onions
Carrots
Baked Potatoes
Sprouting Broccoli
Fresh Fruit
–
Sustaining Salad and Stuffed Egg
Copenhagen Apple Layer Pudding

Sunday
Rabbit Casserole
Baked Potatoes
Spring Greens
Carrots
Prune Swizz

–

Soup
Moroccan Salad with Cold Lambs Heart
Apple Cracknel

Week 2 – Summer

Monday	**Tuesday**
Wholemeal Spaghetti Bolognaise	*Ruth's Favourite Cheese and*
Peas	*Tomato Pie*
Summer Lettuce	*Spinach*
Carrots	*Courgettes*
Strawberries with Honey	*Raspberries with RA Reddell's*
and Orange Juice	*Cottage Cream*
–	–
Kedgeree	*Golden Fruit and Nut Salad*
Apple and Carrot Jewel Salad	*Gooseberry Fool*
Yoghurt and Fruit	

Wednesday	**Thursday**
Layered Liver	*Grilled Mackerel*
Carrots with Parsley	*Mashed Potato*
Runner Beans	*Tomato and Watercress*
Pommes Dauphinoise	*Fresh Peaches*
Strawberries with Gran's Cream	–
–	*Lebanese Salad with Cheese*
Herring Roes on Wholemeal Toast	*Pancakes with 'Strawberry' Sauce*
Prune Salad	
Rhubarb Snow	

Friday	**Saturday**
Beanburgers	*Lamb Chops*
Ratatouille	*Brown Rice*
Green Salad	*Spinach*
Raspberries with Pineapple Juice	*Onions*
–	*Beetroot*
Strawberry Shake	*Summer Pudding*
(Meal in a Glass)	–
	Courgette Salad with Cold
	Beanburgers
	Pineapple Cheesecake

Sunday
Keith's Super Spiced Chicken with Brown Rice
Courgettes
French Beans
Green Salad
Fresh Fruit Salad

Black and White Salad
Orange Ice Cream

Week 3 – Autumn

Monday	**Tuesday**
Shepherds Pie	*Sicilian Quiche*
Spinach Beet	*Leeks*
Carrots	*Marrow*
Melon	*Cabbage*
	Grapes

Sweetcorn
Carrot, Egg and Beetroot Salad   *Nutcase Baked Potatoes*
Copenhagen Apple Layer Pudding   *Blackberry and Apple Crumble*

Wednesday	**Thursday**
Irish Stew	*Vegetarian Moussaka*
Ratatouille	*Baked Potatoes*
Crunchy Mashed Potatoes	*Carrots*
Apples	*Watercress*
	Fresh Pears

Sweetcorn
Colourful Date and Apple Salad   *Chicory and Orange Salad*
with Cold Quiche   *with Cottage Cheese*
Yoghurt   *Toasted Betty*

Friday	**Saturday**
Vegetable Soup	*Chicken Bermudian*
Grilled Sprats with	*Roast Potatoes*
Wholemeal Bread	*Spinach Beet*
Mushroom Salad	*Swede*
Grapes	*Cauliflower*
	Fresh Peaches

Grilled Kidneys
Tabbouleh Salad   *Aubergine Pizza*
Yoghurt   *Cauliflower Salad*
                                    Apple Tart with Cashew Cream

Sunday
Pot Roast Brisket of Beef
Beetroot
Baked Marrow
Brussel Sprouts
Grapes

Creole Rice Salad
Apple Crumble in a Hurry

Week 4 – Winter

Monday
Wholemeal Spaghetti Milanaise
Cabbage
Carrots
Banana Fluff

Herring Roes on Wholemeal Toast
Coleslaw
Watercress
Apple Pie

Wednesday
Sweetbreads with Mushrooms
Brussel Sprouts
Mashed Parsnip and Potato
Baked Bananas
–
Nigels Avocado Egg
Wholemeal Toast
Watercress
Compote

Friday
Baked Haddock
Crunchy Mashed Potato
Tomatoes
Baked Apples
–
Ruth's Favourite Supper Dish
Green Salad
Yoghurt

Tuesday
Sardine Pizza
Cauliflower
Spinach Beet
Apple Crumble
–
Nut Case Baked Potatoes
Christmas Custard

Thursday
Egg Cutlets
Artichokes
Cabbage
Swede
Warm Barley Pudding with
Apricots
–
Brains on Wholemeal Toast
Mushroom and Beansprout Salad
Ripe Bananas

Saturday
Tender Chicken from Ancient
Boiler or boiled Chicken
Brown Rice
Brussel Sprouts
Swede
Onion
Surprise Apple Tart
–
Cauliflower Cheese
Baked Potato
Watercress
Winter Vitality Fruit Salad

Sunday
Roast Lamb with Rosemary
Roast Potatoes
Mashed Parsnips and Carrots
Sprouting Broccoli
Bran and Apple Pudding
–
Soup
Apple and Carrot Jewel Salad
Banana Cheesecake

Breakfast Suggestions
Fresh Fruit Muesli – large bowlful!
Cereal and dried fruit muesli with milk or apple juice. Fresh fruit.
Wholegrain unsugared cereals with milk or apple juice. Fresh or stewed fruit.
Wholegrain toast with free-range egg – boiled, poached, scrambled or coddled. Fresh or stewed fruit.
Wholewheat toast with peanut butter, Houmous, Tahini or cheese; fruit.
Natural yoghurt with wheatgerm or oatgerm and honey, prunes or apricots.
Nuts and raisins with fresh fruit.
Meal in a Glass (see 'Drinks' page 169).
Oat, barley or potato porridge with milk, molasses, molasses sugar or Muscovado sugar or with apple juice.
Kruska (page 108) or Kasha (page 108).
Cornflakes, wheatgerm or oatgerm, bran, Frugrains and milk or apple juice. Fruit.
Ripe bananas, orange, sunflower seeds.
Wheatgerm with stewed fruit, fresh fruit.
Mushrooms, egg, tomato, ham, potato or brown rice.
   Breakfast may be a quick meal, but it is an important start to the day.

The Effects of Omitting Breakfast
1. Less alert
2. Shorter attention span
3. Slower reaction time
4. Decreased efficiency
5. More social and emotional problems in school children
6. Poorer school results
7. Low blood sugar, which encourages greater consumption of sugar-laden snacks and caffeinated drinks.

CHAPTER 5

Flavour

Healthy foods should be full of flavour as well as goodness. Cutting back on salt and sugar should not leave tasteless foods – but open up the spectrum of the natural flavours in vegetables and herbs, grains, fruits and spices, meats, fish, poultry and dairy products.

Organically produced foods are the ideal – but some may be unobtainable to many of us. Cutting down on meat and poultry is one economy which will help the budget stretch to include the wholegrains, free range eggs and extra vegetables, fruit and salads that we recommend (see chapter on proteins).

In addition to using fresh wholesome produce, flavour in savoury dishes is improved by the use of good stocks and occasionally some wine. Read the ingredient list of most stock cubes, and you will realise why stock-making recipes are included! As salt used in excess is a poison to the body, the answer to making foods tasty lies in the judicious use of herbs and spices. The accent is on the word judicious – too much spice (and of some herbs) is not good for us either! Their use should be so subtle that the delighted eater cannot isolate the illusive fragrance or flavour which so enhances the dish.

The Selective Use of Herbs and Spices
As a general rule, when you wish to emphasize the sweetness of a dish, use: allspice, coriander, cinnamon, mace, cloves, nutmeg, cardamon, mint and curry. For well seasoned foods, experiment with: garlic, oregano, sage, basil, parsley, thyme, marjoram, dill, cumin, black pepper, mustard and bay leaves. Mixed spice may contain nutmeg, coriander, cinnamon, cassis, caraway, cloves, mace and ginger. Garam Masala is an Indian blend of spices specially selected for curries and savoury dishes. It is made from coriander, cumin, ginger, black pepper, cinnamon, pimento, cardamon, bay leaves, cloves and nutmeg. Using a pinch of this in a dish could be an easy introduction to the enhancement a little spice can add to a recipe.
Caution: Some herbs and spices are so very strong that they will irritate tender skin – so wash your hands very thoroughly before picking up baby or rubbing your eyes!

While it is difficult to draw the line between some herbs and spices, here are lists of both, with suggestions for their use:

HERBS and their Suggested Uses:

APPLE MINT – fruit sorbets

BASIL – liver, stews, soups, tomato, pasta, eggs, fish and salads

BAY LEAVES – good with sweet milk custards as well as most savoury dishes

BORAGE – salads, eggs, cucumber, and in cider or claret cup or lemonade

BOUQUET GARNI – contains parsley, thyme, marjoram and bay leaf tied in muslin. See page 30 also.

CHERVIL – fish and egg dishes, salads, as garnish on pork chops, steak, tomatoes, carrots and peas

CHIVES – (mild onion flavour) good with egg, attractive garnish – best used fresh

DILL WEED – the leaves are good in salads, meat, fish and in prawn sauces

DILL Seeds – bruised (stronger flavour) pork, boiled potatoes

FENNEL – use leaves with fish, soups and stuffings, fresh root in salads

GARLIC – strong onion flavour which helps many savoury dishes – also useful for its health-giving, blood-purifying properties

HORSERADISH – grated root used in sauce, vinegar, and egg sandwiches

LEMON BALM – salad dressings, soups, sauces, chicken dishes

LEMON THYME – stuffings, fish dishes

LOVAGE – (strong celery flavour) soups, stuffings, stews

MINT – salads, peas, sauce, jelly and tea – savoury and sweet recipes

MARJORAM – (similar but milder than oregano) game, chicken, beef

NASTURTIUM – leaves and flowers in salads

OREGANO – eggs, cheese, fish, mushrooms, tomatoes, minced pork and beef, pizzas and all Italian dishes

PARSLEY – all savoury dishes, hot and cold, salads, garnish, sauces (most flavour is in the stems for soups, stews, casseroles, etc.)

PEPPERMINT – tea, fruit cup, fruit salads

ROSEMARY – roast lamb, pork and chicken, casseroles, soups, marinades, and many Italian dishes

SAGE – stews and shepherds pie, stuffings, patés, egg, pork, poultry, game

SUMMER SAVORY – stuffings, sausages, game

SWEET CICELY – fresh leaves cooked with sour fruit to lessen sugar needed

TARRAGON – fish, eggs, chicken, sauces, vinegar and herb butter

THYME – game stews, roasts, chicken, stuffings and tomato sauce

SPICES and their Suggested Uses:

ALLSPICE – marinades, pickling fruits and vegetables, curries, biscuits

ANISE (aniseed) – sauces, breads, cakes and biscuits

BLACK PEPPER – best freshly ground in peppermill – all savoury dishes

CARAWAY – seeds for cabbage, salads, cakes and breads

CARDAMON – seeds need to be bruised – casseroles, roasts, sauces, curries, also good in ice-cream (lemony flavour)

CAYENNE – (very hot) use sparingly in egg and cheese dishes

CHILLIES – (if using the pods, remove the seeds, which are even hotter.) Powdered, it is a hot pepper. Curries. Wash hands *many* times after handling!

CINNAMON – roast lamb and duck, in chicken and lamb casseroles – with apples, – ground in cakes and biscuits

CLOVES – whole: pickles, savoury and sweet dishes, with apples; powdered in baking.

CORIANDER – ingredient of pickling spice; stews, soups, curries and fancy breads and biscuits

CUMIN – curry, lamb, meatballs

GINGER – ground, in cakes, curries, stews and dips. Fresh root (peel and chop finely) also in curries and savoury dishes

JUNIPER – crushed berries used in sauerkraut, game, marinades, stuffings

LEMON RIND (zest) – fish, sauces, stuffings, cakes and sweet dishes

MACE – (husk of nutmeg) stews, chicken, chutneys, on swede, tomato soup

MUSTARD – pickling, salad dressings, sauces

NUTMEG – (a gently flavoured spice, best freshly grated from a whole nutmeg) sauces, soups, creamed potato and swede, spinach and cream cheese, mushrooms; also sweet egg custard

PAPRIKA – (mildest of the peppers with good flavour and beautiful red colour) Pork, chicken, egg and cheese dishes, good garnish

TURMERIC – curries and pickles (has a lovely yellow colour which also stains fingers and work surfaces!)

VANILLA – well-known flavour for sweet sauces, ice-cream (take care to buy pure vanilla pods or extract, not the imitation product, vanillin)

HERB BUTTERS

The basic proportion is is 2 oz (50 g) of soft butter to one tablespoon of finely chopped fresh herbs (or substitute ½ teaspoon dried herbs) and 2 teaspoons fresh lemon juice.

Cream the butter, mix in the herb, add the lemon juice and beat well. Prepare several hours in advance for the herb flavour to be released. Chives, watercress, basil, chervil, rosemary, parsley, thyme, garlic, mint, marjoram, dill and fennel are all suitable for herb butter. Use for special sandwiches, in the preparation of egg dishes or for topping meat, savoury or vegetable dishes, just before serving and when grilling fish.

Maitre D'Hotel Butter

4 tablespoons butter   ⅛ teaspoon pepper
4 teaspoons lemon juice   ¼ teaspoon minced onion or shallot
1 tablespoon finely chopped parsley

Cream butter until very soft, add herbs and lemon juice very slowly, stirring constantly.

Suggested combinations for you to try:

Vegetable:	Herb and Spice:
Mushrooms	– Nutmeg
Peas	– Cook with mint or serve with mint or Maitre d'Hotel butter
Potato	– Dill, nutmeg, parsley, mint, paprika
Broad Beans	
French Beans and Runner Beans	– Serve with parsley or Maitre d'Hotel butter or cook with summer savory
Swede	– Mash the cooked swede with mace or nutmeg
Spinach	– Grate on a little nutmeg just before serving or serve with butter and lemon juice
Tomatoes	– Raw with basil or cooked with oregano or mace
Cucumber	– With dill
Carrots	– Raw with fresh chopped mint or cooked with rosemary
Courgettes	– Cooked with garlic, or dill
Eggs	– Basil, marjoram, chervil, savory, thyme, rosemary, chives, cayenne, paprika
Fish	– Fennel, dill, bay leaves, basil, chervil, mint or tarragon, lemon peel
Soups	– Rosemary, lavender, thyme, chervil, savory, marjoram or basil, lovage, garlic, celery seeds, cloves, paprika
Poultry	– Bay leaves, basil, sage, thyme, tarragon, marjoram, rosemary, chervil, lovage, parsley, lemon rind, mace, cloves, cinnamon, ginger
Beef	– Lovage, sage, thyme, garlic, basil, summer savory, savory, marjoram, celery seed, cumin
Lamb	– Rosemary, garlic, spearmint, summer savory, chives, marjoram, tarragon, thyme, lovage, celery seed, oregano, bay leaves, cumin

Pork   Garlic, cumin seed, parsley, sage,
                                     bay leaves, lovage, rosemary, mustard

Bouquet Garni
This is a little bunch of fresh herbs tied together, or dried herbs tied in a
muslin bag, cooked with the dish and removed before serving. Choose 3
or 4 from such herbs as parsley, thyme, tarragon, sage, celery stem,
lovage, chervil, basil – according to the character of the dish.

Vegetable Stock
Vegetable stock gives more flavour and nutritional value than water in
soups, sauces, pastas and rice dishes. All stock in which vegetables
have been cooked (except sprouts and savoys which, though nutritious,
really smell unpleasant), should be saved and used – even potato stock,
though this does not keep so long.

When more stock is required than is available from the conservative
cooking of vegetables, e.g. for making soup or cooking rice or pasta,
make up a stock pot using the outer coarser leaves of vegetables that
would normally be wasted. Wash thoroughly, chop small and immerse
immediately in cold water in the stock pot. When potatoes, swedes, etc.
are to be peeled, scrub them well first and the peelings can join the
mixture in the stock pot.

Simmer the mixed vegetables in sufficient water to cover for about an
hour, to extract the mineral salts into the water. Cool and refrigerate the
stock until needed. (Will keep for up to 4 days.) Ensure this stock is
thoroughly boiled for at least 5 minutes before serving. Leek tops,
carrot ends, coarse outer celery stalks and leaves, pea pods, mushroom
stalks and parsley stalks are all especially useful in giving a good
flavour. Enhance this with fresh or dried herbs and careful seasoning
when making up the final soup or savoury dish.

Chicken Stock

*Necks, wings, giblets of 2 chickens OR raw carcass, neck, wings, giblets from
1 bird*

1½ pints (1 1) water	*2-3 onions, sliced*
1 carrot, scrubbed and sliced	*1 bay leaf*
outer stalks of celery, scrubbed and sliced	*freshly ground black pepper*
parsley (stems if possible)	*salty seasoning*

Cover the chicken pieces with cold water and bring to the boil,
skimming off the scum as necessary. Add the other ingredients and
simmer, covered, for 2-3 hours (longer for an older bird). Strain the
stock, and use as required. Any surplus can be cooled and then deep
frozen for later use.

Potassium Broth

An alkalinising hot drink, high in potassium or a good-flavoured vegetable stock, or soup.

2-3 lbs (1 k) old potatoes,
well scrubbed
2-4 parsley stems or parsley sprigs
1 carrot, chopped
1-2 onions, chopped
paprika

2 pts (1.2 l) water
1 clove garlic, crushed
1 celery stalk, chopped
salty seasoning
sweet basil or bay leaf

Peel potatoes THICKLY. It is the peel needed for this recipe – use the potatoes separately. Put into cold water in a large saucepan and add other ingredients. Cover and simmer for 1-1½ hours. Strain. Good for those feeling "off their food", or with "acidity".

Beef Stock

3-4 lbs (1,275-1.75 k) beef marrow
bones
2 carrots, scrubbed and sliced
parsley (stems if possible)

water
2-3 large onions, sliced
outer stalks of celery, chopped
salty seasoning and black pepper

Buy the marrow bones sawn into 1-2″ slices, if possible. Cover these with cold water in a large saucepan. Bring to the boil, skimming off the scum as it forms on the surface. Simmer for 2½-3 hours, then add remaining ingredients and simmer for further hour. Strain the stock and use as required. Any surplus can be cooled then deep frozen for later use.

Summer Vegetable Stock

If you need a brown stock, saute ½ cup finely chopped onion in 2 tablespoons oil till brown OR add brown onions skins and remove them later.

add:

a dash of white pepper
½ teaspoon salty seasoning
2 cups diced celery and yellow leaves
1 cup shredded lettuce
mushroom or tomato skins
1 leek, chopped
1 slice of turnip and parsnip, chopped
cold water to cover

a dash of cayenne
a bouquet garni (3 sprigs parsley/
chervil, ½ bay leaf, 2 sprigs
fresh thyme)
1 small onion, studded with 2
cloves
1 carrot, chopped

Bring to the boil, cover and simmer until the vegetables are very tender. Strain and chill till needed.

Winter Vegetable Stockpot

1 large onion	*2 Jerusalem artichokes*
2 carrots	*1 turnip or swede*
outer stalks celery	*green part of leeks*
parsley stems	*salty seasoning*

Into a large heavy enamel or stainless stell saucepan put two pints (1200 ml) of cold water, adding the vegetables as prepared. Scrub the root vegetables well and remove blight but do not peel. Chop finely all the vegetables to allow maximum release of flavour to the water. Add more water if necessary to cover the vegetables well. Simmer for 2-3 hours. Strain. Cool and refrigerate till needed (within 5 days).

CHAPTER 6

Salads

Salad Ideas

The best salad ingredients are those grown organically, locally, in their own season, picked fresh, washed and prepared just before eating. Never leave to soak in water – some of the water soluble vitamins and minerals will be lost through cut edges.

Start with simple salads of four or five ingredients, twice weekly. Gradually increase the number of salad meals a week, and the diversification of ingredients as the digestion adapts to accept living foods. If troubled with 'wind', eat simpler salads with no dried or raw fruit at the same meal, chewing extra thoroughly. Do not rush a salad meal, sit down and enjoy it!

A salad is not just the usual lettuce, tomatoes, cucumber and beetroot – so many vegetables are delicious raw in salad. Be adventurous. Try to incorporate sprouted seeds into salads for their extra high vitamins B and C and amino acids (protein) content. Vary dressings to add variety. All the following can be used raw in salads:

ASPARAGUS – choose young green spears

AVOCADO – cubed and dressed

BEETROOT – grate finely the young fresh beets – older stored beets
  can be cooked

BROCCOLI LEAVES – finely chopped

BRUSSEL SPROUTS – cut in thin slices – introduce gradually as they
  can be wind-provoking

CABBAGE – green, white and red, finely shredded

CARROT – grated or sliced – or eaten whole when young

CAULIFLOWER – in florets or chopped – delicious and very high in
  vitamin C

CELERIAC – thin slices marinated to prevent discolouration

CELERY – by stalk or chopped – eat the leaves too

CHICORY – bitter

CHINESE LEAVES – chopped

CHIVES – chop – a wonderful addition to egg

COURGETTES – delicious sliced in ¼″ slices or cubed

CUCUMBER – slice or cube leaving the peel on – it contains enzymes
  making it more easily digested

DANDELION LEAVES – chop for chlorophyll – use sparingly

ENDIVE – bitter
FRENCH BEANS – eat young
JERUSALEM ARTICHOKES – deliciously nutty – scrub, dice and
   marinate in a dressing
KALE LEAVES – finely chopped
KHOL RABI – young – cubed
LEEKS – finely sliced or chopped and used sparingly at first as they can
   repeat
LETTUCE – whole leaves or chopped in large pieces
MUSHROOMS – (cultivated) wash well and slice
MUSTARD AND CRESS – leave growing till last moment
NASTURTIUM LEAVES, flowers and seeds – all edible and hot!
ONIONS – finely sliced or chopped – use sparingly until appreciation
   grows
PARSLEY – chopped or in sprigs
PEAS – eat young
RADISH – whole, made into flowers or sliced
RED AND GREEN PEPPER – slice, discarding seeds
RUNNER BEANS – eat young – delicious straight off the plant
SPINACH LEAVES – chop for chlorophyll – use sparingly (see page
   66)
SPRING ONION – whole or chopped
SPROUTED GRAINS, seeds and legumes – whole or chopped – see
   section on sprouting seeds
TOMATOES – keep their flavour best uncut – wash well if bought
TURNIP AND SWEDE – young – cubed or grated
WATERCRESS – chop as little as possible – it is such a nutritious food.
   Soak for 10 minutes in cold salted water to kill any river flukes, then
   rinse thoroughly in fresh water. Store loosely covered.

Salad Combinations To Enjoy
1. Sliced tomato, cauliflower florets, bulgar wheat and chopped parsley
   in a yoghurt dressing.
2. Grated carrot, alfalfa sprouts, mung beansprouts and sliced, raw
   mushroom in a dressing flavoured with Tabasco.
3. Finely shredded cabbage, grated nuts, pineapple pieces, sultanas or
   raisins in an oil and lemon dressing.
4. Sliced mushrooms, diced tomato, beansprouts, coarsely chopped
   parsley in French or vinaigrette dressing.
5. Finely shredded cabbage, little chopped mint, chopped fresh peeled
   orange slices in pineapple juice – no seasoning needed.
6. Sliced tomato with chopped fresh basil and parsley and a sprinkling
   of cider vinegar and salty seasoning.

SIDE SALADS

Caraway Cabbage Slaw

½ lb (225 gm) white cabbage,
finely shredded

1 Bramley apple, peeled and diced

1 stick celery, finely chopped
Caraway dressing
(see page 46)
sprouted fenugreek

Mix all ingredients with the caraway dressing and decorate with sprouted fenugreek.

Avocado Salad

Toss peeled, cubed ripe avocado in orange juice.

Cucumber Salad

1 cucumber
Slimmers garlic dressing

2 stalks of mint
paprika

Cut the cucumber into ½″ cubes and cover with the dressing. Dust with paprika and decorate with thin cucumber slices and the mint leaves.

Carrot Salads

Wash and scrub the carrots but do not peel, similarly use the peel of apples and pears if organically grown.
1. Mix together: Finely grated carrot and grated rind and juice of an orange.
2. Mix together: Finely grated carrot, coarsely grated apple, raisins and a little lemon or orange juice.
3. Combine in equal proportions: Finely grated carrot and grated cheese.
4. Mix together: Finely grated carrot, chopped celery, coarsely grated or chopped apple, finely chopped mint, little lemon or orange juice.

Colourful Date and Apple Salad

3 cups finely sliced cabbage
½-1 cup chopped red or green pepper
chopped hard dates to taste

1 cup chopped celery
1 cup coarsely grated cooking apple
lemon juice dressing

Combine all ingredients and mix in lemon juice dressing.

Raw Beetroot Salads

Choose small freshly pulled beetroot, organically grown. Wash carefully but do not peel.
1. Mix together: Finely grated beetroot, coarsely grated apple, little lemon juice.
2. Mix together: Finely grated beetroot, chopped fresh pears, little lemon juice.
3. Mix together: Finely grated beetroot, finely chopped mint, little lemon juice.

Apple and Carrot Jewel Salad

Orange juice
diced raw apple
chopped red and green peppers
lettuce leaves

grated carrot
finely chopped celery
raisins

Line dish with lettuce leaves, mix other ingredients well together in the orange juice and pile in the centre.

Baked Beans and Celery Salad

1 tin baked beans – Heinz
sprouted Mung beans or sprouted
alfalfa

fresh crisp celery

Choose a brand free from colouring and flavouring, e.g. Heinz. Wash and chop the celery and stir into the baked beans. Stir in the mung bean sprouts or decorate with the fine alfalfa sprouts.

Tomato Salad

Tomatoes
black pepper
onion rings

basil (fresh or dried)
oil and lemon juice dressing

Slice the washed tomatoes and arrange a layer on the serving dish. Sprinkle lightly with basil and black pepper. Repeat layers of tomato and seasoning till filled. Pour over dressing and decorate with onion rings and serve.

Cauliflower Salad – high in vitamin C

1 cup natural yoghurt, mixed with:-
2 cups chopped cabbage
2 tablespoons red pepper, chopped
4 tablespoons chopped spring onion

2 teaspoons thin honey
2 cups chopped cauliflower
4 tablespoons chopped parsley
½ avocado, cut in strips into lemon juice

Mix all chopped ingredients well into the yoghurt, and decorate with the avocado.

Fennel Salad

1 fennel root
2 tablespoons chopped parsley

1 hard boiled egg, chopped
oil and lemon juice dressing

Chill the fennel root in ice water for ½-1 hour to crisp it. Slice finely and combine with the chopped egg and parsley. Sprinkle with an oil and lemon dressing and serve.

Bulgarian Salad

1 lb (450 gm) new young carrots   2 teaspoons chopped chives
1 teaspoon honey   salty seasoning and paprika
1 clove garlic, pressed   ¼ pint (150 ml) natural yoghurt
2 teaspoons chopped parsley

Wash carrots and simmer whole in a very little water with the honey, until just tender. Cool and cut into cubes. Cream the pressed garlic with a little of the yoghurt to blend evenly, and add herbs and seasonings and a little of the carrot stock. Marinate the carrots in the herb dressing in the refrigerator for 1-2 hours before serving cold.

Chicory and Orange Salad

1 head of chicory   3-4 oranges

Wash and separate the chicory leaves. Peel and cut the oranges into slices. Arrange decoratively.

Lebanese Salad

1 bunch spring onions   ½ cucumber
1 tablespoon finely chopped mint   1 tablespoon chopped chives
½ lb (225 gm) sweet tomatoes   ¼ pint (150 ml) natural yoghurt
black pepper

Clean the spring onions and chop them all, including the green. Wash cucumber and tomatoes and cut into cubes. Mix into the yoghurt with the herbs and a little freshly ground black pepper to taste.

Ratatouille Salad

Left-over ratatouille makes a delicious salad served with other green salad ingredients.

Courgette Salad

2-3 courgettes   6-8 fresh radishes
½ small red pepper   2 teaspoons chopped chives
2 teaspoons chopped parsley   1 teaspoon chopped mint
¼ pint (150 ml) natural yoghurt   salty seasoning to taste

Wash the courgettes, radishes and pepper and slice thinly. Mix together in the yoghurt, reserving a little to decorate top.

Provencal Salad

courgettes, raw diced   onion, thinly sliced
tomatoes, quartered   green peppers, thinly sliced
Combine and mix in garlic dressing.

Banana Salad

1 banana, sliced
½ cup finely chopped parsley

4 cups cabbage, shredded finely
2 tablespoons finely chopped mint

Mix salad ingredients and toss in avocado dressing.

Prune Salad

1 cup prunes, soaked for 24 hours
½ cup grated carrot

1 cup diced raw apple
1 cup finely shredded cabbage

Chop and combine ingredients.

Water Melon Salad

Watermelon
fresh mint sprigs

½ cucumber

Wash the melon. Decide which way the watermelon is most stable and cut off the top quarter. Scoop out the flesh with a parisienne cutter to make neat balls, discarding the pips. Wash the cucumber and cut into cubes and mix with the melon balls. Pile back into the melon shell and decorate the top with mint sprigs.

QUICK SNACK SALAD MEALS OR HORS D'OEUVRES

French Bean Salad

1 lb (450 gm) young French beans
French dressing
Smokey Snaps

1 small onion, chopped finely
1-4 hard boiled eggs
chopped parsley

Steam the beans till they are barely cooked. Pour over the dressing and chopped onion, stir well and cool. When cold, decorate with hard-boiled egg slices and the Smokey Snaps and parsley.

Tabbouleh – a Lebanese salad

¼ lb (100 gm) sprouted wheat
2 bunches parsley
1 bunch fresh mint
½ cucumber
½ lb (225 gm) tomatoes
1 cos lettuce

4-5 spring onions or chives or
small onion
3 tablespoons fresh lemon juice
6 tablespoons sunflower oil
2 cloves garlic, crushed
seasoning optional

Sprout wheat ahead. Wash parsley and mint and chop finely. Cut cucumber and tomato into cubes and slice spring onions. Mix with chopped herbs. Mix dressing ingredients together and add the sprouted wheat and other ingredients. Stir well. Wash and dry the separated leaves of the cos lettuce and arrange on a shallow dish. Pile tabbouleh onto the leaves and serve.

Fresh Pear and Grape Salad

ripe raw pears   cottage cheese
black grapes   crisp lettuce
2 oranges   watercress (see page 34)
alfalfa sprouts   sunflower seeds

Squeeze one orange for juice. Peel and cut the pears into slices and toss in the orange juice. Wash the grapes, lettuce and watercress well. Peel and cut the other orange into segments. Mix the sunflower seeds into the cottage cheese. With the lettuce as a base, put the cottage cheese in the centre, with the sliced pears, orange, grapes, alfalfa sprouts and watercress decoratively arranged over and around it.

Blackberry and Apple Salad

3 tablespoons natural yoghurt   3 tablespoons orange juice
2-3 teaspoons honey   ½ cup diced cooking apple
½ cup blackberries, fresh or   2 tablespoons desiccated coconut
frozen (raw)
1 cup cold cooked brown rice   lettuce leaves

Blend honey, yoghurt and orange juice together in a basin. Add diced apple and blackberries and coconut and stir well. Stir in brown rice and serve on bed of lettuce leaves.

Golden Fruit and Nut Salad

4 bananas, sliced   2 oranges, sliced
½ cup walnuts, cashews or pecan nuts   ½ cup coconut flakes
1 small ripe pineapple, chopped   juice of extra orange
lettuce or endive

Toss the sliced banana in the orange juice and add all other ingredients. Arrange on a bed of crisp lettuce or endive.

Tropicana Salad

3 parts Adzuki beansprouts   1 part raisins
1 part dried apricots, soaked   1 part peanuts or cashew nuts
and chopped

Mix together in given proportions and serve with a green salad.

Waldorf Salad

½ lb (225 gm) white cabbage   ½ pint (300 ml) yoghurt dressing
1 red sweet apple   2 tablespoons chopped walnuts
1 green Bramley apple   2 tablespoons raisins, well washed
1-2 sticks celery   1 cup alfalfa sprouts
2 oz (50 gm) black grapes

Well wash the apple skins with hot and cold water and dry them. Core the apples, but leave the skins on and cut them in neat wedges or cubes, covering with dressing to prevent oxidation. Wash and coarsely chop the celery, finely shred the cabbage and add to the apples, together with the nuts and raisins. Stir well to distribute the ingredients. Wash, halve and de-pip the grapes and use to decorate the top of the salad. Arrange the alfalfa sprouts around the edge of the dish.

Egg and Beetroot Salad

boiled eggs, chopped coarsely   *boiled potatoes, diced*
spring onions, chopped   *beetroot, just cooked and diced*

Combine with mayonnaise with a little horseradish sauce.

Date and Walnut Salad

4 oz (100 gm) stoned dates, chopped   *2 oz (50 gm) walnut pieces*
3 sticks celery   *2 sweet red apples*
1 cup mung beansprouts   *1 small lettuce*
yoghurt and honey dressing

Wash and separate the lettuce leaves and arrange as a base. Finely chop the celery. Thoroughly wash the apple and cut into cubes, dropping straight into the yoghurt dressing. Add celery, chopped dates, walnuts and beansprouts and mix well. Pile onto the lettuce and serve.

Rollmop and Orange Salad

8 rollmops (pickled herrings)   *6 tomatoes*
1 large orange   *2 cups alfalfa sprouts*
½ bunch watercress (see page 34)   *1 onion*

Peel the orange and cut into eight halfmoons. Well wash and quarter the tomatoes. Cut the onion into rings. Make a base of the alfalfa sprouts and arrange the drained rollmops, orange and tomato sections and watercress in a satisfying pattern. Garnish with the onion rings.

HEARTY SALADS
Black and White Salad

1 lb (450 gm) potatoes (waxy varieties
are best)   *or finely shredded white cabbage*
¾ lb (350 gm) cold cooked chicken   *or broken cashew nuts or almonds*
1 bunch spring onions   *8 oz (225 gm) black grapes*
2 oz (50 gm) black olives (optional)   *2 oz (50 gm) raisins (seedless, washed)*
1 ripe cooking apple   *6 fl. oz (175 ml) home-made mayonnaise*
freshly ground black pepper

Steam or boil the scrubbed potatoes till just cooked. Then peel, cool and dice them. Chop the white part only of the spring onions (use the green tops for stock or another salad dish). Cut the chicken into bite-sized pieces, halve and remove stones from olives. When halving and removing pips from grapes, divide into two and reserve half for decoration, with a few olives. Peel and cut the apple into dice, mixing immediately with some of the mayonnaise to prevent discolouration. Mix in the other ingredients, check seasoning, and put into serving dish, coated with remaining mayonnaise. Decorate with reserved grapes and olives.

Creole Rice Salad

Creole Dressing

¾ cup vegetable oil	4 tablespoons lemon juice
2 teaspoons thin honey	1 teaspoon Tamari (soy sauce)
1 teaspoon garam masala	3 tablespoons chopped parsley
herb salt	

. . . .

3 cups cooked brown rice	1 cup finely chopped celery
1 green pepper, finely chopped	1 onion, finely chopped
3 fresh peaches or nectarines,	½ cup sunflower seeds (soaked
skinned and cubed	overnight) or slivers of cooked
½ cup raisins or sultanas	chicken

Dressing: Mix garam masala to a paste with Tamari, honey and lemon juice, then blend in oil, herbs and seasoning. Shake well in screw-top jar. Mix other ingredients together and combine with dressing.

Banana and Nut Salad

6 oz (175 gm) brown rice, long grain	2 bananas
½-1 cucumber	zest and juice of 1 small lemon
3-4 oz (75-100 gm) broken cashews,	4 tablespoons washed sultanas
walnuts or almonds	or seedless raisins
2 tablespoons sunflower oil or	¼ teaspoon garam masala
safflower oil	1 teaspoon honey

Cook the brown rice for 40-50 minutes till tender (see page 109) and drain and cool. Slice the peeled bananas into the lemon juice. Slice the washed cucumber and add. Drain off the lemon juice and whisk with the oil, honey and spices. Add all other ingredients and leave in cool place for one hour for flavours to mix before serving.

Seafood Salad Special

1 cos lettuce	1 lb (450 gm) cooked prawns
1 bunch watercress (see page 34)	1lb (450 gm) white fish
½ cucumber	1 tin crabmeat
6 tomatoes	6 hard-boiled eggs
1 bunch spring onions	home-made mayonnaise
1 cup alfalfa sprouts	2 tablespoons chopped chives

Steam the white fish with a little butter and milk (or poach it in a court bouillon). Cool and remove skin and bones. Thin the mayonnaise with a little of the fish stock and add to the flaked fish, with the chopped egg, crab pieces and chives. Mix well. Wash the salad ingredients and arrange the lettuce as a base around a large shallow platter, with the seafood mixture in the centre. Add the other ingredients to make the dish a delight to the eye.

Avocado and Crab Salad with Herb Mayonnaise

1 lb (450 gm) cooked crabmeat	2 ripe avocados
lemon juice	6 tomatoes, quartered
1 lettuce	black grapes
1 cup alfalfa sprouts	
Herb Mayonnaise	
½ pint (300 ml) home-made mayonnaise	1 hard boiled egg, chopped
2 teaspoons finely chopped fresh tarragon or ¼ teaspoon	1 tablespoon finely chopped parsley
dried tarragon	1 clove garlic, pressed

Combine the ingredients of the herb mayonnaise. Remove any shell from the crabmeat. Thoroughly wash the lettuce, tomatoes and grapes. Arrange the lettuce leaves to form a base on the large serving platter, with the prepared crabmeat in the centre. Halve and de-pip the grapes. Peel the avocados and cut into long slices, gently rubbing lemon juice over every cut surface to prevent discolouration. Arrange the avocado slices, alfalfa sprouts, tomato quarters and halved grapes to look attractive. Serve with the herb mayonnaise.

Salad Nicoise

1 tin tuna fish	black olives
cooked French beans	tomatoes, quartered
hard-boiled eggs, quartered	lots of chopped parsley or chives
cos lettuce	watercress (see page 34)

Break the fish into pieces. On a bed of torn lettuce leaves and watercress, arrange the other ingredients. Sprinkle with the tuna fish oil and a French dressing.

Moroccan Salad

Cold roast lamb	fresh mint
cooked beetroot	spring onions
lettuce	

Cut the sliced roast lamb into bite-sized pieces. Chop the fresh mint and toss with the lamb. Arrange lettuce leaves around a salad bowl, with a circle of beetroot slices and the minted lamb in the centre, decorated with the spring onions.

Sustaining Salad

1 cup sprouted wheat
3 sharp ripe apples
½ cup orange juice
pinch of paprika

1 cup sprouted sunflower seeds
4 tablespoons natural yoghurt
½ cup washed raisins or sultanas
½ bunch watercress

Sprout the wheat and sunflower seeds (see chapter on sprouting). Combine the yoghurt and orange juice in a bowl. Thoroughly wash apples and dice, mix into the dressing. Thoroughly wash watercress. Add sprouts and raisins to the bowl and mix well, adding a touch of paprika to taste. Arrange in serving bowl with border of watercress.

SALAD DRESSINGS
Blue Cheese Dressing – For Slimmers

¼ pint (150 ml) natural yoghurt
½ teaspoon Worcester sauce,
tamari or shoyu

¼ pint (150 ml) crumbled blue cheese
½ teaspoon salty seasoning
1 clove garlic, pressed

Blend all ingredients together in a liquidiser. If too thick, add a little whey or milk.

Thousand Island Dressing

½ pint (300 ml) home-made
mayonnaise
½ teaspoon dried basil
1 teaspoon garlic salt
1 teaspoon honey

½ teaspoon Worcester sauce

½ teaspoon dried oregano
1 teaspoon kelp powder
3 hard-boiled eggs

Mash the hard-boiled eggs and mix in all the other ingredients. Store in a closed jar in the refrigerator. Finely chopped fresh herbs may be substituted for the dried.

Herb Vinaigrette

½ pint (300 ml) safflower oil
2 tablespoons lemon juice
1 teaspoon dried oregano
½ teaspoon dried marjoram
1 teaspoon kelp powder

¼ pint (150 ml) apple cider vinegar
2 tablespoons tamari or shoyu
1 teaspoon dried thyme
½ teaspoon rosemary
2 tablespoons sesame seeds

Shake all the ingredients together in a screw-top jar with a secure lid, or liquidise in a blender.

Green Cucumber Dressing – For Slimmers

1 cucumber	juice of 1 lemon
6-10 fl oz (175-300ml) natural yoghurt	1 clove garlic, pressed
¾ teaspoon kelp powder	¼ teaspoon dried dillweed
¼ teaspoon dried basil	

Wash cucumber and remove ends. Chop coarsely and put in blender with other ingredients. Liquidise. Substitute fresh herbs if available.

Tahini Dressing

4 tablespoons tahini	4 tablespoons natural yoghurt
6 tablespoons mayonnaise	½ teaspoon Worcester sauce
1 clove garlic, pressed	½ teaspoon salty seasoning
pinch oregano	

Mix all ingredients together adding a little whey if too thick.

Herb Dressing – For Slimmers

2 tablespoons natural yoghurt	¼ teaspoon honey
2 tablespoons safflower oil	2 teaspoons cider or white wine vinegar
1 tablespoon fresh dill, chopped	1 tablespoon fresh tarragon, chopped
1 tablespoon chopped chives	black pepper and salty seasoning

Blend the honey into the yoghurt. Add other ingredients in a screw-top jar and shake all together (or liquidise). Good for a mixed green salad, or on raw cubed kohlrabi or celeriac salad.

Vegan Mayonnaise

¼ pint (150 ml) tahini	⅛ pint (75 ml) safflower oil
½ pint (300 ml) lemon juice	1 teaspoon honey
½ teaspoon kelp powder	

Liquidise all ingredients together in a blender. Check seasoning, and add salty seasoning if necessary.

Slimmer's Apple Dressing

½ cup cider vinegar	¼-½ cup water
¼ teaspoon garlic powder	1 teaspoon apple juice concentrate
pinch garam masala or	
powdered mustard	

Whisk all together.

Slimmer's Tomato Dressing (or Sauce)

1 tin of peeled tomatoes (15 oz)	1 shallot or small onion
2 teaspoons cider vinegar	pinch cayenne
¼ teaspoon basil or oregano	2 ripe tomatoes, peeled

Finely chop the raw and tinned tomatoes and the onion and mix in other ingredients. Good with salads, pasta, rice or baked potatoes.

Yoghurt and Honey Dressing

2 tablespoons plain yoghurt   2 tablespoons orange juice
½ teaspoon thin honey

Mix together.

Cole Slaw Dressing

1 tablespoon Barbados or   1 cup natural yoghurt
demerara sugar
¼ teaspoon salty seasoning   1-2 tablespoons lemon juice
⅛ teaspoon dry mustard   1 tablespoon sunflower/safflower oil
                                     (optional)

Dissolve the sugar in the yoghurt. Dissolve the salt and incorporate the mustard. Add remaining ingredients and whisk lightly together.

Salt-Free Vinaigrette Dressing

¼ teaspoon dry mustard   10 tablespoons sunflower oil
1 teaspoon honey   ½ teaspoon kelp powder
5 tablespoons apple cider vinegar   ¼ teaspoon paprika

Blend mustard in honey. Place all ingredients in screw-top jar with efficient lid. Shake to combine well.

Simple Tasty Salad Dressing

2 tablespoons thin honey   2 tablespoons cider vinegar
2 tablespoons warm water
Dissolve honey in water and mix with the vinegar.

Garlic and Mint Salad Dressing

3 tablespoons sunflower oil   1-2 cloves garlic
1 tablespoon lemon juice   2 teaspoons fresh mint, chopped
1 tablespoon thin honey

Put oil and lemon juice in a screw-top jar, with honey and mint. Add crushed garlic and shake well.

Lemon Juice Salad Dressing

2 tablespoons lemon juice   1 teaspoon thin honey
5 tablespoons sunflower oil   ¼ teaspoon salty seasoning

Put all ingredients in screw-top jar and shake well to combine.

SALADS

Slimmer's Garlic Dressing

2 cloves garlic
salty seasoning

½ pint (300 ml) natural yoghurt
4 sprigs fresh mint

Crush the garlic into the yoghurt and blend with finely chopped mint. Season to taste.

Caraway Dressing

1 tablespoon lemon juice
1 cup natural yoghurt
1 teaspoon caraway seeds

2 teaspoons sesame seeds, roasted
¼ teaspoon powdered nutmeg

Shake all ingredients together in a screw-top jar and refrigerate for 24 hours before using to allow yoghurt to take up the spice flavours. Suitable for slimmers.

Mayonnaise

1 small pickling onion or shallot
1 tablespoon raw brown sugar
1 teaspoon dry mustard
1 teaspoon paprika
1 teaspoon salty seasoning

or ½ clove garlic
1 large egg
½ pint (300 ml) sunflower oil
2 tablespoons lemon juice
1 tablespoon cider vinegar

Chop the onion or garlic and put in blender with herbs and seasonings, and liquidise at slow speed with egg. Gradually add oil very slowly until thick again. Stir in the vinegar and lemon juice. Store in screw-top jars in refrigerator.

Quick French Dressing

½ teaspoon French mustard
½ teaspoon clear honey
6 tablespoons sunflower/safflower/
soya oil

¼ teaspoon salty seasoning
3 tablespoons apple cider vinegar

Into a small screw-top jar, put all ingredients. Replace lid firmly and shake vigourously to mix the ingredients thoroughly. Add to a green salad just before serving.

Variations to French Dressing

1. Add a small clove of garlic, whole or crushed.
2. Add 1 teaspoon of salad herbs to the dressing.
3. Use lemon juice in place of cider vinegar.
4. Add 2 teaspoons of chopped parsley.
5. Add 2 teaspoons of chopped mint.
6. Add 2 teaspoons of chopped chives.
7. Use half quantity of powdered mustard in place of French mustard.

Vinaigrette Dressing for Avocado

½ teaspoon French mustard
1 teaspoon clear honey
5 tablespoons sunflower/safflower/soya oil

1 tablespoon hot water
2 tablespoons apple cider vinegar or lemon juice
½ teaspoon salty seasoning

Mix together honey, mustard and salt and dissolve in the hot water. Add vinegar or lemon juice and oil and whisk briskly. This dressing is gentler and milder than French dressing and more suited to the delicate flavour of a ripe avocado.

Garlic Vinaigrette Dressing

6 tablespoons sunflower oil
3 tablespoons cider vinegar
1 teaspoon dry or 2 teaspoons French mustard

2-4 cloves garlic, pressed
salty seasoning
paprika

Blend together in a liquidiser or shake well together in a screw-top jar.

Mild Dressing for Salads with Fruits

2 tablespoons cider vinegar
3 tablespoons lemon juice
2 tablespoons water or apple juice
4 tablespoons sunflower or safflower oil

pinch salty seasoning
pinch paprika
pinch dried tarragon, basil & marjoram or steep fresh herbs

Blend together in liquidiser or shake well together in a screw-top jar. If fresh herbs are available, steep them in the prepared dressing for 24 hours before serving.

Enton Hall Salad Cream

1 pint (600 ml) milk
2 tablespoons cornflour
2 teaspoons raw Barbados sugar

1 teaspoon dry mustard
4 fl oz (125 ml) cider vinegar
salty seasoning

Mix the dry ingredients to a creamy paste with a little of the cold milk. Heat the remaining milk in a double saucepan. Whisk the boiling milk into cornflour mixture and return to double boiler to cook for 8-10 minutes, stirring occasionally. Cool. Beat in vinegar and add seasoning to taste.

(This tasty salad dressing contains very little fat or gluten, if gluten-free cornflour and mustard are used.)

Foresight Coleslaw Dressing

1 cup natural yoghurt   1 tablespoon raw Barbados sugar
1 tablespoon lemon juice   ¼ teaspoon French mustard
1 dessertspoon sunflower oil   ¼ teaspoon salty seasoning

Mix the dry ingredients to a smooth paste with the oil, then whisk in all
the other ingredients – or use liquidiser.

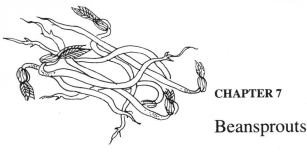

CHAPTER 7

Beansprouts

Sprouted beans, seeds and grains are the most nutritious foods you can possibly prepare and eat – the only food you can readily eat every day while it is alive and still growing. Think of the natural foods wild animals eat. The most intelligent animals that work for man include the horse, the donkey, the ox and the elephant. Do they need bacon and eggs for breakfast? Where do they find their protein? Their protein comes from living vegetation, and from dried grains. For optimum health man also needs living food and sprouted seeds are ideal for his different digestive system.

Buy fresh seeds, beans and grains, organically produced where possible, and check that they are suitable for human consumption (i.e. that they are not treated with fungicides). Besides health food shops, more and more supermarkets are now stocking the more popular seeds.

Try the following:

Triticale (a wheat-rye hybrid)
Organic wheat
Organic brown rice
Buckwheat (unroasted)
Mung beans (the usual Chinese beansprouts)
Adzuki beans (red Japanese beans)
Chick peas
Brown lentils
Corn (maize)

Alfalfa seeds
Sunflower seeds (hulled)
Sesame seeds
Radish seeds

Chinese lettuce seeds
Spinach seeds
Fenugreek

Successful sprouting can be achieved without any special sprouting equipment. All you need is:
Wide-necked clean glass jar – coffee jars are excellent.
Piece of cheesecloth, muttoncloth, net or buttermuslin large enough to clamp over the open neck of the jar with a rubber band (double thickness if necessary).

Basic Method:
1. Take about 2 tablespoons of the selected grain or pulse (more of the larger chick peas, or less – say 2 teaspoons – of the fine seeds, like alfalfa). Wash well in cold water in a sieve.
2. Put to soak in a basin well covered with cold water, for 8-10 hours for seeds and grains, 10-24 hours for pulses – until softened and

almost doubled in size. Strain off the soaking water (it is full of enzymes, so you could drink it! – see rejuvelac).

3. Transfer soaked seeds to the sprouting jar and cover with the net or cheesecloth, and secure with the rubber band.
4. Pour cold water *through* the net or muslin, into the jar to fill it, and then immediately drain it *all* off through the muslin. This is to humidify the air in the jar. Drain thoroughly – any excess water left after the initial soaking period is liable to cause rotting of the seeds.
5. Leave the jar in a relatively warm place (below blood heat) – the kitchen windowsill is fine. (Or it could be left in a warm dark cupboard for the first day or two, during the germination period – as is done for bought beansprouts. Mung beans can be bitter if sprouted in the light).
6. Rinse the growing seeds twice daily (wheat and triticale are the exceptions – see page 51) with cool water, *gently*, as the newly emerging shoots are very soft and vulnerable. The cool water washes away any waste produce, prevents the seeds from sticking together, and re-humidifies the air.

Depending on the variety and the temperature, the sprouts will be ready to eat in 2 to 7 days.

Chick peas are the fastest legume, adzuki beans one of the slowest. Bought Chinese beansprouts are grown in the dark in a very warm atmosphere. But light is advisable for the later stage of growth to enable the sprouts to develop chlorophyll in their green shoots. Generally, the sprouts are ready to eat when the root is 2-5 times the length of the seed, and any uneaten then should be stored in a closed container in the refrigerator, to retard the growth rate – otherwise the food-store of the seed would be exhausted, and the sprouts would spoil. Poor germination rate indicates old seed, drying out or waterlogging.

All these sprouted foods are an excellent source of vitamins A, B complex, C and K, minerals and amino acids.

SUNFLOWER SEEDS are best eaten after being soaked in the minimum of water overnight (as suggested in the muesli recipes). They will not grow large sprouts satisfactorily after being hulled – and are very irksome to detatch from their shells if sprouted whole. Soaked overnight, they are a useful source of vitamin D, B6 and B12 and all the essential amino acids. As they are so rich in protein, do not eat more than 2 oz a day.

SESAME SEEDS are especially rich in calcium, iron, phosphorus and methionine.

ALFALFA SEEDS after seven days growth in sunlight are an excellent source of chlorophyll, and rich in iron, calcium and phosphorus – nutrients needed to help rebuild decaying teeth.

BUCKWHEAT SPROUTS are rich in rutin and lecithin, helpful for healthy blood circulation.

WHEAT SPROUTED is much more nutritious and health-giving than cooked wheat (bread). Much of the starch is transformed into simple sugars (i.e. 'predigested'), the vitamin C content is increased by 600% and the vitamin B complex shows increases of from 20%-1200%. Wheat sprouts can grow long and tough, so eat while the sprouts are tiny, chew well – or mince the young wheatsprouts just before eating.

Method for sprouting wheat and triticale. After soaking the organic wheat in cold water overnight, drain, rinse, and transfer to sprouting jar, muslin-covered, for the daytime. Rinse and put to soak again the next night. Repeat the sequence of days in the sprouting jar, drained, and nights soaking in cold water, until the sprout is $1/8''$ long, when it is ready to eat. Then refrigerate, drained, to retard further growth.

PULSES OR LEGUMES cooked traditionally are sometimes difficult to digest, and raw (soaked but unsprouted) or inadequately cooked tend to be poisonous – but sprouting transforms them into first class nourishment. They are natural protectors from toxic metals.

MUNG BEANSPROUTS are now a well-known and generally accepted salad ingredient and are very easy and economical to grow yourself – so are recommended for your first adventure in sprouting.

The maximum nutritional value from your sprouted seeds, beans and grains is obtained only when you eat them raw and freshly grown. Heating destroys many of the B vitamins and vitamin C and kills the vital life-force in the enzymes and amino acids, which have multiplied up to 1300 times during the germination and sprouting period. If you want them hot for a change, try the Chinese stir-fry method of cooking till hot but still crisp, which is less destructive of their nutrient content.

Use beansprouts in salads, sandwiches, omelettes and as a raw garnish.

CHAPTER 8

Vegetables

Raw and cooked vegetables, with fruits, are 'protective' foods, which should form 45% to 65% of our daily diet. To obtain the maximum nutritional value from vegetables:–

1. Buy as fresh as possible those vegetables in season, locally grown and store in a cool, shady, ventilated place. Choose organically grown produce whenever possible. Next best are those grown without pesticides.
2. Prepare vegetables just before cooking (except whole root vegetables, which can be cleaned ahead) and do not leave cut vegetables soaking in water for long.
3. Use the minimum amount of water in the saucepan, and boil it before adding the prepared vegetables. (Remember that steam is just as hot as boiling water and cooks equally efficiently!)
4. Season sparingly and keep the lid on while cooking to prevent evaporation.
5. Cook till just done – don't overcook. This is **conservative cooking.**
6. Strain off the cooking liquid and retain it. Most of the water-soluble minerals and vitamins are in this stock. Use it in gravy, sauce, soup – or drink it!
7. Vitamins of the B complex group are lost by heating (and in refining). Vitamin C is lost in storage, wilting, by oxidation when cut up and exposed to air, by bruising and cutting with blunt knives, by cooking and keeping hot. No wonder so many of us are short of these vitamins – the little left at the end of the cooking process is often tipped down the sink!
8. When preparing root vegetables, wash them thoroughly (or scrub) rather than peel them. It saves time as well as nutrients! New potatoes boiled or steamed in their skins have much better flavour, and the skin alone is easily discarded when eating by those who object! Potatoes retain most nutrients when baked in their jackets either in the oven or in a 'Gourmette' type pan which uses a low gas flame to produce a 'mini-oven'.
9. Succulent vegetables like spring greens, cos lettuce, celery and watercress keep fresh longer if just the tips of their stems stand in fresh water – pretend they are cut flowers! Similarly freshly dug carrots, spring onions and beetroot benefit from giving their tip roots a drink of fresh water.

ASPARAGUS. When very young, try a little in your salad, raw. Cook by steaming or boiling, after washing throughly and tying up in bundles.

JERUSALEM ARTICHOKES – Scrub well. Steamed or boiled, they have a subtle flavour. Cook them till barely tender, so that they do not mush. Any left-overs make a delicious soup base with its own stock.

AUBERGINES. (egg-plant). Wash and slice in ¼″ slices, retaining the purple skin, and to reduce bitterness, sprinkle slices with salt, leave ½ hour, then wipe off salt and excess moisture. Sweat in a little oil.

Ratatouille

1 aubergine, sliced	*2 onions, sliced*
2 cloves garlic, crushed or	*4 tomatoes, skinned and chopped*
finely chopped	*2 courgettes, sliced*
2 green peppers, de-seeded and sliced	*Salty seasoning to taste*
3 tablespoons olive or soya oil	*little freshly ground black pepper*

Sweat the onions and garlic in the hot oil. Add the tomatoes, green peppers, aubergine and courgettes, and cook gently in a covered saucepan for about 15 minutes, giving an occasional stir to prevent sticking – if necessary, add a very little water. Adjust seasoning to taste. Serve hot or cold.

Ratatouille may also be made omitting either the courgettes or the green pepper, according to preferrence or availability. Omission of the aubergine also gives a delicious dish, though this should no longer truly be called a 'ratatouille'.

BEANS being legumes, contain more protein than other vegetables. Traditionally, beans were often served with a little bacon (see chapter on proteins for maximising their protein value). See also Pulses.
FRENCH BEANS are best picked young, when they need only topping and tailing, and conservative cooking till just tender.

Quick Bean Supper Dish

1½ lb (700 gm) French beans	*4 oz (100 gm) mild ham slices OR 4 oz*
2 hard boiled eggs	*(100 gm) prepared ham-flavoured*
little summer savory	*TVP*

Simmer the prepared beans with the summer savory. Combine with the other ingredients and heat through if required hot, serving with a little butter or vegetable oil to glaze. OR drain the beans, cool, and toss in French dressing before adding the egg slices and ham. Serve with wholemeal bread and butter.
NB   Grow your summer savory with your beans as it discourages black-fly!

RUNNER BEANS need stringing, and retain more flavour if chopped into half inch slices instead of shredding finely in a bean slicer. This is a vital point when preparing them for freezing, too. Young beans are good eaten raw.

Herbed Beans with Rice

1 lb (450 gm) runner or French beans   *4 oz (100 gm) cooked brown rice*
4 tablespoons oil or butter   *shoyu or tamari to taste*
1 clove garlic, pressed   *½ teaspoon summer savory*
½ teaspoon marjoram

Conservatively cook the prepared green beans, adding the cooked rice for the final five minutes cooking time. Heat the oil. Add garlic, herbs, drained beans and rice. Cook gently for few minutes. Add shoyu or tamari to taste, and serve.

BROAD BEANS. If you grow your own, cook the broad bean tops snipped off when fully flowering – they have a flavour between spinach and asparagus. When the earlier beans appear and the pods are only 3-4 inches long, the whole bean, pod and all, can be cooked and eaten with parsley sauce. Normally, broad beans are nicer if individually peeled after podding, before being cooked conservatively.

BEETROOT. Young tender beetroots are good to eat raw when grated – they are good blood-builders. Young beetroot leaves, cooked, are like beautiful spinach and very nutritious. Russian Borscht soups are different and good. To cook beetroot, wash very carefully, taking care not to puncture the skin or cut the root. Leave stubbs when cutting the leaves – beetroots 'bleed' when the skin is broken, leaking out colour, flavour and nutrients. After cooking, the stock needs to be strained through a sieve lined with kitchen paper, to remove all the grit. The cooked beetroot are easy to peel – and stain! Beetroot may be served hot with a glaze made from its own stock thickened with arrowroot, with a little lemon juice or cider vinegar added to taste. For salad use, marinate in this dressing:

1½ cups strained beetroot stock   *½ cup cider vinegar*
2 tablespoons honey or *dark*
muscovado sugar

Dissolve honey or raw sugar in the warm beetroot stock, add vinegar and pour over the sliced cooked beetroot. Beetroot may also be roasted in hot fat.

BROCCOLI or CALABRESE. Conservatively cooked and served with a little butter, these make a delectable dish on their own, eaten like asparagus. High in vitamin C.

BRUSSEL SPROUTS are rich in vitamin C. Conservatively cooked and served immediately, they are completely different from the foul smelling khaki-coloured mush which can result from over-cooking and long waiting! Finely sliced raw Brussel sprouts provide useful greens in a winter salad – introduce them slowly, as they tend to be 'windy'. *CABBAGE* also is high in vitamin C. Like Brussel sprouts, cabbage can be delicious or detestable, depending on how it is cooked! The greener the leaves, the more nutritious, so be sparing to the waste bucket! The chopped outer leaves can be cooked longer by putting them in the boiling water a few minutes before the rest. Cook conservatively till just done – or stir fry, so that they are not mushy. Raw outer green cabbage leaves are helpful as a poultice too (see Maurice Mességué's "Of Men and Plants").

Sauerkraut

Sauerkraut is traditionally made from just white cabbage and salt, with a few juniper berries, relying on the salt to preserve it. Here is a healthier alternative. It is a slow process which is made worth-while when all the vegetables and herbs have been organically grown and freshly picked.

8 lb (4 Kg) white cabbage
1 tablespoon caraway seed
2 teaspoons fine salty seasoning
1 lb (450 gm) fresh carrots
Fresh herbs as available –
parsley, tarragon, marjoram,
basil, bay leaves.

1 tablespoon juniper berries
1 tablespoon dill seed
1 tablespoon celery seed
1 lb (450 gm) fresh beetroot

These quantities will vary depending upon availability and the size of your chosen container, which should be a large glass, china, earthenware or stainless steel jar, at least 8″ deep, with neck wide enough to permit your fist to reach comfortably to the bottom. If pottery, make sure that it has a safe glaze unaffected by acid. Under no circumstances use aluminium. Wash the jar thoroughly and sterilise it with boiling water. An old shop glass sweet jar is ideal.

Enlist a friend to help you and choose a time when you need not be hurried, as the long operation must be completed at one go! If possible, secure mechanical help in the form of an electric shredder and mincer.

Crush the spice seeds in a pestle and mortar, and bruise the juniper berries. (Do not put in a liquidiser with a plastic container, or the flavour will permanently impregnate the container!) Wash the herbs and dry in a cloth. Wash the vegetables and drain well.

Finely mince or grate some white cabbage and pack it tightly into the jar, to form a layer about 1½″ deep. Punch it down so that no air bubbles remain and it becomes covered with its own juice. Sprinkle over with salty seasoning. Finely chop some of the mixed herbs, using bay leaves whole, and sprinkle right across the cabbage layer, pressing down firmly again. Finely grate some carrot and beetroot, and add a layer to bring the total depth up to 2″, again punching down firmly to remove all air. Then sprinkle over juniper berries and about half a teaspoon of the mixed spices.

Continue with these layers in the same order, adjusting the depth so that the final layer is of cabbage sprinkled with salt, and add a few spices as well. Check that all is thoroughly punched down and no air bubbles are trapped.

Cover with a large cabbage leaf, then a clean cotton cloth, weighted down by a large clean oval stone. Stand the jar in a large clean basin to catch any overspill, and put in a warm place where the temperature will not fall below 70°F (the airing cupboard?). Fermentation will soon start and continue for some weeks, during which time the juice may overflow. Check the top regularly, washing the cloth and stone, and removing foam and possible midlew from the top. Leave the sauerkraut in this warm environment for 3-4 weeks, then transfer to a cool, dry, dark, airy storage place. It will be ready for eating within a week, or will store untouched for several months. Once a jar is started, the top layer may spoil and need to be discarded (as with opened jam).

Sauerkraut is a very nutritious food, which should be eaten raw in order to enjoy its full health-giving potential, high in natural lactic acid and enzymes which aid the digestion of grains and counteract cravings for sugar.

CARROTS. When cooking carrots, scrub rather than peel them, and cut lengthwise rather than in rounds, as this helps speed the cooking time. High in vitamin A.

CAULIFLOWER. When steaming or boiling, cut the cauliflower into serving size pieces to aid faster cooking of the stem. A crust of bread on top of the cauliflower will minimise the cooking smell.

CELERIAC and CELERY. Celeriac makes a good alternative to celery, having a similar flavour, but no strings. Cut off the fibrous skin and chop into dice for cooking, putting straight into cold water and then boiling when ready (as it oxidises). Both are good as vegetables on their own or in soups and stews. Celeriac looks better served with a white sauce made from some of its own stock – or mash it with potato.

CELERY: The tougher outer stems are delicious cooked and greatly enhance casseroles and stews. Scrub well and cut into short lengths. Sweat in a little oil before adding water and simmer till tender. Do not discard the celery leaves – they add flavour to the stockpot and casserole, or to a salad.

CORN ON THE COB is best when young and pale yellow in colour, needing only five minutes cooking. Strip off the husks and silk, and cut back the stem before boiling. Older sweetcorn (deeper yellow) may need simmering up to fifteen minutes. Serve with butter.

COURGETTES. Young courgettes do not need peeling. Slice them and cook conservatively either in a little water, diluted wine or grape juice; or sweat them in a little butter in a tightly closed saucepan or casserole. *FENNEL* leaf fronds are used as a herb for flavouring fish. The root, finely sliced raw, is useful in salads, and for cooking

Cooked Fennel

2 heads of fennel	*1 tablespoon chopped fresh dill*
½ lb (225 gm) small tomatoes	*salty seasoning*
soya oil or corn oil	*freshly ground black pepper*

Thinly slice the fennel and sweat in the hot oil, until nearly done. Slice the tomatoes and carefully cook them with the fennel. Season and sprinkle with dill. Serve cold several hours after preparing to allow the flavours to blend.

KOHL RABI is a mild flavoured root vegetable. Remove the tough skin, dice and cook conservatively till tender. May be served with parsley or cheese sauce.
LEEKS with their gently onion flavour need careful washing to remove any trapped grit. Discard outer damaged leaves, but use as much of the green part as you can – or reserve it for the stockpot. Conservatively cook about 20 minutes till tender. Or sweat in a little butter in a tightly lidded saucepan or casserole. Leeks are also good braised: put prepared leeks in a closed casserole with a little stock and oil for about an hour.

Leeks Provencal

1 lb (450 gm) leeks	*2 tablespoons butter or oil*
2 cloves garlic	*2 tomatoes, skinned and chopped*
3 oz (75 gm) mushrooms	

Stand leeks upside down in a jug of luke-warm water for 10 minutes to remove sand. Melt butter and add crushed garlic. Add leeks cut in ½″ slices, placing separately over base of the pan. Cover and cook for 3-4 minutes. Turn each piece and add tomatoes. Slice the washed mushrooms finely and add. Simmer for further 8-10 minutes, covered. Carefully transfer leeks to a serving dish and pour over the Provencal sauce.

Leeks Vinaigrette

1 lb (450 gm) fresh leeks	*1 tablespoon butter or oil*
1 small glass white wine or *vegetable stock*	*vinaigrette dressing*
	1 tablespoon chopped parsley

Put leeks in a jug of luke-warm water, upside down, to remove sand. Cut sections 2″ long and halve lengthwise. Heat pan, add butter and leeks, shaking to glaze them all over. Add wine or stock, and simmer till barely cooked. Cool. Pour over vinaigrette dressing and sprinkle with parsley.

LETTUCE. If you grow your own lettuce and so know it is pesticide-free (bought lettuces may have been sprayed up to fourteen times, and so are not recommended in this book!) you may have a surplus. This is Norman's way of using them at Enton Hall:

Summer Lettuce

2-4 lettuce	*1 tablespoon butter or oil*
1 clove garlic, pressed	*1 small onion, finely chopped*
2-6 ripe tomatoes, skinned and chopped	

Wash lettuce and drain. Blanch. Heat pan, add butter and sweat the garlic and onion. Add tomato. Cut lettuces in half and add, cut side down. Put on lid and simmer for 10-12 minutes, till tender. Serve hot covered with its tomato stock poured over.

MARROW when young can be peeled and cooked like courgettes, including the seeds. Being a watery vegetable which readily loses its flavour into the cooking water, braising is advisable: grease a covered casserole and lay the peeled pieces of marrow across, season lightly, and bake till tender. Alternatively, remove the seeds only, cut and roast the marrow in its skin.

Vegetarian Stuffed Marrow

1 marrow, washed	*5 oz (150 gm) lotus TVP mince*
½ pint (300 ml) vegetable stock	*(beef-like flavoured soya granules)*
1 cup wholemeal breadcrumbs	*or 8 oz (225 gm) cooked Adzuki beans*
1 onion, finely chopped	*or brown lentils, well flavoured*
1 tablespoon butter or corn oil	*1 clove garlic, pressed*
2-3 tablespoons chopped parsley	*sprig rosemary*
little Tastex	

Soak the TVP in stock for ten minutes. Bring to boil and simmer for ten minutes. Sweat the onion and garlic in the fat. Combine and add herbs, breadcrumbs and Tastex to taste. Cut marrow in half lengthwise, remove seeds and fill with the stuffing. Place in baking tin with very little water. Bake 1-1½ hours in moderate oven till marrow is tender.

MUSHROOMS. The large open mushrooms have more flavour than button mushrooms. Field mushrooms excel in flavour, need several washings to remove grit from the gills, and should always be cooked. To serve as a vegetable: chop the mushroom stems and place in a saucepan with half an inch depth of water. Place the largest mushrooms in a layer over these, cup side uppermost. Pour a little melted dripping, butter or oil into each 'cup'. Sprinkle with fine seasalt, and a little grated nutmeg. Continue the mushroom layers in this way, cover and cook. They will steam from below while cooking in the fat; you will have a delicious mushroom stock for making soup with the stems and any left-over mushrooms – and mushrooms which are neither too fatty nor shrunken as your vegetable. Alternatively grill them with a drizzle of oil in the 'cup' or simmer in milk.

ONIONS are the most useful of vegetables. Conservatively cooked onions are delicious as a vegetable on their own, or with a sauce made partly with their own stock. Braised onions are tasty. Onion slices placed over fish or meat before grilling add to the dish. Stuffings, stews, soup, stock, casseroles – all gain from the inclusion of onions. If properly washed, the outer brown skins will add colour to the stock before discarding. See vegetarian dishes.

PARSNIPS combine well with carrots, conservatively cooked together, or mashed together. For roasting, par-boil the parsnips for five minutes before putting to roast. As I prefer to roast meat 'long and slow', I put the par-boiled parsnips and potatoes in a baking tin with dripping at the top of the oven when the joint is put to roast at the bottom; the oven set at 300-325°F, Gas 2-3. Turn the parsnips and potatoes once during cooking, and drain off the fat twenty minutes before end of cooking time, to facilitate a crisp golden finish.

PEAS. Let the children eat the youngest raw peas as they help you pod them – raw baby peas are a real delicacy. Cook peas conservatively with a sprig of bruised mint, or simmer in milk. Fresh peas are better nutritionally than commercially frozen peas and beans which are chemically treated to retain their bright colour. Cold cooked peas are good in salads with seafoods. Like beans, peas contain more protein than most vegetables.

POTATOES cooked whole are a good, satisfying, alkaline food – not especially fattening if cooked without fat. Whenever possible, cook potatoes in their skins – folic acid is present immediately beneath the skin and is readily lost in peeling.

Pommes Dauphinoise

1 lb (450 gm) potatoes	*3-6 cloves garlic*
6 oz (150 gm) Edam Cheese	*¼ pint (150 ml) milk*

Par-boil the scrubbed potatoes in their skins. Peel and slice. Finely chop the garlic and arrange layers of potato and garlic in a greased casserole with the grated cheese. Pour over the milk and bake in moderate oven till golden brown, about 1-1¼ hours.

Crunchy Mashed Potatoes with Beansprouts

hot boiled potato (unpeeled)   *butter or vegetable margarine or oil*

hot milk or potato stock
paprika   grated cheese – Lancashire or Parmesan
sprouted mung or adzuki beans
   (fresh and raw)

Remove the skins from the hot cooked potato and mash well with the
butter, hot fluid and paprika until smooth and creamy. Add grated
cheese to taste and incorporate well. Keep hot. When serving, add a
good spoonful (heaped) of raw beansprouts to each portion of hot potato
and fold in. Thus the beansprouts are not cooked and retain their high
nutritional value, while adding flavour and interest to the dish.

Jacket Potatoes. Potatoes are an excellent source of complex
carbohydrate and especially nutritious when oven baked in their skins,
so no nutrients are leaked out. They contain vitamin C, some B vitamins
and trace minerals, including iron. The skins provide added fibre and
cooked this way are not fattening – only 24 calories per ounce,
compared with 93 calories per ounce for pasta. Just scrub them well and
remove any small blemishes and prick whole skins to prevent bursting.
Bake about an hour to an hour and a quarter at 375°F, 190°C, Gas 5,
until soft in the centre. Besides serving with butter or cottage cheese
with a salad, they make delicious easy snack meals filled with many
combinations which you will enjoy devising. Here are a few
suggestions:

Smoked Cod's Roe Potatoes

large freshly baked potatoes   1 tablespoon home-made mayonnaise
2 oz (50 gm) smoked cod's roe   1 tablespoon tomato purée
watercress (see page 34)

Cut potato in half and remove pulp into a basin. Mash in the next three
ingredients and pile back into the potato skins. Reheat and serve with
fresh watercress.

Potato Eggs

large freshly baked potatoes   chopped chives
free range eggs   salty seasoning and paprika
butter or vegetable margarine or oil   alfalfa sprouts

Halve the large baked potatoes and scoop out egg-sized indentations in
each half. Into each hollow put butter, a little seasoning and chopped
chives and then the raw egg. Return to the oven until just nicely set.
Decorate with more chopped chives and a sprinkling of paprika on the
egg. Serve with alfalfa sprouts and a tomato.

Nut Case Potatoes

freshly baked potatoes
1 teaspoon Tastex
1 teaspoon sesame seeds
tossed green salad

2 tablespoons Harmony crunchy
    peanut butter
2 tablespoon vegetable stock

Dissolve the Tastex in the hot stock. Halve potato and mash the flesh with the stock and peanut butter and sesame seeds. Pile back in skins and reheat. Serve with a tossed green salad.

Sardine Specials

freshly baked potatoes
tinned sardines in olive oil
mung bean sprouts
wedges of lemon

natural yoghurt
tomato purée
freshly ground black pepper
crisp green salad

Blend the sardine oil with the yoghurt, tomato purée and black pepper. Rough chop the bean sprouts if longer than ¾", and mix in with the potato and yoghurt mixture. Flake the sardines and add. Correct seasoning and pile back into skins and reheat. Garnish with lemon wedges and serve with crisp green salad.

Horseradish Scramble Potatoes

freshly baked potatoes
horseradish cream
scrambled egg

vegetable stock or milk
parsley sprigs
tomato and onion salad

Mash a little hot vegetable stock or milk into the potato flesh and add a little horseradish cream. Reheat. Scramble the egg and pile over. Serve with parsley garnish, and tomato and onion salad.

Garlic and Cheese Potatoes

freshly baked potatoes
garlic cloves, pressed
curd cheese
sea salt and paprika

fresh parsley, chives, mint, basil,
    as available
parsley sprigs
beansprout and mushroom salad

Cut potatoes in half and mash flesh with the curd cheese, blended with the seasonings, crushed garlic and chopped fresh herbs. Pile back into skins, reheat and serve garnished with parsley sprigs and beansprout and mushroom salad.

Chutney Cheese Potatoes

freshly baked potatoes
home made chutney
golden salad

natural yoghurt
grated cheddar cheese
watercress (see page 34)

Halve the potatoes. Mash the flesh with natural yoghurt blended with chutney to taste. Refill skins with alternating layers of enriched potato and grated cheese, finishing with the cheese. Reheat until the cheese melts and browns on top. Garnish with watercress and serve with golden salad.

French Bean Bakes

freshly baked potatoes   *vinaigrette dressing*
French beans   *vegetable stock*
grilled streaky bacon   *tomatoes*

Conservatively cook small French beans until just tender. Grill the bacon and cut in strips. Mash the potato with a little hot stock and the bacon fat. Put back in skins. Toss the beans and bacon in vinaigrette dressing and pile on top. Reheat and serve with whole tomatoes.

Pulses: Tips for Cooking Dried Beans, Peas and Lentils

1. Plan ahead – most beans need to be soaked overnight, and need long cooking. Soya and lima beans are better soaked for twenty-four hours.
2. As a compromise when you cannot soak overnight: add three cups of water to each cup of beans (not soya or butterbeans), bring to the boil and boil rapidly for two minutes. Remove from the heat and leave standing for an hour. Again bring to the boil, boil rapidly for 10 minutes, then simmer until cooked.
3. Never add salt until the beans are almost cooked – salt will prevent the proper absorption of water during cooking.
4. Choose mung beans, brown, green and orange lentils, split peas and black-eyed beans when you need beans in a hurry. These can be cooked satisfactorily without the need to soak them.
5. Use the soaking water for cooking the beans, or you will lose the water-soluble vitamins and minerals. Use sufficient water so that the beans are covered when you start cooking, and do not allow them to dry out.
6. Five cooking methods:
    a) Long slow cooking in a slow oven about 300°F, if you have an Aga or Raeburn. First boil for 10 minutes to inactivate potentially poisonous enzymes blockers in beans.
    b) Rapid boil and then simmer in heavy saucepan with close fitting lid.
    c) Economise on fuel by transferring the beans (after soaking and rapid boiling for ten minutes) and their boiling stock into a heated wide-necked vacuum jar. Leave them in this for 6-8 hours or overnight, when they should be cooked.
    d) Use a slow cooking pot in the same way as a) or c).

e) Use a pressure cooker, to speed up the cooking process.
7. To avoid the mealy taste of beans, add a very little oil or fat to the cooking water.
8. Add to the flavour of your dish by using herbs and spices such as basil, oregano, bay leaves, onion, garlic, etc., and kombu.
9. Cook more than you need now – beans re-heat beautifully.
10. Remember to keep a stock of the dried beans, peas and lentils you like best. They store well and are good emergency rations when the hoardes descend and you do not have time to get out to the shops. Remember that soya beans are high in good value protein, and that other beans or peas when served with grains also produce a dish high in protein (see chapter on proteins). Beans added to a little meat can make a meaty dish which goes a long way.
11. Beans are high in fibre and make good filling meals for those watching their weight – and their pocket!
12. Louise always adds a 4"-6" strip of Kombu (sea vegetable) to her beans during cooking. This adds trace minerals, helps soften beans, brings out their flavour and makes them more digestible.
13. Adzukis, blackeye beans, brown and green lentils, cooked with wholegrains and vegetables, are recommended for enjoyable cheap complete protein meals (see Proteins page 195).
14. Soya beans tend to be a) the least tasty, and b) the least digestible of the pulses. Overcome a) by mixing cooked soya beans with other recipe ingredients the day before, to allow time for other flavours to be absorbed. Cooking with sea vegetables will help offset b).
15. Fish and pulses together make an indigestible combination.
More recipes are given in Chapter 11.

Cooking Guide for Pulses

(After pre-soaking the chosen beans, boil rapidly for 10 minutes, then simmer for approximate time given, or pressure cook for time indicated (using methods given in 6 b) and e) on page 62).

Chosen pulse, soaked	cooking time	pressure cooking time
Adzuki beans	1½ – 2 hours	(unsuitable method)
Chick peas (garbanzos)	3 hours	1 hour
Brown and green lentils	½ – 1 hour	15 – 20 minutes
Blackeye beans	1½ hours	35 minutes
Butterbeans (lima beans)	1½ – 2 hours	35 – 40 minutes
Haricot beans (navy beans)	1½ – 2 hours	35 – 40 minutes
Red kidney beans	1½ – 2 hours	35 – 40 minutes
Split peas	1 hour	(unsuitable method)
Soya beans (soy beans)	3 – 4 hours	1 hour

Boston Baked Beans

8 oz (225 gm) haricot beans   1 tablespoon molasses
1 large onion
For sauce:
2 oz (50 gm) butter or 4 tablespoons   1 onion, finely chopped
vegetable oil   ½ teaspoon mustard
1 tablespoon cider vinegar   1 tablespoon molasses
1 oz (25 gm) wholemeal flour   little of the bean stock
salty seasoning to taste   little honey if desired

Soak the beans overnight in plenty of water. Cook them slowly in this
water with the chopped onion and molasses. Drain and reserve stock for
the sauce. Sweat the finely chopped onion in the butter or oil, stir in the
mustard and the flour and gradually stir in enough bean stock to make a
smooth sauce. Add the vinegar and the molasses and simmer for five
minutes, stirring. Add the beans and heat through. Taste and add salt as
desired, and possibly a little honey.

Houmous – Chick Pea Paté

8 oz (225 gm) chick peas   1 pint (600 ml) water
1 clove garlic

Soak the chick peas in the cold water overnight. Add the crushed clove
of garlic and simmer till soft, adding more water if necessary. Drain,
mash and measure the mashed peas, adding 5 parts of the peas to 2 parts
of Tahini Dip, made as follows:

Tahini Dip

5 tablespoons lemon juice   ¼ pint (150 ml) Tahini (sesame seed
1-3 cloves garlic, crushed   cream)
salty seasoning to taste   ½ teaspoon ground cumin
7 tablespoons finely chopped parsley

Mix all the ingredients together, adding a little chick pea stock or water
if needed to give the consistency of smooth cream. Adjust quantities of
salt, cumin and lemon juice to taste. This dip is tasty to use as it is.
Combine it with the puréed chick peas to produce **Houmous** in the
proportions given above. Houmous makes a nutritious dip for crudités
for a party, or for a lunchbox, or a good filling for sandwiches and
baked potatoes.

Dhal – Indian Curried Lentils

2 cups red lentils   4½ cups water
1 bayleaf   2 onions, sliced
2 cloves garlic, crushed   2 tablespoons vegetable oil
1 lb (450 gm) tomatoes   1 teaspoon each of turmeric & coriander
1 tablespoon fresh lemon juice   ½ teaspoon each of cumin, chilli,
                                        ginger, mustard seed

Soak the lentils overnight in the water, then cook them gently with the bay leaf till soft. Sweat the onions in the oil with the mustard seeds. Add quartered tomatoes, spices, and cook gently for ten minutes. Add to the lentil mixture and simmer ten minutes more. Stir in the lemon juice. Serve with lots of boiled brown rice, vegetables and natural yoghurt.

Pease Pudding

1 lb (450 gm) split yellow peas
2 sage leaves
1 tablespoon wholemeal flour
salty seasoning

1 large onion, sliced
1 oz (25 gm) butter or oil
1 egg
freshly ground black pepper

Soak the peas overnight in plenty of water. Add the sage and onion and cook gently until soft. Remove sage leaves and strain. Liquidise while hot with the onion, butter or oil, egg and flour to produce a smooth paste. Adjust seasoning. Grease a pudding bowl, fill with the purée, cover and steam for one hour.

RED CABBAGE is a delicious hot cooked vegetable cooked this way:

1 lb (450 gm) red cabbage
1-2 teaspoons muscovado sugar
¼ teaspoon allspice
¼ teaspoon paprika

1 large cooking apple
juice of ½ lemon or 1 teaspoon
   apple cider vinegar
1 small onion, finely chopped

Wash and chop the cabbage and apple. Add other ingredients and just sufficient water to cook conservatively without boiling dry. Cook about 20 minutes, until just done; don't allow it to become mushy.

RED AND GREEN PEPPERS are very high in vitamin C. Steam, bake or sauté green peppers, reserving the seeds to add to stock or recipes to boost their vitamin C content. Peppers lend themselves to baking, filled with your favourite stuffing, and add unique flavour to many dishes.

SEAWEEDS OR SEA VEGETABLES are very high in trace minerals and are a good source of iodine. Valuable for their protective value, sea vegetables deserve greater use in soups, stews and pulse dishes (see page 189).

Wakame Soup

½ lb (225 gm) onions
2 pints (1200 ml) water
freshly ground black pepper

2 tablespoons dried wakame
tamari or miso to taste

Soak the dried wakame in the cold water for fifteen minutes. Chop the onion and add. Simmer till tender. Add tamari or miso and black pepper to taste.

Kombu (Vegetable)

Boil the kombu in water for about five minutes, reserving stock for soup if the kombu is served as a vegetable. Include when cooking pulses to enhance flavour and digestibility.

Arame or Hiziki (Vegetable)

Wash well in cold water and then soak for 20-30 minutes (reserve the soaking water). Cut into strips and sweat in a little hot vegetable oil. Add tamari and the reserved water and simmer for about one hour.

Nori (Garnish)

Toast the thin sheets briefly in a hot oven or above a gas flame. Crumble them for use in soups or with salads.

SPINACH is rich in vitamin A, E and folic acid, but also contains oxalic acid. For this reason it is an exception to the conservative cooking rule. After thorough washing to remove all grit, cook spinach leaves in plenty of boiling water till tender. Drain well in colander or sieve. Serve with little butter or squeeze of lemon juice, or little grated nutmeg. Good with poached egg, in quiches, or 'creamed' by liquidising with a little white sauce.

TOMATOES are good raw, grilled, baked, stewed or stuffed; used in grills, soups, stews, casseroles or with fish. Juice and purée are useful too! Freeze whole for winter cooking use. Tomatoes contain some vitamin C. (Unsuitable for those with arthritis, skin problems and digestive disorders).

WATERCRESS is especially nutritious – high in iron, vitamins C, A and folic acid. Use as garnish and in hot and cold soups. (See page 34).

CHAPTER 9

Soups

Soups can be a warming starter to a winter salad meal, a flavourful blend of nutritious vegetables subtly enhanced with herbs and spices. Soups are useful in bringing good nutrients to reluctant vegetable eaters and are economical in using up left-overs. Hearty thick soups and broths can be a meal on their own with wholemeal bread or dumplings, followed by fresh fruit or celery and cheese.

When a soup is to be liquidised in a blender, the vegetables need only be cooked till just tender and all their own stock incorporated. Take care to avoid over-long simmering when the soup is ready. Add any chopped parsley at the last moment.

See also the recipes for meat and vegetable stocks given in chapter 5.

Bouquet Garni is useful in preparing soups. Choose your own blend of the stronger flavoured herbs: Rosemary, thyme, bay leaves and parsley stems; add a piece of lemon rind and a clove or two and put in a little muslin bag to cook in the soup. Remove just before serving – or 10 minutes before, when the final delicate flavouring herbs are added.

When *sautéing* vegetables for soup, sweat them carefully in the oil or fat without browning them, to extract the flavour into the fat and soften the vegetables. Root vegetables take longer and should be added before garlic, leeks, mushrooms, etc.

If milk, yoghurt or cream is to be added to the soup, add it at the end and reheat without boiling, or it will curdle.

To *thicken* soup, remember extra cooked vegetables liquidised with the soup are a good alternative to the use of cornflour or wholewheat flour; or use leftover cooked wholegrains – brown rice, oats, barley, millet, etc. For slimmers, sprinkle in rice, oat or soya bran flakes occasionally.

Imaginative Vegetarian Soups

Contrary to the expectations of traditional cooks, vegetable soups can be easy to prepare and quickly made using left-over vegetables with their own stock, remains of savoury dishes and sauces, liquidised in a blender. When brought to the boil and then simmered together, check the flavour and add herbs, soy-sauce, tomato juice, Tastex, shoyu, tamari, miso, Worcester Sauce or a little grated cheese or grated lemon rind to enhance the flavour. Or use a vegetable Bouillon cube.

Starting from scratch, a good vegetable stock can easily be produced from chosen root and leafy green vegetables – carrots, onions, leeks, celery, potato, parsnip and parsley, spinach, broccoli, watercress, spring greens, pea pods, young dandelion leaves and nettletops, leek greens. Choose small quantities of the stronger flavoured vegetables (turnip, swede, dandelion leaves and parsnip) so that they do not predominate. Beetroot, carrot and turnip tops can also be used. Wash and chop the vegetables finely and put immediately into cold water in a tightly lidded saucepan. Bring to the boil and then reduce heat to allow the vegetables to simmer slowly for about ¾ hour, till the flavour is well extracted into the liquid. This vegetable stock, strained, is a good basis for soup, sauces and for cooking wholegrain pastas, pulses, brown rice etc., seasoning with yeast extract or Bio-salt, herbs, etc., 5-10 minutes before serving.

Norman's Secret Ingredient in soup-making is butter. While not strictly health food cookery, using extra butter in which to sweat the vegetables imparts an epicurean touch to a smooth liquidised soup.

Doris Grant's Recipe for Mushroom Soup

½ lb (225 gm) large mushrooms
  (open, dark gilled mushrooms
  have the best flavour)
1 pint (600 ml) water   *1 small onion, chopped*
1 medium sized carrot, sliced   *1 stick celery, sliced*
1 oz (25 gm) butter   *4 tablespoons double cream*
salty seasoning   *freshly ground black pepper*
freshly ground nutmeg   *3 teaspoons yeast extract*

Melt the butter in a saucepan, add the chopped onion and cook gently till a pale golden brown. Then add the vegetables, mushrooms, yeast extract and water. Bring to the boil, then turn heat to simmering point and cook for approximately 15 minutes, or until the vegetables are tender. Place in electric blender for 30 seconds, till smooth, then return them to saucepan. Re-heat, add a miserly pinch of finely grated nutmeg (this is a 'must' – it gives the soup a subtle flavour and greatly enhances the mushroom flavour), and season to taste. Just before serving add the double cream. For special occasions, a dab of whipped cream with a pinch of paprika on top makes a decorative finish.

Cream of Green Tomato Soup
Also suitable for slimmers

1 lb (450 gm) green tomatoes   *1 large onion*
1 pint (600 ml) vegetable or meat stock *3 tablespoons butter or vegetable*
1 small potato   *margarine*
salty seasoning and black pepper   *1 teaspoon oregano*

¼ pint (150 ml) natural yoghurt   honey
2-3 tablespoons chopped chives
  or parsley

Skin and quarter the green tomatoes and slice the onions. Sweat the onion in the hot butter and then add the tomatoes and cook for a further five minutes. Add oregano and seasoning to the stock with a scrubbed thinly sliced potato. Cook till potato is done, then liquidise and check seasoning, adding honey to taste. Reheat, then stir in the yoghurt and serve, garnished with chives or parsley.

Cream of Leek Soup
Also suitable for slimmers

3 leeks   2 bay leaves
1 potato   salty seasoning and black pepper
¼-½ pint (150-300ml) milk   1½ pints (900 ml) water or stock
2 tablespoons chives or parsley

Wash the leeks well to remove all grit and chop, using as much of the green as possible. Scrub and slice the potato. Cook these together in the stock or water with bay leaves and a little sea salt until just cooked. Remove bay leaves. Put through mouli or liquidise. Add milk and adjust seasoning. Re-heat and serve garnished with chives or parsley.

Green Leek-Top Soup
Also suitable for slimmers
When using up the top, dark green part of leeks for soup, cook with parsnip (to counterbalance the bitterness of the leeks) in place of the potato and proceed as for cream of leek soup.

Tomato Soup
Also suitable for slimmers.

½ lb (225 gm) carrots   ½ teaspoon dried basil or oregano
1 large onion, chopped   1½ pints (900 ml) water or stock
2 sticks celery, chopped   salty seasoning and paprika
2 tablespoons margarine or oil   freshly ground black pepper
1 large can tomatoes   ½ teaspoon honey – optional

Sweat the onion and celery in the hot fat until softened without browning. Add other ingredients, bring to boil and simmer until just cooked. Liquidise or rub through a sieve and check seasoning, adding a little honey if liked. Reheat and serve.

Cream of Artichoke Soup
Also suitable for slimmers

1 lb (450 g) Jerusalem artichokes   salty seasoning
½ lb (225 g) potatoes   paprika

1 pint (600 ml) water or stock   *¼-½ pint (150-300 ml) milk*
chopped parsley

Cook the sliced artichokes and potatoes in the water with a little seasoning until just tender. Liquidise with the milk. Heat and serve with chopped parsley to garnish.

Cream of Runner Bean Soup
Also suitable for slimmers

1 lb (450 g) runner beans   *1½ lb (675 g) potatoes*
2 pints (1200 ml) water   *4 cloves garlic*
salty seasoning   *2 tablespoons butter or vegetable*
½ pint (300 ml) natural yoghurt *margarine (optional)*

String the washed beans and chop into thick slices. Scrub the potatoes and cut into 2-3 slices. Boil together in the water with the butter, seasoning and chopped garlic till tender. Remove potato skins when cooked, if preferred. Liquidise the vegetables with their stock and the yoghurt. Reheat without boiling and serve.

Special Sea Green Soup

2 tablespoons hiziki (dried sea vegetable)1¾ pints (1 litre) water
2 tablespoons soya oil   *1-2 onions, chopped*
1-2 carrots, chopped   *1 cooking apple, chopped*
½ cup almonds   *1 tablespoons raisins*
¼ cup buckwheat macaroni *2 teaspoons miso (soya paste)*
1 bunch watercress, chopped *3 tablespoons chopped parsley*
2 tablespoons toasted sesame seeds *salty seasoning*

Soak the hiziki in cold water for 10 minutes. Sweat the onion and carrot in the hot oil till softened a little, then add the apple, water and drained sea vegetable (reserving the soaking liquid), raisins and almonds and cook a few more minutes. Cook the buckwheat pasta in most of the sea vegetable liquid till almost tender, then add the chopped watercress and cook just one minute more. Combine the onion mixture with the watercress soup. Mix the miso with a little cool stock and stir into the soup. Reheat without boiling, and adjust seasoning to taste. Garnish with chopped parsley and sesame seeds.

French Onion Soup

1½ lb (675 gm) onions, sliced *2-4 cloves garlic, pressed*
¼ teaspoon paprika   *4 tablespoons butter or vegetable oil*
grated nutmeg   *2 pints (1200 ml) water or stock*
shoyu or tamari to taste   *1 tablespoon Muscovado or raw brown*
2-3 slices wholemeal toast, diced or *sugar (optional)*
croutons   *Parmesan cheese*
freshly ground black pepper

Sweat the onions and garlic in the butter till transparent. Add Muscovado, spices, shoyu and water and boil for a few minutes. Serve very hot with the wholemeal toast ('croutons') and a sprinkling of Parmesan cheese.

Swede and Parsnip Soup
Also suitable for slimmers

2 onions, chopped	2 pints (1200 ml) water or stock
1 swede, sliced	salty seasoning
1 parsnip, sliced	little powdered mace

Sweat the onion in a little oil. Add the stock and other vegetables and simmer until just cooked. Liquidise, add mace and correct seasoning.

Sauerkraut and Mushroom Soup
Also suitable for slimmers

8 oz (225 g) sauerkraut	12 oz (350 g) mushrooms
1½ pints (900 ml) meat or vegetable stock	3 tablespoons butter or vegetable
2 pints (1200 ml) tomato juice	margarine
freshly ground black pepper	

Wash and slice the mushrooms, and sweat them in the butter for a few minutes. Add to the stock with sauerkraut and seasoning. Simmer for one hour, without allowing to boil. Add the tomato juice, stir, reheat, and serve piping hot.

Spanish Summer Soup
Also suitable for slimmers

1 pint (600 ml) tomato juice	oregano
½ pint (300 ml) chicken stock	tomatoes
2-3 tablespoons cider vinegar	cucumber
1 small onion, chopped	red and/or green pepper
spring onions	

Mix together the tomato juice, stock and vinegar, blending with a little raw chopped onion and oregano to taste. Chill. Prepare separate dishes of diced tomatoes, cucumber, pepper and spring onions and chill. Serve the chilled soup and hand the salad garnishes separately.

Provencal Summer Vegetable Soup (serves 8)

6 oz (175 g) courgettes, cut in ½" slices	6 oz (175 g) French beans, cut in ½"
1 onion, chopped	slices
2 young carrots, chopped	2 small leeks, chopped
3 tablespoons olive or sunflower oil	10 oz (275 g) tomatoes, skinned and
2 pints (1200 ml) water or vegetable stock	quartered
sea salt and black pepper	2 tablespoons fresh basil, finely
1-3 cloves garlic, pressed	chopped
2 oz (50 g) grated Parmesan cheese	4 oz (100 g) cooked French beans
2 oz (50 g) wholewheat or buckwheat macaroni	

Prepare the vegetables, leaving the courgettes unpeeled. In the hot oil, sweat the onion and leeks until soft. Add the water, French beans, carrots and seasoning and simmer about ¾ hour. Add the tomatoes, courgettes and macaroni and continue cooking for 15-20 minutes. Serve with grated Parmesan cheese.

Chicken Broth

1 boiling fowl (including feet)   *3-4 pints (2 litres) water*
outer celery leaves finely chopped   *3 large onions*
2-3 large carrots   *2 tablespoons Worcester sauce*
1 leek   *fresh or dried herbs as available:*
½ cup pot barley or brown rice or soup *(see page 29)*
mixture or lentils, etc.

Into a large preserving pan put the cold water, Worcester sauce, cleaned fowl and giblets. Bring to the boil and skim. Add barley or soup mixture and simmer for 1 hour. Clean and chop the celery, onions, leek and carrots and add, with the rice or lentils. Return to boil, then simmer with half of the mixed herbs (left whole if fresh). Cover and cook till all is tender. Remove cooked fresh herbs and replace with remaining herbs finely chopped, or add a few more dried herbs. Remove chicken for using for a separate meal (perhaps with supreme sauce made from some of the strained soup). Chop any left-over chicken and add to soup, adjust seasoning, heat through and serve.

Turkey Broth

Make in the same way from the cooked turkey carcass. Soup in excess of immediate requirements can be frozen for later use.

Bone Broth for Babies

Prepare as for beef stock in recipe in Flavour section.

Potassium and Silicon Broth

Tonic health and beauty drink.

4 oz (100 gm) carrots   *4 oz (100 gm) celery, including leaves*
1 bunch parsley including stems   *4 oz (100 g) spinach (leaves and stems)*
few comfrey leaves (optional)   *green lettuce leaves as available*
Tastex, tamari or shoyu   *salty seasoning*

Wash, but do not peel, then chop the vegetables finely and cover with cold water. Simmer gently for 30-40 minutes in covered saucepan. Strain the stock and flavour with Tastex or shoyu or salty seasoning to taste. Drink hot or cold as a revitalising health drink which helps clear the skin, harden the nails, add life to tired hair and tired people. Taken before retiring it helps promote sound sleep. A good tonic to take regularly as a health and beauty drink. Keeps, refrigerated for 2-3 days.

Lentil Soup
Also suitable for slimmers

4 oz (100 g) lentils
2 carrots, chopped
2 onions, chopped
vegetable oil

2 bay leaves
2-3 teaspoons lemon juice (optional)
2 pints (1200 ml) stock OR water
+ 1 teaspoon Tastex

Sweat the carrot and onion in a little oil. Add the stock, bay leaves and washed lentils and simmer until cooked, about 1 hour. Sieve or liquidise and add a little lemon juice and adjust seasoning.

Golden Pea Soup
Nourishing but free from oil, grains, milk and meat.

1 cup split peas
1 large onion
1 small parsnip
1 stick celery
1/2 teaspoon salty seasoning
chives or parsley (optional)

1 pint (600 ml) water
1 large carrot
1-2 tomatoes
little fresh lovage (1 leaf)
1/2 teaspoon paprika
2 pints (1200 ml) vegetable stock
    or water

Wash the peas and soak in one pint of water 24 hours. Scrub celery and chop finely. Prepare and slice the other vegetables and finely chop the lovage. Add stock, paprika and the swollen peas and their soaking water. Boil rapidly 10 minutes then simmer with lid just ajar for about 1 hour, till peas are tender. Add salt. Remove tomato skins. Liquidise or sieve the soup. Serve with chopped chives or parsley, or with a sprinkling of paprika.

Cream of Black Bean Soup

1 1/2 cups black beans (see page 62)
Piece of kombu sea vegetable
2 tablespoons vegetable oil
2 onions
3 sticks celery
1 pint (600 ml) vegetable stock
1 teaspoon lovage

1 bay leaf
black pepper
1 large potato
1/2 teaspoon salty seasoning
zest and juice of 1 lemon
chopped parsley

Wash the beans and kombu and soak in water to cover. Sweat the chopped onion and celery in the oil. Add the beans, their soaking liquid, the stock, lovage, black pepper and bayleaf. Boil rapidly for 10 minutes then simmer for 2 hours. Scrub and slice potato and add. Continue cooking till everything is tender. Discard bay leaf, and remove a few black beans for garnish. Liquidise soup with lemon juice and zest. Reheat the soup, thin with more stock or water if necessary, and check seasoning, adding salt to taste. Garnish with the reserved black beans and parsley.

Chilled Raw Beetroot Soup
Also suitable for slimmers

young beetroot
natural yoghurt
lemon juice as desired

salty seasoning and paprika
chives chopped

Grate the scrubbed beetroot into the yoghurt and liquidise with the seasoning and half the chives. Chill. Serve with swirl of extra yoghurt and the remaining chopped chives.

Chilled Cream of Cucumber Soup
Also suitable for slimmers

2 large cucumbers, peeled and chopped
1 large onion, chopped
3 tablespoons butter
salty seasoning
1 small potato, scrubbed and sliced

1 clove garlic, chopped
1½ pints (900 ml) vegetable or meat stock
zest of 1 lemon
1-2 tablespoons fresh dill
¼ pint (150 ml) natural yoghurt

Sweat the onion and garlic in the hot butter till transparent. Add to the stock with the cucumber, potato, seasoning, and half the fresh dill. Simmer till tender. Remove dill and liquidise or rub through a sieve. Stir in the remaining fresh dill, finely chopped, the lemon zest and yoghurt, and chill.

Watercress Soup
Also suitable for slimmers

½-¾ lb (225-350 g) potatoes
½-¾ lb (225-350 g) onions
1 pint (600 ml) water or stock
½ pint (300ml) milk (optional)

salty seasoning and paprika
1-2 bunches watercress (see page 34)
½ teaspoon dried dill or marjoram

Slice the potatoes and onions and cook in the stock or water with seasoning and herbs. Wash watercress and reserve a few sprigs for garnish. Liquidise remaining watercress in the soup with the milk. Heat through and serve with the watercress garnish. Also good served chilled.

Borscht I
Also suitable for slimmers

1¼ lb (550 g) raw beetroot
2 sticks celery
¼ lb (100 g) tomatoes
paprika
natural yoghurt

1 lb (450 g) carrots
1 large onion
2 pints good vegetable stock
1 teaspoon honey

Scrub thoroughly or peel the vegetables and slice finely into small strips for maximum release of flavour. Add stock, bring to the boil and simmer for ¾ hour adding a little more water if necessary. Liquidise. Serve with blobs of yoghurt.

Borscht II

1 tablespoon sunflower oil
2 large onions, chopped
2-3 large beetroots, grated or finely
  chopped
2 large tomatoes, skinned and
  chopped
½ teaspoon dill weed, dried or ¼
  teaspoon ground allspice
2 bay leaves
½ teaspoon dill weed, dried or ¼
  teaspoon ground allspice
salty seasoning to taste

2 carrots, chopped
1 large potato, peeled and chopped
  OR 1 cup sauerkraut
1 cooking apple, chopped or grated
2½ pints (1500ml) vegetable or meat
  stock OR 1½ pints (900ml) stock
  and 1 pint (600ml) tomato juice
natural yoghurt

Sweat the onions and carrots in the hot oil. Add beetroot, tomatoes, potato (or sauerkraut), apple and stock, and bring to the boil. Simmer till vegetables are almost tender. Add the bay leaves and dill weed and simmer 5 more minutes. Taste and adjust seasoning. Remove bay leaves and liquidise. Reheat and serve with a swirl of natural yoghurt.

Croutons

slices of wholemeal bread
garlic powder

sunflower or soya oil

Use stale bread cut into cubes and leave to dry out at room temperature for 2-3 days or put into cool oven (250°F) till dry. Sprinkle with garlic powder and oil and heat in oven, or deep fry and drain thoroughly.

Bavarian Dumplings

6 oz (175 g) SR 100% wholemeal flour
2 tablespoons chopped chives or onion
½ teaspoon salty seasoning
vegetable stock or soup

2 oz (50 g) vegetable margarine or butter

2 tablespoons grated cheese
¼ teaspoon freshly ground black pepper

Rub the fat into the seasoned flour. Add cheese and herbs, moisten with stock or soup to make a soft dough. Roll into balls about 1" diameter. Cook in boiling soup or wet casserole dish, for about ½ hour, till done (test by removing one and cutting in half). Dumplings add wholesome whole grain body to a soup – turn a soup into a meal!

"Cream of Fridge"
– The one where you always have the ingredients!
This is a common title given when guests ask what soup we are serving! It is made from any remaining vegetables and their stocks and available savoury leftovers in our refrigerator from the day before. They are

liquidised together and seasoned with herbs, perhaps a little Tastex, shoyu or Worcester sauce, or gravy and ends of meat dishes – and are most delicious! Brussels sprouts and savoy cabbage are the sole unsuitable vegetables. A little macaroni cheese does delicous things to a mixture of vegetables.

CHAPTER 10

Main Course and Supper Dishes

FISH

Grilled Whole Plaice

4 small whole plaice
1 teaspoon dried basil or marjoram
freshly ground black pepper
butter or vegetable margarine
2 tomatoes
parsley sprigs

1 large onion, finely chopped
½ teaspoon salty seasoning
3 tablespoons wholewheat flour or
  brown rice flour
1 lemon

Wash, trim and gut the fish and dry with kitchen paper. Mix together the flour, seasoning and herbs and coat fish with it. Remove the rack from the grill pan and generously grease the bottom. Sprinkle half the chopped onion on this, where the fish is to lie, and cover with the plaice, again sprinkled with chopped onion. Dot with small dabs of butter and put under medium hot grill to cook. Add a smear of butter as necessary while cooking and grill until just tender on the underside if very small – or turn and grill on the second side. Serve decorated with tomato slices and parsley sprigs, accompanied by one or two lemon wedges.

Baked Haddock
Also suitable for slimmers

2 lb (900 g) haddock (hake or cod)
1 large tomato
¼ pint (150 ml) fish stock
½ teaspoon dried oregano
freshly ground black pepper
1 tablespoon vegetable oil

1 onion
¼-½ green pepper
1 tablespoon cider vinegar
½ teaspoon dried thyme, or fresh
  sprig
salty seasoning

Clean and gut the fish. Then carefully remove the backbone system. Boil up the heads and backbones in seasoned water for 10 minutes to make the fish stock. Chop the onion and pepper finely and sweat in the hot oil. Remove from heat and add the tomato and dried herbs. Grease a casserole, lay in the fish and cover with the vegetable mixture and thyme. Pour over the fish stock and apple cider vinegar. Cover tightly and bake until just done – about 20 minutes at 300-325°F, 150-160°C, Gas 2-3.

Baked Cod Supreme
Also suitable for slimmers

4 cod steaks	1 bunch spring onions
1 carrot, scrubbed and grated	2 tomatoes, chopped
1 tablespoon fresh parsley or dill	salty seasoning
black pepper	

Prepare the spring onions and chop. Mix with the prepared vegetables, herbs and seasoning and line a greased casserole with half the mixture. Wipe the cod and arrange as second layer, with remaining vegetable mixture over the top. Add 2 tablespoons water, cover and bake till just done, about 20 minutes at 350°F, 180°C, Gas 4.

Oven Baked Fish Steaks
Also suitable for slimmers

4 thick cod or halibut steaks	1-2 carrots, chopped finely
1 green pepper, finely chopped	3 tomatoes, thinly sliced
6 spring onions, chopped	1 tablespoon chopped fresh dill
salty seasoning	freshly ground black pepper
2 teaspoons lemon juice	1/4 cup water
2 tablespoons oil or butter	1 1/2 cups natural yoghurt
lemon wedges and alfalfa sprouts to garnish	

Grease a tightly-lidded casserole with the oil. Mix together the prepared carrots, pepper, tomatoes, spring onions and dill and scatter half over the base of the casserole. Cover with the fish, sprinkle with lemon juice and seasoning to taste. Cover with remaining half of the vegetables. Pour over the water and sprinkle with remaining oil (or dot with butter). Cover closely and bake for 20-30 minutes at 350°F, 180°C, Gas 4 or until fish flakes easily. Pour natural yoghurt over the fish and warm through, for about 5 minutes. Serve with lemon wedges and alfalfa sprouts to garnish.

Fennel Stuffing for Fish
Good for use in grilled or baked fish

1 onion, finely chopped	1/2 oz (10g) butter or vegetable margarine
2 tablespoons chopped fresh fennel leaves OR 1 teaspoon dried fennel OR fennel seed	2 oz (50 g) fresh wholemeal breadcrumbs
freshly ground black pepper	salty seasoning
1 egg, beaten	

Just brown the onion in the hot butter. Remove from the heat and add the breadcrumbs, fennel, seasoning and egg. Stir to mix well.

Grilled Sprats or Sardines

Buy really fresh sprats or sardines to use the same day. Wash thoroughly but leave whole. Place in large grill tray, top to tail and grill under moderately hot grill for 6-10 minutes. They need no seasoning or fat and will cook in their own juices. Serve 6-12 per portion, depending on size and appetite, with paper squares and finger bowls, and eat them Spanish 'tapas' style – holding them in the fingers by the head and the tail, gently pulling off the soft flesh with the lips, so all the bones and the "guts" remain; they can be enjoyed without the difficulty of coping with tiny bones. A squeeze of lemon juice is all that is needed to enhance the delicious flavour – and wholemeal bread and butter. Complete the meal with salad to offset the natural richness of the fish.

Herring Roes on Toast

½ lb (225 g) herring roes	vegetable oil
wholemeal flour or soya flour	4 slices wholemeal toast
salty seasoning	lemon
paprika	tomatoes

Season the flour. Wash and dry the roes, cutting the dark line on the underside skin to help even cooking. Fry on both sides until golden. Drain well and serve on hot toast garnished with lemon and tomato.

Moules Marinières
Also suitable for slimmers

2 lb (900 g) fresh mussels	1 large onion, chopped
bunch of parsley	freshly ground black pepper
glass dry white wine	2 tablespoons butter or oil

Wash the mussels thoroughly to remove grit and beards, discarding those with broken shells and any that float. Sweat the onion in the hot butter, add the chopped parsley stems, wine, pepper and the mussels and add enough water to just cover. Cook over a steady heat until they open (about 7-10 minutes). Serve in large soup bowls, with the liquor poured over, sprinkled with chopped parsley, with wholemeal bread and butter.

Kedgeree

8-12 oz (225-350 g) smoked haddock	1 oz (25 g) butter, margarine or oil
2 cups water	2 eggs, freshly hard-boiled
1 cup brown rice	bunch of parsley
pinch saffron, turmeric or paprika	

Poach haddock in the water for 2-3 minutes. Drain, reserving stock for cooking rice. Remove bones and skin. Boil the rice in the stock with the haddock skins, spice and 1 tablespoon of the butter about 40 minutes, till just done. Remove skin. Flake the fish. Shell and chop the eggs. Chop 2-3 tablespoons parsley, reserving sprigs for garnish. Add remaining butter to the rice and stir in flaked haddock, egg and chopped parsley. Heat through carefully. Check seasoning and serve decorated with parsley sprigs.

MEAT

Pot Roast of Beef
Also suitable for slimmers

2½-3½ lb (1125-1575 g) brisket of beef wholemeal or soya flour
2 cloves garlic (optional)   salty seasoning
¾ pint (400 ml) water or stock   1 large onion, sliced thickly
vegetable oil

Wipe the meat and make small knife slits in the joint and push in slivers of fresh garlic. Coat joint with seasoned flour. Heat a little oil and fry the joint on all sides to seal it. Drain off any surplus fat. Place the beef on onion slices in the saucepan and add the water or stock. Simmer gently with lid tightly closed until tender (about 3-4 hours) or pressure cook for 1 hour at 15 lb pressure. Remove beef and turn under hot grill to dry out the surface before serving.

Pot Roast Brisket of Beef
Gluten and salt-free, low fat

3-4 lb (1,350-1,800 g) fresh brisket of   ¼ teaspoon freshly ground black
beef   pepper
1-2 cloves garlic   ½ teaspoon freshly ground allspice
3 tablespoons brown rice flour for   1 lb (450 g) onions, sliced
coating   1 stick celery, chopped
2 fl oz (50 ml) water   1 teaspoon marjoram

Wipe the meat and trim off the excess fat. Melt this fat in a large heavybased saucepan while you prepare the brisket by making small knife jabs in the surface and pushing in slivers of fresh garlic. Mix half the ground spices with the flour and dust over the brisket joint. Then brown the beef on all sides in its own fat. Remove joint and pour off the fat. Put prepared onions, water and celery in the bottom of the pan, replace brisket on top and sprinkle over remaining spices and dried marjoram. Cover and simmer for about 4 hours, turning and basting occasionally. When tender, remove the joint and strain the stock from the vegetables. Separate off the fat and liquidise the remaining juices with the strained vegetables to make a delicious gravy.

Casseroled Steak with Celery Jervaise
Also suitable for slimmers

12 oz (350 g) stewing steak	*2 cups water*
4oz (100 g) bacon	*1 teaspoon marjoram*
8-12 outer celery sticks	*soya or wholewheat flour*
4 tablespoons tomato purée	*1 tablespoon Worcester sauce or shoyu*

Wipe the beef, cut into inch cubes and coat in the flour mixed with the marjoram. Chop the bacon, wash the celery well and chop fairly finely. Grease a deep casserole and mix together in it the tomato purée, Worcester sauce and water. Stir in the meats and celery. Heat gently to just bring to the boil, then cook in very slow oven (250°F, 120°C, Gas ½) for 2-3 hours. A delicious unfatty dish without the usual onion and garlic flavour.

Spaghetti Bolognaise

8 oz (225 g) minced beef	*2 tablespoons vegetable oil*
1 large onion, chopped	*1 stick celery, chopped*
½ lb (225 g) tomatoes, skinned and chopped	*1 small cooking apple, peeled and finely sliced*
2 tablespoons tomato purée	*freshly ground black pepper*
salty seasoning	*bay leaf*
oregano	*8-10 oz (225-275 g) wholewheat spaghetti, or buckwheat pasta*
1 clove garlic, pressed (optional)	*1 extra tomato for garnish*
2 oz (50 g) grated cheese	

To the hot oil in a pan, add the chopped celery, garlic, onion and beef and fry for a few minutes until beef browns. Add the seasoning, herbs, apple, tomatoes and purée and a little water if too thick. Simmer gently, covered. Boil the pasta in salted water until just tender. Drain and reserve stock for other use. Add half the spaghetti to the cooked Bolognaise sauce and correct seasoning. Serve on a large hot dish surrounded by the extra spaghetti. Sprinkle with grated cheese and decorate with the final sliced tomato. Serve with a green vegetable or side salad.

Norman's Roast Lamb with Rosemary
Better method for slimmers

leg or shoulder of lamb	*1-4 cloves garlic*
1 large onion	*stem fresh rosemary*
wholemeal flour	*salty seasoning and black pepper*

Wipe the joint. Season the flour and rub all over the surface of the meat. Cut the garlic into long slithers. Make jab cuts into the joint with a pointed knife, inserting a garlic slither into each, with a small sprig of rosemary to plug the top. Coarsely chop the onions and place in base of covered baking dish with the lamb on top. Add 3 tablespoons water and cover. Bake at 300-325°F, 150-160°C, Gas 2-3 till tender, removing lid to baste and then crisp surface for the last half hour.

A clay baking 'Römertopf' is helpful in roasting with this method, as the lamb will roast in its own fat, the juices later being poured into a gravy separator to remove the fat and separate the meat juices for the gravy. The onion beneath the joint is a good addition, liquidised, to the gravy.

Irish Stew

2 lb (900 g) neck of mutton or lamb
1 turnip, cubed
1 lb (450 g) carrots, chopped
freshly ground black pepper
bouquet garni
1 tablespoon cider vinegar

2 large onions, chopped
1 lb (450 g) potatoes, scrubbed and halved
¼ lb (100 g) pot barley or pearl barley
1 pint (600 ml) water
salty seasoning

Put all ingredients into a large pan with a tight-fitting lid. Bring to boil and remove scum. Simmer about 2-2½ hours until the meat is tender. Leave to go cold and refrigerate so that fat can be removed from the top and discarded. Take meat off the bones and replace. Remove the bouquet garni, reheat, check seasoning and serve hot with greens.

Boiled Beef Roll

1 lb (450 g) minced beef
1½ cups soft wholemeal breadcrumbs
1 large onion, chopped finely
1 egg, beaten
1 little marjoram

1 tablespoon chopped parsley
1 teaspoon Worcester sauce or shoyu
½ teaspoon salty seasoning
¼ teaspoon freshly ground black pepper
1 tablespoon tomato purée

Thoroughly mix all the ingredients together in a bowl. Turn onto a floured work surface and shape into a long roll. Place on floured pudding cloth and roll up, securing the ends. Boil gently but steadily for 2 hours in stock. Serve hot or cold.

Fricandelles

1 lb (450 g) minced beef
1-2 onions, finely chopped
grated rind of 1 lemon
1 tablespoon chopped parsley
1 large egg
1 teaspoon Worcester sauce or shoyu
4 tablespoons oil

1 clove garlic, crushed
5 oz (150 g) fresh wholemeal breadcrumbs
½ teaspoon dried thyme
3 tablespoons stock or water
black pepper and salty seasoning
little wholemeal flour

In a large bowl whisk together the egg, stock and Worcester sauce. Add mince, garlic, onions, breadcrumbs, lemon zest, parsley, thyme, seasoning and mix to blend thoroughly. Roll into balls and coat with a little flour. Fry in hot oil, rolling them around till light golden on all sides. Drain well on absorbent paper before transferring to serving dish. Serve with tomato sauce.

Beefergine Loaf
Also suitable for slimmers

1 lb (450 g) minced beef	1 large aubergine
3 tablespoons fine bran or oatflakes	2 cloves garlic, crushed
1 tablespoon tamari or shoyu	1 egg
¼ teaspoon garam masala	½ teaspoon salty seasoning
black pepper	1 tablespoon chopped parsley
½ teaspoon dried thyme	Garnish: tomato and parsley

First cook the aubergine: prick it thoroughly, place in greased casserole, bake in oven, 350-375°F, 180-190°C, Gas 4-5 till tender (½-¾ hour). Cut open, remove and chop aubergine flesh and mix with all remaining ingredients. Tranfer to a greased loaf tin, cover with greased butterpapers and bake for 1¼-1½ hours at 350-375°F, 180-190°C, Gas 4-5. Turn out before serving and decorate with tomato slices and parsley.

Tasty Tender Steak Casserole

1 lb (450 g) stewing steak	4 tablespoons tomato purée
1 cup red wine	3 tablespoons vegetable oil
¼ teaspoon ground coriander	¼ inch ginger root, finely chopped
2-3 cloves garlic, finely sliced	3-4 sticks celery, including leaves
black pepper and salty seasoning	

Wipe and cube the stewing steak, removing fatty connective tissue. Mix together the tomato purée, wine, oil, spices, garlic and pepper. Stir in the steak so that each piece is well coated. Leave soaking in marinade 4-24 hours covered, in refrigerator. Wash and finely chop all the celery, stir into the marinade. Add salt. Transfer to casserole with tightly fitting lid (clay baking pot is ideal) and bake slowly, 275°F, 140°C, Gas 1 for about 3 hours, till tender. If the excess fat is spooned off this dish, it is suitable for slimmers. Also suitable for cooking in a slow cooker.

POULTRY

Keith's Super Spiced Chicken
Gluten-and salt-free, low-fat

1 roasting chicken	1-2 cloves garlic
½ inch ginger root	½ teaspoon ground ginger
1 teaspoon coriander seeds	½ teaspoon cumin seeds
½-3 dried chillies	zest and juice of ½ lemon
3 tablespoons natural yoghurt	3 tablespoons vegetable oil

brown rice flour for coating   *1-1½ cups brown long grain rice*
parsley sprigs   *lemon for garnish*

For stock and sauce:

carcase, neck and giblets from   *1 large onion*
  chicken   *1 carrot*
2 scrubbed potatoes   *reserved chilli seeds*
1-1½ pts (600-900 ml) water   *stems from the parsley*
¼ pt (150 ml) natural yoghurt

1. **4-12 hours before cooking:** Wipe and cut the chicken into serving
   pieces and slash the skin. Make the marinade: Crush the sliced
   ginger root, garlic, coriander and cumin seeds (splitting open the
   seeds). Use a pestle and mortar or place between greaseproof paper
   and press hard with a flat heavy knife blade. Carefully remove all
   seeds from the chillies (reserving a third for the chicken stockpot)
   and grind red flesh with the other spices. Add ground ginger, lemon
   juice and yoghurt and mix. Coat chicken pieces with the mixture.
   Leave to marinate, refrigerated, for several hours, preferably
   overnight.
2. **Make chicken stock** with the chicken carcass, neck, giblets,
   prepared onion, carrots and potatoes, reserved chilli seeds, parsley
   stems and water. Use strained stock for cooking the accompanying
   brown rice without salt.
3. **Cooking**: Drain the chicken joints from the marinade, coat in the
   rice flour and seal all over in the hot oil till golden brown. Transfer
   to a greased casserole, add the marinade, cover and bake 1-1¼
   hours at 300-325°F, 150-160°C, Gas 2-3 till tender. Drain off the
   liquid from the chicken, strain out the spices and separate off the fat
   with a saucière (for low fat dish) or simply pour off excess fat,
   keeping chicken warm. Add the extra yoghurt to the de-fatted
   cooking liquor and liquidise with sufficient peeled potato to produce
   a coating consistency. Add the reserved spices to the sauce in the
   pan before reheating without boiling. Arrange chicken on serving
   dish with the sauce and garnish with lemon slices and parsley.

Curried Chicken
(serves 2) Also suitable for slimmers

6-8 oz (175 g) boiled chicken   *½ cup milk*
1 large onion, chopped   *1 cup stock, chicken or vegetable*
1 tablespoon soya oil   *2 tablespoons sultanas*
1-3 teaspoon curry powder   *wholemeal flour or soya flour*
2 tablespoons desiccated coconut

Wash the sultanas in hot water and soak for ½ hour in the stock. Cut up
the chicken. Bring the milk to the boil and pour it over the coconut.

Sweat the onion in the oil until transparent, then add the curry powder and flour and cook it in, stirring. Stir in stock; add sultanas, milk and coconut and chicken pieces and transfer to casserole. The curry flavour will take time to penetrate the other ingredients, so a wait at this stage can be advantageous. Cook in a very slow oven for about 1-1½ hours. Serve with brown rice or lightly cooked white cabbage.

Casseroled Chicken

1 boiling fowl, prepared	½ pint (300 ml) tomato juice or
½ lb (225 g) carrots, sliced	1 can tomatoes
1 lb (450 g) small onions	wholemeal flour
1 clove garlic, finely chopped	salty seasoning
2 stalks celery, finely chopped	vegetable oil

Cut chicken into joints and portions, reserving carcase and giblets for making chicken stock or soup. Coat the chicken portions in seasoned flour and seal in the hot fat until nicely browned. Into a deep casserole, pour the tomatoes, sliced carrots, whole prepared onions, garlic, celery and chicken pieces. Cover tightly and bake in cool oven 275°F, 140°C, Gas 1 for 3-4 hours until tender.

Tender Chicken from a Really Ancient Boiler

1 very elderly boiling fowl, prepared	2 large onions, peeled and thickly
1 cup brown rice, long grain	sliced and 1 small onion
salty seasoning	1 pint (600 ml) milk
pinch mace	freshly ground black pepper
1 eating apple, studded with cloves	little sage (if fowl is rather fat)
1 clove garlic (optional)	1 bay leaf

This method involves cooking all day in a casserole with a close fitting lid, so prepare it at breakfast time for the evening meal. Wipe the fowl inside and out. Dust the cavity with mixed seasoning and herbs. Fill the cavity with the clove-studded apple, small onion and garlic and bay leaf. Into the greased casserole put the washed brown rice, milk, sliced onions and the prepared chicken. Sprinkle with seasoning and cover tightly. Bake in a very slow oven all day. It should not need attention but check that the oven is cool enough to prevent the chicken from becoming dry. This is also a good method for cooking a tough, elderly 'boiling duck' with appropriate changes of herbs.

Chicken Imperial
Rich party dish

1 roasting chicken, portioned	3 oz (75 g) butter or beaten egg
large bunch fresh parsley, chopped	4 oz Edam cheese, grated
1 large onion, finely chopped	freshly ground black pepper
1 cup soft wholemeal breadcrumbs	

Wipe the chicken and cut into joints, separating thighs from drums. Melt the butter. Mix together the finely chopped onion, parsley, cheese and breadcrumbs. Coat the chicken pieces in melted butter or beaten egg, then press a layer of the stuffing mixture all round them. Into a large greased casserole dish arrange the coated chicken and sprinkle any remaining stuffing over the top. Bake 325-350°F, 160-180°C, Gas 3-4 for about 1¼-1¾ hours until tender. This rich dish is a party favourite and needs no gravy or added seasonings.

Caribbean Chicken
Gluten free

1 free range chicken for roasting	*1 tin pineapple in own juice or fresh pineapple*
tarragon	*flaked almonds*
soya flour	*2 cups natural yoghurt*
salty seasoning	*thin honey*
2 onions, sliced	*pineapple or lemon juice*
vegetable margarine or oil	*2-3 cups cooked brown rice*
1 small green pepper	

Wash and dry the chicken. Sprinkle cavity with mixed tarragon, flour and salt and rub over the exterior. Put half onions in the cavity and remainder in the base of the covered roasting tin with the margarine. Roast the chicken slowly till tender. Let cool. Cut into fork sized pieces when ready to assemble dish. Cut pepper into strips. Cut pineapple into small pieces. Lightly roast the almonds and cool.
Dressing:
Blend the yoghurt with a little honey and lemon *or* pineapple juice to taste. Mix together the cold cooked rice, chicken pieces, dressing and 2/3 of the pineapple and green pepper pieces. Spread on a serving dish and decorate the dish with the remaining pineapple and pepper and flaked almonds. Serve cold.

Chicken Bermudian
Gluten free

1 roasting chicken	*1 tablespoon rice flour*
½ cup sultanas	*1 eating apple, quartered*
¼ teaspoon cinnamon	*1 small onion, quartered*
¼ teaspoon allspice	*2 bananas*

Wash sultanas and soak in water several hours. Mix together the spices and rice flour and use to sprinkle inside the cavity and rub all over the surface of the bird. Push apple and onion pieces into the cavity. Roast the chicken slowly till tender. Simmer the sultanas for 5 minutes in their soaking water and then liquidise to make the sauce. Cut the peeled bananas in half lengthwise and then into halves again, dipping each quarter into the sauce to prevent oxidation. Serve the chicken with the hot sauce, garnished with the banana slices.

Chicken with Apricots

1 roasting chicken	3-4 tablespoons cooked brown rice
salty seasoning	½ pint (300 ml) vegetable stock
freshly ground black pepper	1 bay leaf
pinch mace	4 oz (100 g) dried apricots, soaked for
2-4 rashes bacon (optional)	24 hours
2 onions, sliced	parsley

Cut the chicken into portions and season with the herb salt, pepper and mace. Line the bottom of a casserole with the bacon and place the chicken joints on them. Cover with the sliced onions and rice and pour over the stock with the bay leaf. Cover tightly and cook for 1½ hours at 300°F, 150°C, Gas 2 until tender. Gently simmer apricots in their soaking liquid for 5 minutes. Serve the chicken on its bed of rice, decorated with the apricots and sprigs of parsley.

Baked Boiling Fowl or Elderly Duck
Also suitable for slimmers

1 large chicken, oven ready	1 eating apple, quartered
½ teaspoon ground ginger	4 cloves
⅛ teaspoon ground mace	2 lb (900 g) ripe tomatoes, halved
salty seasoning	3 onions, sliced
freshly ground black pepper	bay leaf

Wipe chicken and dust cavity with a little of the mixed seasonings and spices. Stud the apple pieces with a clove and place in the cavity. Choose a suitable casserole with a tight fitting lid and nestle the bird in it, surrounded by the onions and tomatoes. Sprinkle over remaining seasoning. Add no fat or liquid. Bake in moderate oven 350°F, 180°C, Gas 4 for 2-4 hours until tender. Use the tomato liquid to make an accompanying sauce or a delicious soup.

GAME

Foresight Rabbit
Also suitable for slimmers

4 joints of young rabbit, about 1¼-1½ lb (575-675 g) or 1 lb (450 g) raw boned rabbit	1 carrot, sliced
	4 soaked prunes
	½ teaspoon dried marjoram or basil
wholemeal, soya or rice flour	fresh sage
salty seasoning and black pepper	fresh parsley
vegetable oil	fresh thyme
2 large onions, chopped	½-1 cup water
2-4 sticks celery, chopped	½ teaspoon Worcester sauce or shoyu

Coat the rabbit pieces in seasoned flour and seal in the hot oil. Drain. Mix together the prepared raw vegetables and put a third in the bottom of a casserole. Cover with the rabbit and the halved, stoned prunes, and the remaining vegetables. Sprinkle over the dried herbs and nestle the fresh herbs among the top vegetables to facilitate their easy removal before serving. Mix the water with the Worcester sauce and pour over. Bake in slow oven tightly covered till rabbit is tender, about 1¾-2 hours.

Rabbit Fricasse
Also suitable for slimmers.

young rabbit joints	salty seasoning
1 turnip, sliced	freshly ground black pepper
2 onions, sliced	bouquet garni
1 carrot, sliced	chopped parsley
2 tablespoons brown rice, washed	wholemeal toast

Cover rabbit with cold water, bring quickly to the boil then discard the water. Add vegetables, rice, herbs, seasoning and fresh water to cover the rabbit, bring to boil and simmer until tender (about 1 hour). Make a good white sauce from the stock, either traditionally or by liquidising sufficient rabbit stock with the cooked onions and rice and reheating. Serve rabbit covered in its sauce, decorated with carrot slices and chopped parsley sprinkled over. Surround by triangles of wholemeal toast.

Potted Rabbit

1 rabbit	1 teaspoon cider vinegar
2 teaspoons capers	freshly ground black pepper
2 onions, sliced	1 teaspoon zest of lemon
2 carrots, sliced	1 tablespoon parsley, finely chopped
herb salt	melted butter

Cover the rabbit with cold water, bring quickly to the boil and then discard the water. Cover the rabbit with fresh water, add the capers, onions, carrots, herb salt and cider vinegar. Bring to boil and simmer for 1½-3 hours, until quite tender. Cool. Strip the meat off the bones and mince it finely. Season to taste with black pepper, freshly grated lemon rind, parsley and herb salt. Mix in sufficient of its own strained stock to wet it well and transfer to a clean, dry frying pan. Heat, stirring constantly to evaporate the excess water and give a good spreading consistency. Pot into small sterilised jars, press down well and leave to get cold. Run the melted butter over the top to seal out the air. Refrigerate.

Rabbit Casserole

1 young rabbit, jointed	4 oz (100 g) open mushrooms, sliced
salty seasoning	2 large onions, sliced
sage and thyme	vegetable stock or water
wholemeal flour	½ cup pot barley, washed
vegetable oil	1 bay leaf

Season the flour and coat the rabbit pieces with it. Seal in the hot oil. Drain and transfer to large casserole. Add the mushrooms and onions to the hot oil and cook for five minutes. Drain and add to casserole with the other ingredients, with sufficient stock just to cover. Cover tightly and cook slowly for about 2½ hours until the rabbit and barley are tender.

Roast Venison

For roasting, most suitable joint is the haunch (leg and loin together). As venison is an exceptionally lean meat, it would become very dry if roasted in the usual way. Therefore the joint should be rubbed well all over with oil or butter, then sprinkled with seasoned wholemeal flour and herbs of your choice. Either roast the joint slowly in a covered, self-basting roasting tin, or cover the joint with greaseproof paper and use either a clay baking pot or a large casserole with a close fitting lid. Roast in a very cool oven, 250-300°F, 120-150°C, Gas ½-2 for 2-5 hours, depending on size, till tender, basting if necessary.

Casserole of Venison

Venison cuts other than haunch are best casseroled or stewed. Marinate the prepared meat before cooking, using 2 parts red wine to 1 part vegetable oil (or 2 parts oil to 1 part lemon juice). Use sufficient marinade to just cover the prepared meat. Leave covered in a cool place for 3-16 hours, then stew or casserole the venison in the usual way. After draining it from the meat, the marinade is best separated in a saucière. Then the oil can be used for sealing the venison and sweating the onions and the wine or lemon juice (with the meat juices) incorporated into the liquid used in cooking. Venison, being a wild, free-ranging animal, provides meat of the highest nutritional value, with very little saturated fat.

OFFAL

Liver, kidney, brains, heart and sweetbreads are very high in nutritional value and deserve more popularity. (see page 196, note 7).

Grilled Calves Liver

1 lb (450 g) calves liver sliced	1 large onion sliced in rings
freshly ground black pepper	butter or vegetable oil

Season the wiped liver with pepper and place on grill pan, cover with the onion rings and brush with butter or oil. Grill for 5 minutes, turn, replacing onion slices on the second side. Cook for a few minutes more until done.

Layered Liver

1 lb (450 g) sliced liver
2 onions, chopped
½ lb (225 g) ripe tomatoes, halved
* (or tinned tomatoes)*
1½ lb (675 g) potatoes, scrubbed and
* sliced*

½ pt (300 ml) stock or water
salty seasoning
freshly ground black pepper
sage, thyme and basil
½ lb (225 g) streaky bacon rashers
* (optional)*

Into a deep greased casserole, put layers of onion, liver, tomato and potato, seasoning with the herbs judiciously as you go and finishing with a potato layer. Pour over the seasoned stock. Bake covered in a moderate oven, 350°F, 180°C, Gas 4 for 1 hour. Then thicken stock if necessary and cover top with bacon rashers and cook for a further half hour.

Liver Dumplings

12 oz (350 g) minced liver
3 cups wholemeal breadcrumbs
4 eggs
½ teaspoon nutmeg
2-3 onions, finely chopped

1-6 cloves garlic, pressed or finely chopped
3 tablespoons vegetable oil
salty seasoning
wholemeal flour
vegetable soup

Mix well together the first eight ingredients, adding sufficient of the flour to make the mixture quite stiff. Form into balls and drop into fast boiling vegetable soup and cook for 10-15 minutes until cooked. Check by cutting one in half. Serve with the soup.

Caroline's Liver Goulash
Also suitable for slimmers

1 large carrot, grated
1 large turnip, grated or diced
1 large onion, finely chopped
little vegetable oil
wholemeal flour

3-3½ lb (1,575 g) liver in one piece
2-3 cups vegetable stock
salty seasoning
2 bay leaves
1 clove garlic, finely sliced

Brown the vegetables in the oil, blend in the flour and then the stock. Add bayleaves and liver. Simmer for 1¼-1½ hours, till tender.

Really Tender Liver
Buy liver cut in very thin slices. Make a thick coating of wholemeal flour and water, dip the liver in it, coating both sides. Fry briefly in hot

oil, turning once (about 2 minutes altogether). Transfer to a hot casserole containing hot homemade tomato and onion sauce, seasoned with a little seasalt and Worcester sauce. Put in cool oven for 15 minutes. Serve covered with chopped parsley.

Braised Lambs Hearts

2 lambs hearts	vegetable oil
marjoram or tarragon	1 lb (450 g) onions, sliced
wholemeal or rice flour	vegetable stock or water

Wash the hearts in running water. Cut in half and remove clotted blood, veins and arteries. Sprinkle with seasoned flour. Brown in hot oil. Place in deep casserole on bed of onions and half cover with stock. Cover closely and bake slowly at 300°F, 150°C, Gas 2 for about 2 hours, turning after one hour. When tender, thicken stock. Correct seasoning and serve sauce with the hearts.

Grilled Sweetbreads

Soak sweetbreads in cold water for one hour. Drain and discard water. Simmer in fresh water, lightly seasoned with seasalt and a little lemon juice, for 20-25 minutes. Drain and immerse in cold water again. Drain and slit lengthwise. Brush with oil and grill under medium heat for 5 minutes, turning, till golden.

Sweetbreads with Mushrooms
Also suitable for slimmers

1 lb (450 g) sweetbreads	2-3 sprigs parsley, finely chopped
butter or oil	½ lb (225 g) mushrooms, sliced
wholemeal flour	little milk
chives or spring onions,	2 eggs yolks, beaten
finely chopped	4 fl oz (120 ml) natural yoghurt

Pre-cook the sweetbreads, reserving the stock (as in recipe above). Make a sauce from the butter, flour, sweetbread stock, and add sweetbreads, onion and parsley, and simmer for 10 minutes. Meanwhile cook mushrooms in a little milk for 5 minutes. Add mushrooms to sweetbreads. Just before serving, mix egg yolks with yoghurt and add. Stir continuously until heated through, without boiling, and serve immediately.

Kidney Stew

4 kidneys	1 carrot, sliced
salty seasoning	4 oz (100 g) mushrooms, sliced
butter or oil	wholemeal or rice flour
2 onions, sliced	stock
lemon juice	celery seed or lovage

Scald kidneys by plunging into boiling water; remove skin, then soak in cold salted water for half an hour, to remove urates. Halve. Remove the hard tissue and tubes. Cut into slices, season, then satué in oil for 5-7 minutes. Remove kidney from pan. Add prepared vegetables and brown them in the oil, then remove. Add flour and stock, blending into a sauce with a little lemon juice and celery seed or chopped lovage. Transfer all to casserole and cook slowly till tender.

Grilled Kidneys

Prepare kidneys as in previous recipe. Season the kidney halves and grill under a low heat, basting with a little butter. Serve with Maitre d'Hotel butter.

Brains on Toast

1 calf's brain
2 eggs, beaten
1 tablespoon butter
1 large tomato
wholemeal toast

1 teaspoon shoyu or tamari
¼ teaspoon salty seasoning
2-3 tablespoons chopped parsley
2 oz (50 g) mushrooms, sliced

Wash brain thoroughly; remove membranes and blood vessels. Soak in cold water for 1 hour. Drain and cover with fresh water, add salt, bring to boil and simmer slowly for about ½ hour. Cut into slices and keep hot in its stock. Sweat mushroom in the butter, add the mixed egg and shoyu, and stir over low heat until beginning to scramble. Then add the hot, drained brains, and serve immediately on wholemeal toast.

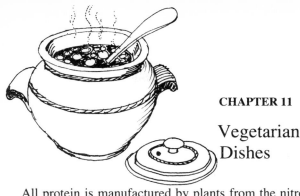

CHAPTER 11

Vegetarian Dishes

All protein is manufactured by plants from the nitrogen in the soil and the carbon dioxide in the air. Animals can obtain their protein by eating plant protein or other animals, as can man. Only 10% of the food given to animals appears as flesh, eggs or milk – 90% is used by the animals for energy. So meat protein is very wasteful of the earth's resources.

There are other reasons, too, for recommending non-meat dishes in the weekly eating plan – nourishment, economy and variety of flavour. Pulse dishes also provide a rest from cholesterol and protection from toxic metals (see chapter 23), so are positive contributors to good health.

Good quality protein is not confined to meat. The only perfectly constituted protein food for man is human protein – as found in breast milk! Meat does not even rate second or third best! (see Proteins, page 196)

Nuts and seeds are Nature's convenience foods. These are good protein foods which may be tastier and more digestible when lightly toasted in the oven, or under the grill, or dry pot-roasted. Dairy products provide excellent nourishment too – see also chapters on Milk Recipes and Health Drinks.

Hotpot of Mixed Beans
Also suitable for slimmers

4 oz (100g) red kidney beans or
  Adzuki beans
4 oz (100g) haricot beans or
  black eyed beans
4 oz (100 g) split yellow peas
1-2 sticks celery, chopped
soya or sunflower oil
½ teaspoon freshly ground allspice
  or ¼ teaspoon mixed spice
1 teaspoon Worcester sauce

2 tablespoons apple cider vinegar
1-2 onions, chopped
1-2 carrots, chopped
1-3 cloves garlic, pressed
1 teaspoon Tastex
2 tablespoons tomato purée
1 tablespoon black treacle or
  molasses (not bitter)
6 oz (175 g) brown rice

Garnish:
3 tablespoons chopped parsley OR
1 cup alfalfa sprouts

Wash the beans and soak in cold water for 24 hours. Boil rapidly 10 minutes then simmer gently for about ¾ hour in a large pan. Cook the

onion, celery and carrot in a little hot oil for a few minutes and add to
the cooking beans. Add pressed garlic, spice and all other ingredients;
stir well, and continue cooking until tender, about 45 minutes. Check
seasoning and serve sprinkled with chopped parsley or surrounded with
alfalfa sprouts. This is a complete protein dish as well as a tasty,
satisfying one. Serves 6-9.
N.B. Tips for cooking dried peas, beans and lentils are given on page
62.

Jay's Nut Roast for Christmas

6 oz (175 g) mixed nuts (excluding
   peanuts)
3 oz (75 g) wholemeal breadcrumbs
3 oz (75 g) grated Cheddar cheese
2 onions, chopped
½ cup vegetable stock or water

1 egg, beaten
1 teaspoon mixed herbs
1 oz (25 g) butter or vegetable
   margarine
½-1 teaspoon Tastex
3 oz (75 g) chopped mushrooms

Rough chop the nuts and mix with the breadcrumbs, cheese and herbs.
Sweat the onions in the hot butter and then add the mushrooms and cook
for a few minutes longer. Dissolve the Tastex in the warm water or
stock. Combine all the ingredients and mix well together. Put in a
greased casserole and bake for 30-40 minutes at 350°F, 180°C Gas 4.
Delicious hot or cold.

Cassoulet – French Casserole
Also suitable for slimmers

1½ lb (700 g) haricot beans
2-4 cloves garlic, chopped
3 tablespoons vegetable oil
1 lb (450 g) Tonabanga TVP 'sausages'
3 onions, sliced

4 tomatoes, sliced
2 oz (50 g) wholemeal breadcrumbs
2 pints (1.2 l) water
bouquet garni
salty seasoning and black pepper

Soak the beans overnight in plenty of cold water. Boil rapidly 10
minutes. Simmer for 1½ hours. Sweat the onion and garlic in the oil.
Pour into the beanpot with the tomatoes and bouquet garni and simmer
for a further half hour. Meanwhile grill the 'sausages'. Rub the inside of
a large casserole with garlic. Remove bouquet garni from the bean
mixture, and transfer to the casserole with the 'sausages'. Season to
taste. Sprinkle breadcrumbs over the top. Cook in slow oven, 325°F,
160°C, Gas 3 for about 1 hour. Also good without the TVP 'sausages'.
Serve with large green salad.

Beanburgers
Suitable for slimmers when baked

2 lb (900 g) cooked mashed beans
1 small onion, finely chopped

2 tablespoons finely chopped parsley
3 tablespoons wheatgerm or oatflakes

2 eggs, beaten   ½ teaspoon basil
tamari or shoyu to taste   freshly ground black pepper

Mix all the ingredients well together and check the seasoning. Shape
into patties and either fry in a little vegetable oil or oven bake on an
oiled baking sheet till done (in a moderate oven). Serve hot or cold.
Good for a change instead of sandwiches in a lunchbox.

Red Beanburgers

8 oz (225 g) Adzuki beans   3-4 sticks celery, finely chopped
piece kombu (sea vegetable)   1 onion, finely chopped
2 carrots, grated   ½ teaspoon oregano
4 oz (100 g) wholemeal flour or   2 eggs, beaten
   oatmeal or buckwheat flour   salty seasoning to taste
½ teaspoon black pepper

The day before, soak the beans and Kombu in plenty of cold water
overnight and cook gently till soft. (see page 63) Drain the beans,
reserving the stock. Add the other ingredients with a little flour and mix
well. Shape into patties and dust in wholemeal flour, oatmeal or
buckwheat flour. Shallow fry in a little vegetable oil, or oven bake on an
oiled baking sheet in a moderate oven till done.

Brown Lentil Savoury – Four Possibilities
Slimmers choose 1,2,4.

4 oz (100 g) brown whole lentils   ½ pt (300 ml) water
1 oz (25 g) margarine or oil   1 onion, finely chopped
1 carrot, finely chopped   1 large clove garlic, crushed
4 tablespoons tomato purée   ¼ teaspoon curry powder
¼ teaspoon kelp powder   ¼ teaspoon mixed herbs
¼ teaspoon paprika   pinch of mace

Wash lentils. Cook gently in the water until lentils are soft and all the
water is absorbed (about ¾ hour). Heat the margarine in a pan and cook
onion and carrot until softened (about 10-15 minutes). Roughly mash
the lentils leaving a few whole. Add the vegetable mixture, garlic,
tomato purée, herbs and seasonings and mix well together.
EITHER:
1. Heat all through in the saucepan and serve immediately.
2. Put into shallow greased casserole and heat through in a cool oven.
3. Roll into small rounds, dip each into beaten egg, then wholemeal
   breadcrumbs, and shallow fry in a little vegetable oil, till golden
   brown.
4. Roll into balls and leave to cool. Serve cold with salad.

Persian Nut Savoury
Gluten free

6 oz (175 g) organic brown rice	*5 oz (150 g) chopped nuts*
1 egg	*¼ pt (150 ml) natural yoghurt*
little grated nutmeg	*salty seasoning*
freshly ground black pepper	*½ oz (10 g) butter*

Cook the rice in boiling stock or water with Tastex till tender, 35-45 minutes. Drain (reserving stock). Beat the egg with the yoghurt and nutmeg and stir in the drained rice. Add seasoning to taste. Grease a casserole and put in layers of rice, then nuts, finishing with nuts. Dot with slithers of butter and bake for about 1 hour at 300°F, 150°C, Gas 2 or in a Bain Marie. (See "Cooking Wholegrains", page 109.)

Quick Hazelnut Roast
Gluten free

5 oz (150 g) grated hazelnuts	*5 oz (150 g) cooked mashed potato*
10 oz (300 g) tomatoes	*1 large onion*
3 oz (75 g) grated cheese	*chopped parsley*
salty seasoning and black pepper	*2 tablespoons vegetable oil*

Chop onion and sweat in hot oil. Skin tomatoes, slice and add. Mix in half the cheese with the other ingredients and put in greased casserole. Sprinkle remaining cheese on top. Bake 30-40 minutes at 375°F, 190°C, Gas 5.

Nut Rissoles or Roast

5 oz (150 g) grated nuts	*4 oz (100 g) wholemeal bread or rolled oats*
1 cup vegetable stock or water	*½ teaspoon Tastex*
1 large onion	*½ teaspoon tarragon*
vegetable oil	

Heat the vegetable stock and dissolve Tastex in it. Pour over crumbled bread or rolled oats and leave to soak. Slice and sauté the onion till soft. Add other ingredients and check seasoning. Pour into a greased casserole and bake for 45 minutes at 375°F, 190°C, Gas 5. Or shape into rissoles, egg and breadcrumb them and place on greased baking tin, dotted with a little butter and bake till brown. Casserole suitable for slimmers.

Aubergine Pizza
Gluten free

vegetable oil	*1 small aubergine*
1 egg	*salty seasoning*
¼ lb (100 g) onions	*4 oz (100 g) Edam or Lancashire cheese*
2 tablespoons tomato purée or 4-6 fresh tomatoes	

Paint the inside of the pie-dish with oil. Beat egg in a basin. Wash and dry the aubergine and slice finely in ⅛" slices. Dip them in the beaten egg and arrange overlapping to cover the base and sides of the dish. Pour remaining egg over and season. Slice the onions finely and sweat in a covered pan with a little oil, without browning, until transparent. Drain well. Grate the cheese and put ⅔ of it over the aubergine base. Pour over the onions. Spread over the tomato paste or the sliced tomatoes. Sprinkle over the remaining grated cheese. Bake in moderate oven, 350°F, 180°C, Gas 4 for about 30-45 minutes, till the aubergine is tender and cheese lightly browned.

PIZZA VARIATIONS

For the topping include: 2 oz (50 g) sautéed mushrooms or *anchovy fillets**
or mashed sardines* or black and green olives
or use crushed clove of garlic in place of the chopped onion

Vegetarian Pizza

1 lb (450 g) wholemeal bread dough	*black olives*
(after the first proving)	*1 onion*
oil	*6 oz (175 g) grated Edam cheese*
tomato paste or skinned tomatoes	*oregano, basil or marjoram*

Divide dough and knead into 2 balls. Roll out into two very thin circles to fit small sandwich tins. Brush tops with oil. Put to rise, covered, in a warm place, till doubled in size. Chop onion finely and scatter over the bases. Cover each with tomato and with the grated cheese. Sprinkle oregano or other herbs. Decorate with olives and slices of tomato. Bake at 375°F, 190°C, Gas 5 for about 20 minutes.

Chestnut Savoury

1 lb (450 g) sweet chestnuts	*6-8 oz (175-225 g) fresh wholemeal*
2 large onions, chopped	*breadcrumbs or rolled oats*
3 sticks, celery, chopped	*2 oz (50 g) mushrooms*
1 tablespoon vegetable oil	*1 egg*
little grated nutmeg	

Wash the chestnuts. Boil for 15 minutes, cool and scoop out the flesh from the skin with a teaspoon. Reserve a few whole peeled chestnuts for decoration. Sweat the onions, celery and mushrooms, in the oil. Rough chop the chestnuts and put into a bowl with all the other ingredients. Mix well and adjust seasoning. Decorate top with reserved chestnuts; put into a greased casserole and bake at 325-350°F, 160-180°C, Gas 3-4 for about 1 hour. Serve with peas or beans to increase the protein value of the meal.

*For not-so-strict vegetarians who eat fish

Caroline's Casserole
Delicious party dish

3 oz (75 g) protoveg TVP chunks OR	2-3 large onions, sliced
8 oz (225 g) cooked black eye beans	2 large potatoes
2 cloves garlic, sliced	3 tablespoons sunflower oil
1 vegetable bouillon cube	½ teaspoon marjoram
tomato purée	6 oz (175 g) mushrooms
3 oz (75g) grated cheese	4 eggs
2 tomatoes	

Parboil the potatoes. Cover the TVP chunks with water to hydrate. Add bouillon cube and 1 teaspoon oil and simmer with the marjoram till water is absorbed. Add tomato pureé to taste. Sweat the onions and garlic in the hot oil until transparent and tranfer to greased casserole. Cover with layer of TVP or cooked beans, then layer of sliced mushrooms and top with the sliced potatoes. Bake, covered, for 45 minutes at 350°F, 180°C, Gas 4. Beat the eggs and add the cheese and pour over the casserole. Slice tomatoes and arrange over the top. Return to oven, uncovered, till cheese melts on the top (about 10 minutes).

Buckwheat Rissoles
Also suitable for slimmers

1 cup unroasted buckwheat	2 cups water
½ teaspoon Tastex	1-2 onions, chopped
1 tablespoon oil	4 oz (100 g) grated cheese
2 eggs, beaten	½ teaspoon marjoram
½ teaspoon basil	buckwheat flour

Dissolve the Tastex in the water and boil the buckwheat for 2 minutes. Then cover tightly and leave standing for 20 minutes. Sweat the onion in the hot oil, then add the buckwheat, herbs, grated cheese and 1 beaten egg to bind. Shape into rissoles, dip in beaten egg and buckwheat flour. Grill or bake in the oven.

Vegetarian Moussaka
Also suitable for slimmers

1 large aubergine, sliced	2-3 onions, chopped
2 cloves garlic, finely chopped	1 lb (450 g) hydrated protoveg mince
2 tablespoons oil	(TVP) or brown lentils (cooked)
3 tablespoons tomato concentrate	½ teaspoon basil
1 teaspoon Tastex	2 bay leaves
2 oz (50 g) grated cheese (Lancashire)	

Hydrate the protoveg as directed. Sweat first the onion and garlic in the hot oil, and then brown the aubergine slices and put on one side. Put vegetable stock, tomato purée, Tastex and basil into the pan and mix well. Add the sautéed onion and garlic and the protoveg and simmer for

10 minutes. In a deep greased casserole, assemble layers of aubergine, mince mixture and grated cheese. Bake until cheese melts and all is heated through.

Egg Cutlets

2 oz (50 g) butter or margarine	3 tablespoons cornflour
½ pint (300 ml) milk	½ teaspoon Tastex
4 hardboiled eggs, chopped	2 tablespoons chopped parsley
salty seasoning and black pepper	little ground mace
1 tablespoon onion, finely chopped	wholemeal flour or oatmeal
vegetable oil	

Melt butter and add cornflour to make a roux, then stir in milk gradually to make a very thick sauce. Cook carefully for 5 minutes, blending in the Tastex. Add chopped eggs, onion, and parsley. Season to taste. Shape into cutlets. Coat with wholemeal flour and fry in hot oil until golden.

Eggs in a Nest
Also suitable for slimmers

2 lb (900 g) potatoes	1 tablespoon chopped chervil
1 oz (25 g) butter or vegetable margarine	1½ cups mung beansprouts
salty seasoning	¼ pt (150 ml) natural yoghurt
3 tablespoons chopped chives	4 – 8 eggs
2 tablespoons chopped parsley	

Scrub the potatoes, slice thickly and boil in water with a little sea salt. Remove skins when cooked and mash the potato with the butter, yoghurt and herbs. Stir in 1 cup of beansprouts. Put in a shallow greased casserole to keep hot while you soft boil and shell the eggs. Put the eggs in the centre of the nest, with the remaining beansprouts around the edge of the nest. Serve immediately.

Stuffed Eggs
Also suitable for slimmers

6 eggs	1 tablespoon chopped tarragon
1 tablespoon natural yoghurt	1 tablespoon chopped dill
1 tablespoon home-made mayonnaise	salty seasoning
2 tablespoons chopped chives	paprika
alfalfa sprouts or lettuce	

Boil the eggs for 8-10 minutes, then immerse in cold water. Shell and cut in half lengthwise. Carefully scoop out the yolks and mash with the mayonnaise and yoghurt until reasonably smooth. Mix in the fresh chopped herbs and add seasoning to taste. Pile the yolk mixture back into the egg whites and dust lightly with paprika. Arrange on a bed of alfalfa sprouts or lettuce leaves.

Nigel's Avocado Eggs

2 large ripe avocados
1 teaspoon lemon juice
4 small onions
2 tablespoons butter or oil
3 sprigs fresh tarragon or
  1 teaspoon dried tarragon
black pepper and salty seasoning

2 sprigs fresh chervil or
  1 teaspoon dried chervil
2 tablespoons potato flour or
  wholemeal flour
vegetable stock or water
4 free range eggs

Halve the avocados and brush with lemon juice. Put in very cool oven at 150°F, Gas ⅛, with the plates to warm gently, while making the sauce. Chop onions finely and sweat till tender in the hot butter, together with one tarragon and chevril sprig finely chopped (or half of each of the dried herbs). Remove onions when tender, drain and keep warm. Make a roux with the flour and remaining butter and add vegetable stock or water. Simmer for 5 minutes then add seasoning, remaining finely chopped (or dry) herbs and the onions. Cover while poaching the eggs in water containing 1 sprig of tarragon. Serve the warm avocado halves with the poached eggs in the centre, with the sauce.

Rice and Egg Casserole

1 cup brown rice
6 oz (175 g) mushrooms, sliced
1 oz (25 g) butter or sunflower oil
3 tablespoons chopped parsley
3 tablespoons chopped chervil

6 oz (175 g) French beans
2 bunches spring onions, sliced
salty seasoning and paprika
3 tablespoons chopped chives
4 hardboiled eggs, shelled and sliced

Boil the brown rice in 4 cups water with one large unsliced onion and herb salt and soy sauce, for about 40 minutes till just tender. Drain and reserve stock, onion and 3 tablespoons of the cooked rice. Cut the beans into ½″ lengths and cook in a little of the rice stock until just tender. Sweat the spring onions and the mushrooms in the hot butter until tender. Add the rice, beans and 2 tablespoons of the herbs and mix well. Transfer to a greased casserole, arranging most of the sliced eggs in the middle of rice mixture. Make a sauce from the reserved rice and bean stock and whole onion by liquidising these together with sufficient of the reserved cooked rice to thicken. Add the remaining parsley, chives and chervil and blend with the sauce. Heat the herb sauce, taste and adjust seasoning. Pour over the rice casserole and heat through. Garnish with reserved slices of hardboiled eggs and parsley sprigs.

Curried Eggs

1 oz (25 g) butter
1 oz (25 g) wholemeal flour or
½ oz (15 g) cornflour
1 teaspoon curry powder

4 hardboiled eggs
salty seasoning
wholemeal toast or hot brown rice
½ pt (300 ml) vegetable stock

Melt butter, add flour and curry powder and cook, stirring. Add stock slowly, whisking to make a smooth sauce. Simmer for 5 minutes. Add sliced eggs and season to taste. Heat through and serve on toast or brown rice.

Stuffed Marrow
Also suitable for slimmers

1 small marrow	*½-1 teaspoon dried sage*
2 large onions, chopped	*½ cup stock or water*
2 oz (50 g) margarine or oil	*4 oz (100 g) hazelnuts, grated*
4 oz (100 g) fresh wholemeal breadcrumbs	*salty seasoning*
1 egg	*black pepper*
3 oz (75 g) sliced mushrooms	

Sweat the mushrooms and onion in the margarine. Add the other ingredients and cook for a few minutes. Check seasoning. Cut marrow lengthwise and remove seeds. Fill with the nut stuffing. Put in greased casserole with 2 tablespoons of water and cover with a piece of buttered greaseproof paper. Bake at 325-350°F, 160-180°C, Gas 3-4 for about 1 hour, until marrow is tender.

Ruth's Favourite Cheese, Tomato and Onion Pie
Also suitable for slimmers

slices of wholemeal bread, buttered	*sliced tomatoes*
onions, sliced thinly	*grated cheese*

In a deep greased casserole, line the bottom with bread slices. Cover with a layer of onions, then tomatoes and then cheese. Repeat the layers of onion, tomato and cheese and top with the bread, buttered side up and more grated cheese. Add a little water or stock. Bake at 350°F, 180°C, Gas 4 for ¾-1 hour, till nicely browned on the top.

Ruth's Favourite Supper Dish
Also suitable for slimmers

onions	*Lancashire cheese, grated*
wholemeal bread and butter	*salty seasoning*

Slice onions thickly (or cut in half if small) and simmer till barely done in a little more water than normally necessary in conservative cooking. Serve in a large soup bowl covered in grated cheese, the onion stock poured over to melt the cheese. Eat with soup spoons and fingers of wholemeal bread and butter.

Cauliflower Au Gratin
Also suitable for slimmers

cauliflower   1 oz (25 g) margarine or butter
1 oz (25 g) wholemeal flour   ½ pt (300 ml) stock
¼ pt (150 ml) milk   4 oz (100 g) grated cheese
pinch mustard powder   salty seasoning and paprika
2 tablespoons wholemeal breadcrumbs 1 oz (25 g) extra grated cheese

Wash thoroughly the cauliflower, discarding only the tough leaves, and cut into serving size florets. Steam until just tender (10-15 minutes), retaining stock. Keep hot. Melt margarine and make a roux with the flour and milk and stock. Cook, stirring for 5 minutes. Add cheese and seasonings to taste and pour over hot cauliflower in casserole dish. Mix together extra cheese and breadcrumbs and scatter over the top. Brown under the grill. Leeks, celery, artichokes, marrow or broad beans are all delicious as au gratin dishes, made in the same way.

Cheese Pie

2 large beaten eggs   ½ pt (300 ml) soft wholemeal breadcrumbs
salty seasoning   OR barley kernels OR Scotts porridge oats
pinch cayenne pepper   6-8 oz (175 g) grated cheese
1 pt (600 ml) milk   ½ teaspoon Tastex
butter or oil.

Dissolve the Tastex in the milk and soak the breadcrumbs, barley kernels or rolled oats in it for ½-1 hour. Mix in the beaten eggs, seasoning and grated cheese, beating well together. Grease well a pie dish with butter and fill with the mixture. Bake at 275°F, 140°C, Gas 1 for about 1 hour until well set and nicely browned.

Cheese Soufflé
Also suitable for slimmers

2 eggs   6 oz (175 g) tasty cheese, grated
1½ oz (40 g) margarine, butter or oil   1 small onion, finely chopped
1 oz (25 g) cornflour   OR 2 tablespoons chopped chives
½ pt (300 ml) milk   ¼ teaspoon dry mustard

Make a thick roux with the butter, cornflour and milk and cook, stirring, until thick. Remove from heat. Beat in the egg yolks and other ingredients. Whisk the egg whites until stiff and fold into the mixture. Turn into greased deep soufflé dish and bake in moderate oven for about 30 minutes. Serve immediately it is ready. Flaked fish, meat (for non-vegetarians) or vegetables may be used in place of the cheese and mustard.

CHAPTER 12

Muesli and Grain Dishes

Muesli or Wholemeal Bread?

Both are made from whole grains, but one is raw and the other cooked – so which is better? Muesli! When made from raw ingredients, with the grains and seeds soaked overnight, muesli is a living food full of enzymes, amino-acids, vitamins and minerals, and should be eaten every day.

Muesli is the ideal quickly prepared meal, and should be considered for packed lunches, snack meals, home suppers as well as breakfasts, especially when salads are not eaten daily. When time is pressing, muesli can be made without adding the fruit – and fresh fruit eaten separately.

Where a milk allergy exists, muesli can be made with a little soya milk or nut milk (see page 173), or made with fruit juice only.

Choose a muesli base composed of organically grown grains, free from sugar, milk powder and maize. Organically grown whole grains, sprouted (see page 51), are ideal inclusions and are preferable to crushed, cooked grains not organically produced.

Soak the crushed muesli grains overnight in just sufficient water to wet them. The growth enzymes will develop and multiply, increasing the amino-acids (pre-digested protein) and overcoming the phytic acid present in the bran (which otherwise binds the calcium, iron and zinc). So the effort of soaking for 8-24 hours in a cool place rewards us with many extra nutrients otherwise unavailable!

Buy the flaked raw grains separately, and blend your mixture to help overcome specific mineral deficiencies. You can even produce a nutritious gluten-free muesli, individually tailored. Here is a list to help you choose the ingredients you need:

Muesli ingredient:	Rich in:
Almonds	Magnesium, potassium, vits. E, B complex
Apricots	Magnesium, iron, A
Alfalfa & other sprouts	Many vits. (especially B and C), minerals, enzymes, amino-acids
††Barley	Silica, manganese, molybdenum
Brazil nuts	Selenium
*Brewers yeast	Many minerals, vits, B complex, chromium
Buckwheat (raw, soaked)	Manganese, B1, B5, B6, molybdenum

Caraway seeds	Silica
Cashew nuts	Magnesium, zinc, A, B5
Coconut	Manganese
Hard figs	Silica
Fresh fruits	Vitamins C and P
Hazel nuts	Magnesium, potassium, manganese, A, B2, E
Honey	Enzymes and trace minerals
*Kelp powder	Iodine and trace minerals
*Lecithin granules	B1, choline, inositol
Linseed (soaked)	Potassium (mucillaginous laxative)
Maize flakes	Zinc
Millet (whole soaked)	Potassium, magnesium, iron, B1, B2
††Oats (crushed or sprouted)	Zinc, molybdenum, fibre
Peanuts (raw)	Potassium, manganese, E, magnesium
Pecans	Manganese
Pumpkin seeds (soaked)	Iron, folic acid
Raisins and Sultanas	Potassium, magnesium, iron
Brown rice flakes	Manganese, zinc
Rice bran (polishings)	Manganese, B1, Niacin, fibre
Brown Rice (sprouted)	Selenium, zinc, manganese
††Rye flakes (or whole sprouted)	Potassium, folic acid, zinc
Sesame seeds (soaked)	Calcium, magnesium, niacin
Soya flour or flakes	Potassium, molybdenum, magnesium
Soya Bran	Potassium, fibre
*Spirulina	Iron, B12, F
Sunflower seeds (soaked)	Potassium, iron, B1, molybdenum
Walnuts	Vitamin F, manganese
††Wheat bran	Zinc, iron, potassium, fibre, manganese
††Wheatgerm	Selenium, zinc, iron, molybdenum
††Wholewheat (sprouted)	Selenium, zinc, iron, calcium, manganese
Natural yoghurt	Lactic acid

*Food supplements – to be used sparingly, if at all.
††Best avoided if on a gluten-free diet.

(Sources: "Nutrition Almanac" – Nutrition Search, Inc.; "Mental and Elemental Nutrients" by Carl C. Pfeiffer, Ph. D., M.D.)

Whenever possible include oats (or oatmeal) which has a particularly health-promoting form of fibre.

Original Bircher-Benner Muesli

2 tablespoons raw rolled oats
2 tablespoons raw wheatgerm   Ruth's Changes:
4 tablespoons water
2 tablespoons sweetened condensed   *4 teaspoons nut cream and*
    milk   *2 teaspoons honey*
½ lemon
2 apples
2 tablespoons chopped hazel nuts

Soak the oatflakes and wheatgerm overnight in the water. Next morning add the fresh lemon juice, condensed milk and mix well. Coarsely grate in the apples (unpeeled but well washed), stirring well. Add nuts and serve immediately. The author (now a granny) was brought up on this breakfast – devised before the horrors of white sugar were realised! For my own children, I used honey and nut cream instead of the condensed milk. Now we have many more enterprising recipes, using the Swiss doctor's principles of combining raw cereal grains and fresh fruit for a healthy start to the day. But for reluctant muesli eaters, the original recipe is a good introduction to better breakfasts. The important factors with muesli are the pre-soaking, the higher proportion of fruit to grain and ample chewing – seldom practised by packet muesli eaters.

Ruth's Basic Muesli Recipe

4 tablespoons muesli base – of raw crushed cereal grains, unsugared
1 tablespoon sunflower seeds   *1 teaspoon millet*

These dry ingredients are soaked overnight in 5 tablespoons cold water. Next morning add:

½ cup orange juice   *2-4 tablespoons natural yoghurt*
2 teaspoons honey (or to taste)

Then stir all well together to mix the honey in thoroughly, then grate in:

1 cooking apple (Bramley)   *1 large eating apple*

and stir well together. Use a coarse, stainless steel grater, or chop the apples – it should be necessary to chew the muesli.
    To this basic muesli, add variations of choice; choose from:

1 tablespoon desiccated coconut   *1 tablespoon chopped nuts*
1 tablespoon raisins or sultanas   *1 tablespoon chopped hard dates*
½-1 ripe banana, sliced
Add any other fresh fruit available: e.g. blackberries, strawberries, raspberries,
blackcurrants, redcurrants, cherries, grapes; sliced pears, apricots, peaches or
plums.

Similarly in winter a few home frozen fruits can be added occasionally. If really needed, powdered supplements such as kelp can be added judiciously – personally I prefer to keep them separate as muesli is too delicious a dish to be spoilt!

Pearl Reddell's Dried Muesli

8 oz (250 g) jumbo oat flakes
8 oz (250 g) rolled barley
4 oz (125 g) sunflower seeds
4 oz (125 g) dried figs, chopped
8 oz (250 g) sultanas or raisins
4 oz (125 g) dried bananas, chopped

8 oz (250 g) rolled wheat
8 oz (250 g) rolled rye
2 oz (50 g) whole millet
4 oz (125 g) hard dates, chopped
4 oz (125 g) dried apricots, chopped
or minced

Mix all ingredients together. Sufficient for each meal should be soaked ahead in just sufficient water to cover. This comprehensive muesli may then be used as in the basic recipe with fruit, or eaten alone with apple juice or milk, with the fresh fruit eaten separately. In order to add a crisp element, add a little grape nuts, almonds, peanuts or coconut when serving.

Dutch Harnett's Gently Laxative Muesli

1 cup muesli base (unsweetened)
½ cup oat bran
½ cup chopped nuts

½ cup wheatgerm (raw)
½ cup mixed dried fruits

Mix all together. Soak serving overnight. Eat with milk or apple juice, or make into basic fruit muesli.

Gluten-Free Muesli For One

1 tablespoon soyabean flakes
1 teaspoon rice bran
1 teaspoon desiccated coconut
dried fruit to taste

1 tablespoon brown rice flakes
1 teaspoon ground almonds
1 teaspoon sunflower seeds

Muesli Rich in Manganese and Selenium*

4 tablespoons barley kernels or rolled
  barley or wheat
1 tablespoon coconut

1 tablespoon sprouted wheat
1 tablespoon walnuts, chopped

Grown the wheatsprouts. Soak the rolled barley and wheat overnight. Add other ingredients and make as basic muesli recipe.

Muesli Rich in Iron*

Use wholewheat flakes, wheatgerm, apricots, raisins, millet, sunflower seeds, soaked overnight. Add orange or lemon juice and sprouted wheat before serving, with apples.

Muesli Rich in Magnesium*

Use soya flour or soya flakes, soya bran, peanuts, almonds, cashews, hazel nuts, millet, raisins and apricots, soaking the last three.

Puréed Smooth Muesli

½ cup natural yoghurt
½ cup orange juice
1 teaspoon cold-pressed safflower
  oil OR *All Blend oil*
2 teaspoons honey

2 sweet eating apples
½ cup alfalfa sprouts
4 tablespoons raw wheatgerm
2 tablespoons sunflower seeds OR
  broken nuts cashew nuts

Soak sunflower seeds overnight. Put liquid ingredients into liquidiser, and add sliced apples and honey. Liquidise. Add alfalfa sprouts and liquidise. Stir in wheatgerm. Serve with the soaked sunflower seeds or cashew nuts to encourage chewing.

High Protein Muesli (Gluten-Free)

3 tablespoons sunflower seeds
½ cup natural yoghurt
4 good flavoured apples
Honey to taste
sultanas or raisins to taste

1 tablespoon whole millet
½ cup orange juice
½ cup broken cashew nuts
2 cups beansprouts or *alfalfa sprouts*

Soak the millet and sunflower seeds overnight. Add wet ingredients and grate in the apples, stirring. Add other ingredients; stir well and add honey and raisins to taste.

Variations: Use lemon juice instead of orange. Add ripe sliced banana, blackberries or any other available fresh or dried fruits.

Slimmer's Muesli

Any of these fresh fruit muesli recipes, with the proportions adjusted, are suitable for slimmers. The wholegrain cereal base, yoghurt and juice remain unchanged. Choose eating apples with a good flavour so that less honey and dried fruits are needed – tasteless apples spoil muesli. Add a squeeze of fresh lemon juice if liked. Add extra protein with soaked millet and sunflower seeds, sprouted wheat, alfalfa and beansprouts in preference to the calorie laden nuts.

A large bowl of fresh fruit muesli makes a filling, satisfying start to the day and is a meal in itself at any time.

Cold Weather Recipes

If the weather is cold and a warming breakfast is needed, there are variations on the traditional porridge theme:

*Food samples vary, depending on the soil and production methods (see page 10).

Five Grain Kruska

1 tablespoon whole wheat	*1 tablespoon whole rye*
1 tablespoon whole millet	*1 tablespoon whole barley*
1 tablespoon whole oats	*1 tablespoon wheat bran*
1 tablespoon wheatgerm	*2 tablespoons raisins or sultanas*

Buy organically produced grains if possible – otherwise ensure that you have untreated grains, suitable for human consumption. Coarsely grind them in a grain mill, coffee grinder or Moulinex chopper. Soak overnight in about a cup of cold water. In the morning just bring to the boil, then transfer immediately to a heated thermos jar for ½ hour for the completion of cooking at a lower temperature. The exact quantity of water will depend on the dryness of the grains – experiment to produce kruska with the consistency of thick porridge. It should not be mushy. Serve hot with milk and/or stewed apples or apricots.

This Scandinavian version of muesli is also full of vital nutrients. Eat it alone as a complete meal.

Rice Kruska
Gluten Free

3 tablespoons brown rice	*1-2 dried figs* (or *prunes*)
¾ pt (450 ml) water	

Soak the organic brown rice with the dried fruit overnight. In the morning bring to the boil and simmer 15 minutes. Transfer to heated vacuum jar for further 30 minutes cooking. Gluten-free.

Mr Amundsen's Oat Kruska

½ cup cracked oats	*¼ cup wheat, oat or soya bran*
½ cup raisins	

Soak all together overnight. Bring to boil and transfer to heated thermos to continue cooking slowly for 30-40 minutes more.

Kasha

1 cup raw buckwheat	*1-2 dried figs or prunes (optional)*
2 cups water	

Soak the buckwheat and dried fruit overnight. Bring to the boil, simmer five minutes. Transfer to heated thermos for final 30 minutes cooking. Serve with little sunflower oil.

Potato Porridge
Gluten and grain free

Boil about 2 cups water. Scrub a large potato thoroughly. Grate it into the boiling water. Stir and boil till the porridge thickens. This highly alkaline and cleansing dish is surprisingly good to eat with milk and perhaps a little molasses.

Packet Cereal Eaters
Choose whole-grain, unsugared cereals, free of chemical additives: e.g. Shredded Wheat, Shreddies, Weetabix, GrapeNuts – and fruit and nut muesli! If serving cornflakes, add raw wheatgerm and Frugrains, dried fruit, honey or molasses to sweeten. Most commercial cereals are wheat based. In American unsweetened puffed whole brown rice, millet and corn (maize) cereals are available – we should press for these here!

Guide to Cooking Wholegrains
Sometimes a simple dish of one wholegrain may be better tolerated by those with allergies than compound preparations such as shop-bought wholemeal bread. For this may have some chemical additives (and yeast!) and may be made from high gluten flour, inorganically grown.

Buy organically produced grain whenever possible, and wash in cold water. For savoury dishes, stock is preferable to water, measured by volume in the general proportion of 2:1 (i.e. 2 cups of stock to 1 cup brown rice). See table below.

1. *Boiling:* boil the measured fluid, add the grains, bring back to the boil, stir once only. Then simmer, covered, until all the fluid is absorbed, and the grain is tender but not mushy.

2. *Sautéing* produces a nuttier flavour, and is traditionally used in cooking Spanish rice dishes, buckwheat and bulgar wheat. After washing and draining the grain, place in a dry saucepan and heat gently, stirring till dry. Add just sufficient oil to coat the grains and sauté them gently, stirring, until golden. Then add boiling stock or water and continue as for boiling, above.

Guide to quantities and cooking times

Wholegrain	Water needed	Simmer for
8 oz (225 g) wheat	3 pt (1.8 1)	2 hours
8 oz (225 g) barley	3 pt (1.8 1)	2 hours
8 oz (225 g) rye	3 pt (1.8 1)	2 hours
8 oz (225 g) oats	3 pt (1.8 1)	2 hours
8 oz (225 g) brown rice	1½ pt (900 ml)	40-50 minutes
8 oz (225 g) buckwheat	2½ pt (1.5 1)	20-30 minutes
8 oz (225 g) millet	2½ pt (1.5 1)	½ hour
8 oz (225 g) Bulgar wheat	2 pt (1.2 1)	½ hour

Boil the water, add ½ teaspoon Biosalt or sea salt and stir in the clean grain. Do *not* stir again to prevent it from sticking. Double boilers are ideal to avoid burning (or use a heavy saucepan). Serve with leafy vegetables, tomatoes, mushrooms, onions; i.e. use in place of potatoes or bread.

3. *Vacuum Flask* method is a fuel saving way of cooking the quicker grains, which preserves more of the vital nutrients and avoids the danger of boiling dry and burnt saucepans! Soak the grains in cold water overnight. Bring to the boil then quickly transfer to a well heated vacuum jar for the completion of cooking at a lower temperature. Exact water quantity depends on dryness of grains – experiment to produce a cooked grain that has absorbed all the fluid but is not mushy. This method is recommended for Kruska and Kasha.

Savoury Brown Rice

2 tomatoes, sliced	*1 green pepper, sliced*
2 onions, sliced	*1½ tablespoons vegetable oil*
1 cup brown rice	*1 teaspoon Tastex*
2½ cups boiling water	

Sauté the tomatoes, pepper and onions gently in the oil to soften. Add washed rice and stir till glazed. Add boiling water and Tastex, bring back to the boil, stir once and cover tightly. Simmer gently till cooked (about ¾ hour) checking that it does not burn, but absorbs all the water (remove lid towards end of cooking time if needed to evaporate excess water). Stir once and serve.

CHAPTER 13

Breadmaking

Breadmaking is a very satisfying activity. It is an art which may take a week or two to perfect. Persist, and you will be rewarded with the delectable aroma of nutty, delicious, satisfying bread.

Where 100% wholewheat bread, free from chemical additives, cannot be bought, it is logical to bake it at home, freezing extra loaves till required. Ideally, choose organically grown, stone-ground, 100% wholemeal flour. I like to go one step further and grind my own flour from bio-dynamically produced grain, as I need it. The flavour is magnificent!

Practical notes to breadmakers:
Flour varies in its water content, so the exact proportion of water to flour must be flexible. Canadian 'hard' wheat, high in gluten, is not necessary for good home-made bread. Using the slow, cool overnight 'setting the sponge' or 'batter' method (as in many of these recipes) allows good gluten strand formation even with 'soft' English flours. With increasing incidence of gluten allergy this seems better sense to me.

Do not keep working in extra flour to the elastic kneaded dough – it will make the bread dry.

Different batches of bread will turn out differently. Active dried yeast does not keep indefinitely – if it does not froth up well in 10 minutes, you could need a fresh supply. Fresh yeast can be kept in the refrigerator for a few days or successfully frozen. Then it needs slow defrosting at room temperature and to be used immediately, in twice the quantity given for dried yeast.

Proving time varies also, depending on the yeast, the flour, the kneading and the humidity as well as the temperature. Sourdough bread is very much slower to rise. So choose to make your bread when you have other jobs to do around the house and you do not have to watch the clock for a deadline.

The dough-hook of an electric mixer, used at slow speed, is a useful energy saver – although I enjoy sharing the kneading with it.

Loaf tins need to be greased well, especially into the corners, preferably with salt-free butter. Fill the tins about two-thirds full to produce a nicely rounded loaf risen about an inch above the rim.

Bread is cooked when it sounds hollow when tapped. Usually I remove the loaves from their tins when they appear cooked on top, reversing them in the oven for their final 5-10 minutes, till sounding hollow when tapped on the bottom too. Then I like to wrap them in a clean damp tea-towel, on a cake rack, to prevent too hard a crust. Choose a good bread-knife which will slice your good home-made bread without tearing it into crumbs.

To refresh an uncut loaf which is not fresh enough, or to produce quickly 'steaming fresh bread' from the freezer, wet the crust all over and put in a cool oven 15-20 minutes for stale bread, 30-45 minutes for frozen bread.

Remedies for Specific Problems

If the loaf has collapsed and slices reveal doughy sticky streaks, the second proving was probably too long, allowing the loaves to collapse when put into the oven. If the slices of bread reveal small, hard lumps, the original dough was not sufficiently well mixed. If the top crust separates away, the loaf was not sufficiently well kneaded into shape.

If your bread has large holes it indicates overlong kneading or overlong rising.

If a slice of bread is soggy with a sagging crust, the dough probably was too wet and needed more kneading.

Soda Bread

Soda bread is not included, as bicarbonate of soda destroys B vitamins – it is better to make yeast breads or use baking powder in scone mixtures.

Quick Wholemeal Bread – and Pizza Base

2 lb (900 gm) plain 100% wholemeal flour 2 teaspoons raw brown sugar
½ pint (300 ml) very hot water   2 teaspoons salty seasoning
1 tablespoon dried yeast   ½ pint (300 ml) additional water
2 tablespoons vegetable oil   (See page 97 for toppings.)

Warm the flour and put into a large bowl and make a well in the centre. Dissolve the sugar and salty seasoning in the very hot water in a basin and add the additional ½ pint to give 1 pint (600 ml) of solution at blood heat. Sprinkle the dried yeast on the warm water and leave in a warm place till frothy (about 10 minutes). Tip a little of the yeast water into the well in the flour, stirring in the flour from the edges. Add the oil and the remainder of the warm yeast water, mixing continuously. If necessary, add a very little additional warm water, to incorporate all the flour into a dough.

Turn on to a floured board and knead till the dough is firm and elastic (3-5 minutes).

Divide into loaves, and knead into loaves (or 1 loaf and 4 large pizza bases). Knead into shape. Put into greased tins and put to prove in a warm place until doubled in size (about 1 hour). Bake at 350°F, 180°C, Gas 4 for 30 minutes, for 1 lb loaf, 20 minutes for the pizza bases.

Foresight Five Grain Bread
Also suitable for slimmers

1 teaspoon honey
1 pint (600 ml) warm water
3 oz (75 g) rye flour
3 oz (75 g) buckwheat flour
1 tablespoon sunflower oil

1½ tablespoon dried yeast
1¼ lb (550 g) 100% wholewheat flour
3 oz (75 g) cornmeal
3 oz (75 g) soya flour
2 teaspoons salty seasoning

In the evening: Dissolve the honey in ½ pint (300 ml) of the warm water, sprinkle over the yeast and leave to fluff up. Mix together all the flours well and divide into two, putting half into a large bowl. Pour in the yeast water and the remaining warm water and oil and whisk to form a smooth thick batter. Cover with a greased plastic film and leave in a cool place overnight to 'set the sponge'.

Next morning: Mix the salty seasoning with the remaining flour and gently stir into the 'sponge' to form a soft dough, adding more water or flour if necessary. Knead thoroughly on floured surface till smooth and elastic. Shape into 3 loaves and put in well-greased 1 lb loaf tins. Leave to prove (till risen by 75%). Bake at 350°F, 180°C, Gas 4 for 30-40 minutes. A good-flavoured, dark bread.

Slimmer's Wholemeal Bread – High Fibre

6 oz (160 g) fine oat bran
1 teaspoon honey
1½-1¾ pt (900-1000 ml) warm water
2 tablespoons dried yeast or
2 oz (50g) fresh yeast

3 lb (1350 g) plain 100% wholemeal flour
2 tablespoons vegetable oil
1 tablespoon salty seasoning including little kelp powder

In the evening: Put the bran and flour into a large bowl and make a well in the centre. Dissolve the honey in 1½ pints (900 ml) warm water and pour into the well. Sprinkle over the dried yeast. After 10-15 minutes (when the yeast is fluffing up) gradually work the yeasty water into the top flour, to make a thick batter (there should be no lumps but dry flour left underneath). Cover and leave in a cool place.

Next morning: Add the oil and seasoning and work all ingredients together, adding a little more water if necessary. Turn onto floured table and knead for 3-5 minutes. Divide into 2 large and 1 small loaves (or 4 small) and put into greased tins. Allow to rise, covered with greased sheet, till double in size (½-1½ hours). Bake for about 35 minutes for large loaves, 23-30 minutes for small loaves, at 400°F, 200°C, Gas 6.

Rye Bread
(with sourdough) Also suitable for slimmer's bread and rusks

1 lb (450 g) 100% wholewheat flour
1¼ pints (750 ml) tepid water

1½ cups sour-dough starter

In the evening: Mix the flour and water to a smooth thick batter in a large bowl (not metal). Add the starter and stir well. Cover with cloth and leave in a warm place overnight.

Next morning: Remove 1½ cups of batter from the bowl and return to the sourdough starter crock.

½ lb (225 g) rye flour	*2 tablespoons sunflower oil*
1 tablespoon salty seasoning	*1 lb (450 g) 100% wholewheat flour*
2 tablespoons molasses	

To the remainder add the molasses, rye flour, oil and salt and fold in gently, adding sufficient of the extra wholemeal flour to produce a soft dough. Turn the mixture gently with long movements of the wooden spoon to avoid breaking up the gluten strands which have formed overnight.

Scatter the remaining flour thickly over the clean dry work surface, and turn the dough on it. Knead gently for about 2-3 minutes till evenly worked; till soft and moist, but not sticky – do not attempt to incorporate all the flour. Shape into loaf. Quickly brush the warmed 2 lb (large) loaf tin with oil, and put the soft loaf in, to come about 2/3 up the sides. Slash the top with a sharp knife to release any large bubbles which may form. Paint top with little water. Cover with greased polythene and put to prove in a warm draught-free place for 4-5 hours, till risen by ⅓. Bake at 375°F, 190°C, Gas 5 for 30-35 minutes. This loaf keeps well in a cake tin for over a week. Delicious sliced thinly and spread with butter and Barmene or Tastex.

Light Rye Bread
(with sourdough and yeast) Also suitable for slimmers

Quick sourdough starter – prepare 7 days before needed:

1 teaspoon dried baker's yeast	*½ pint (300 ml) warm water (100-110°F)*
½ lb (225 g) plain 100% wholewheat flour	

Sprinkle the dried yeast on the warm water and leave to froth up (about 10 minutes). Mix into the flour to make a smooth thick batter. Put in a large glass screw-top jar (leaving plenty of headspace) and put to stand in a warm place for 48 hours. Then refrigerate for 5 days, when it will be ready for use. After use, add more plain flour and water to the remaining starter to make up to the original volume, leave in a warm place for 24 hours, then refrigerate till needed.

12 oz (350 g) rye flour	*¾ pint (400 ml) warm water (100-110°F)*
1 cup sourdough starter	

The evening before: Mix the rye flour to a thick batter with the warm water and whisk in the starter. Cover the bowl and leave overnight at room temperature.

1 teaspoon honey
1 tablespoon dried yeast
1¼ lb (575 g) plain 100% wholewheat
   flour
3 tablespoons vegetable oil

¼ pt (150 ml) warm water
   (100-110°F)
1 tablespoon salty seasoning
1 teaspoon poppy seeds
1 teaspoon caraway seeds

The next morning: Dissolve the honey in the ¼ pint (150 ml) warm water, sprinkle on the yeast and leave to froth up. Add the salt and seeds, the wholewheat flour, 2 tablespoons oil and frothing yeast to the rye mixture and work together to a soft dough. Knead for 10 minutes.
  Pour the remaining 1 tablespoon of oil into a large mixing bowl and grease the sides with it. Put the ball of dough in the bowl and roll it around to coat the sides with the oil. Cover with greased film and leave in a warm place to prove (about 2 hours). Grease 2 × 2 lb (large) loaf tins. Knead the dough again and divide and knead into 2 loaves, place in the tins, cover again and leave to rise until doubled in bulk (about 1 hour in warm place).
  Bake for 30-35 minutes at 350°F, 180°C, Gas 4 until nicely browned and hollow sounding when tapped. Wrap in damp cloth on wire rack while cooling. Good with smoked fish and for sandwiches. Keeps well.
  The replenished starter will be ready for more breadmaking one or two weeks later.

Quick Wholemeal Loaf or Rolls with Vitamin C

1 × 25 mg vitamin C tablet
2 tablespoons sunflower oil
2 oz (50 g) fresh yeast
1½ teaspoons salty seasoning

1½ lb (675 g) wholewheat flour at room
   temperature
¾ pint (450 ml) water (100°F)
½ teaspoon kelp powder

Crush the vitamin tablet and then cream into the fresh yeast. Add the tepid water and leave to foam. Mix together the flour, kelp and salt. Make a well in the centre and pour on yeast liquid and oil. Mix into a soft dough ball. Tip onto floured table and knead for 3-5 minutes.
A. Divide into 2½ oz- 4 oz pieces and work into rolls, well spaced out on greased baking tray and cover while rising. When proved, paint top lightly with beaten egg and bake for about 15 minutes.
B. Divide into two loaves, knead and put into greased tins. Cover with greased polythene sheet and put to rise till doubled in size. Bake for 22-25 minutes at 400°F, 200°C, Gas 6.

Light Spongy Wholemeal Bread

½ lb (225 g) potatoes and	to give 1 cup mashed potato and
½ pt (300 ml) water	to give 1 cup potato stock
2 tablespoons raw brown sugar	1 cup warm water (100-110°F)
2 tablespoons dried yeast	2 eggs
¼ pt (150 ml) vegetable oil	4 teaspoons salty seasoning
2½ lb (1125 g) 100% plain	1 tablespoon soft butter or
wholemeal flour	extra oil
Glaze: (optional)	1 tablespoon egg white (reserved
1 tablespoon cold water	from the eggs)

Scrub potatoes thoroughly and slice each in three. Cook in the water till tender then drain, reserving the stock; peel the potatoes and mash thoroughly. Dissolve the sugar in the warm water in a basin and sprinkle on the yeast. Leave to froth up. In another basin, beat the eggs (reserve 1 tablespoon egg white for the glaze if required) and add the cool potato stock, the mashed potato and the oil. Whisk together well.

Stir the salt into the flour in a large mixing bowl and make a well in the centre. Pour in the yeast and potato mixtures and blend together, gradually working in the flour, to make a firm dough. Turn out on to floured board and knead for about 10 minutes. Generously grease a large bowl with the butter and put the dough in it, rolling the dough around to coat it with butter all over. Cover with a greased plastic film and place in refrigerator to rise slowly. When doubled in size, remove and punch down to original size. Rest the dough for about 5 minutes while you thoroughly grease two 2 lb (large) tins, then knead for about 5 minutes. Divide into two and knead into two loaves. Cover and leave to rise until doubled in size (it may be slow rising, so keep an eye on it). Gently brush on the egg glaze (made by combining the egg white and water) and bake for 35-45 minutes at 375°F, 190°C, Gas 5.

Remove loaves from tins for the final 5-10 minutes of baking to colour the crust. Cool thoroughly before cutting. This bread keeps very well and is very good toasted. It is slow to make but appeals to those accustomed to the soft 'sponginess' of English white bread.

Doris Grant has kindly sent her recipe for:

The Grant Loaf – no kneading – easier to make than a mud pie!

3 lb (1350 ml) stone-ground 100% wholewheat flour	2 teaspoons salt (according to taste)
	2 pt (1200 ml) water at blood heat
3 teaspoons dried yeast or 1 oz (25 g) fresh yeast	6 teaspoons Barbados sugar or honey or black molasses

If using fresh yeast, mix it in a small bowl with 4 teaspoons Barbados sugar, honey or black molasses and add ¼ pint (150 ml) water at blood heat. Leave for 10 minutes or so to froth up before adding to the flour with the rest of the water. To make 1 loaf, use a scant ½ oz fresh yeast mixed with 2 teaspoons sugar, etc. with about 8 tablespoons water.

Method: Mix the salt with flour (in very cold weather, warm flour slightly – enough to take off the chill). Place in a cup 3 tablespoons of the water at blood heat; the temperature is important – it is best to check with a cooking thermometer which should register 35-38°C. Sprinkle the dried yeast on top. Leave for 2 minutes or so for the yeast to soak, then add the sugar, honey or black molasses. In about 10-15 minutes this should have produced a thick, creamy froth. Pour this into the flour and add the rest of the water. Mix well – by hand is best – for a minute or so, working from sides to middle, till the dough feels elastic and leaves the sides of the mixing bowl clean; this helps to make a well-built loaf. (To test if the dough is of the right consistency, hold a handful above the basin – it should drop slowly back into the basin. The tendency is to make the mixture too dry). Divide the dough into three 2-pint tins which have been warmed and greased. Put the tins in a warm place, cover with a cloth and leave for about 20 minutes or *until the dough is within half an inch of the top of the tins.* Bake in a fairly hot oven (400°F, 200°C, Gas 6) for approximately 35-40 minutes.

Quantities for 1 loaf

1 lb (450 g) flour	*13 fl. oz (375 ml) water at blood heat*
1 teaspoon salt (to taste)	*2 teaspoons Barbados sugar, honey*
1 teaspoon dried yeast	*or black molasses*

Miss Woolf's Chewy Wheat Bread
Also suitable for slimmers

8 oz (225 g) whole wheat or bulgar	*3 oz (75 g) oat bran*
3 lb (1350 g) 100% wholewheat flour	*2 tablespoons honey*
1 tablespoon salty seasoning	*1 oz (25 g) sunflower margarine*
2 oz (50 g) fresh yeast	*1¾ pints (1 ltr) water approx.*
little cracked wheat	*2 × 2 lb and 2 × 1 lb loaf tins*

Boil ½ pint (300 ml) water and pour over wholewheat. Leave till tepid, adding most of the honey. In another bowl, whisk together fresh yeast with one teaspoon honey and ½ pint (300 ml) warm water (100°F). Mix salt with flour and lightly rub in the margarine. Strain water from whole wheat and make up to 1¼ pints (750 ml) liquid. Mix wheat and bran into flour before adding total liquid. Mix into dough ball and knead till dough is elastic. Put in greased bowl, cover with greased polythene sheet and prove until doubled in size. Knock back the dough, divide and knead into loaves. Cover and prove again. Brush with milk and egg wash and sprinkle with cracked wheat. Bake at 425°F, 220°C, Gas 7 for 30-40 minutes. Remove from tins and bake 5 further minutes inverted.

Soya Bread

22 fl oz (650 ml) warm water	4 teaspoons honey
1¼ teaspoons salty seasoning	1 oz (25 g) dried yeast
2 tablespoons sunflower or safflower oil	1¾ lb (800 g) 100% wholemeal flour
6 oz (175 g) soya flour	3 × 1 lb (small) loaf tins

Make sure flours are warm (not hot). Dissolve the honey and salt in half the water heating a little if necessary. Add remaining water to adjust temperature to blood heat. Sprinkle the yeast over the warm liquid and leave to froth up (about 10 minutes). Add the oil to the yeast water. Mix the warm wheat and soya flours together and sift to aerate, throwing the bran back in, and put into a large mixing bowl. Make a well in the centre. Pour the frothy warm yeast liquid into the well and mix well to incorporate all the dry ingredients (add a little more tepid water if necessary).

Knead thoroughly on floured board for about 5 minutes. Oil a clean large mixing bowl and place the dough in it, covering it with greased polythene, and set it in a warm place to rise till double in bulk (about 2 hours). Grease and flour loaf tins. Knead dough again for further 5 minutes, divide into 3 loaves, and press down well into prepared tins. Cover with greased polythene and put to rise again till doubled in size (about 1 hour in a warm place). Bake for 30-35 minutes at 375-400°F, 190-200°C, Gas 5-6.

Juliana's Popular Wholemeal Rolls or Loaves

3 lb (1350 g) 100% wholemeal flour (approximately)	4 tablespoons raw brown sugar
	¾ pt (450 ml) boiling water
1 oz (25g) butter or vegetable margarine	¾ pt (450 ml) chilled milk
	2 oz (50 g) fresh yeast OR
4 teaspoons salty seasoning	2 tablespoons dried yeast
little cracked wheat	2 eggs beaten

Dissolve the sugar and butter in the water in a large mixing bowl. Add cold milk to give fluid at blood heat. Add yeast and leave to froth. Add eggs. Mix salt with some of the flour, and mix in gradually to produce a smooth batter. Beat in sufficient extra flour to produce a soft dough which leaves the sides of the bowl clean. Tip onto working surface liberally sprinkled with wholemeal flour, and knead thoroughly, about 7-10 minutes. Put in greased bowl, covered with greased polythene film, to prove until doubled in volume. Knock back the dough and knead thoroughly into rolls or loaves, rolling their surface in cracked wheat. Put into greased tins, cover, and leave to rise again. Bake 400°F, 200°C, Gas 6, about 15-20 minutes for rolls, 25-35 minutes for loaves. A sweet-flavoured, softer wholemeal bread popular with all the family.

Enriched Bread – Higher Protein I
Also suitable for slimmers

1 teaspoon honey	1¾ lb (800 g) 100% wholewheat flour
1 pt (600 ml) warm water	3 oz (75 g) dried milk powder
1 tablespoon dried yeast or	2 oz (50 g) soya flour
2 tablespoons fresh yeast	3 teaspoons salty seasoning
3 oz (75 g) wheatgerm	2 tablespoons vegetable oil

In the evening: Dissolve the honey in the warm water and sprinkle the yeast over the top. Leave to fluff up. Put 1 lb (450 g) of the wholewheat flour in a large bowl and mix to a smooth thick batter with the yeast water. Cover and leave overnight in a cool place to 'set the sponge'.
Next morning: Mix the remaining flour with the wheat germ, milk powder, soya flour and salt. Add the oil to the 'sponge' and gradually work in the dry flours to give a soft dough, adding more flour or water as necessary. Knead thoroughly and put into greased bowl to prove. Knead and shape into 3 loaves. Put in well greased loaf tins, cover with greased plastic film and leave to prove again till nearly double in size. Bake at 350°F, 180°C, Gas 4 for 30 minutes then reduce the heat to 325°F, 160°C, Gas 3 until cooked (about 45-60 minutes altogether).

Enriched Bread – Higher Protein II
Also suitable for slimmers

1 teaspoon honey	4 oz (100 g) wheatgerm
½ pt (300 ml) warm water	8 oz (225 g) chick pea flour
2 tablespoons dried yeast	12 oz (350 g) wholewheat flour
1½ lb (675 g) plain 100%	4 teaspoons salty seasoning
wholewheat flour	2 tablespoons sunflower oil
1 pt (600 ml) tepid milk	

In the evening: Dissolve the honey in the water, sprinkle over the yeast and leave to fluff up. Mix into the 1½ lb (675 g) wholewheat flour with the tepid milk to produce a smooth thick batter, cover with a greased plastic film and leave overnight to 'set the sponge'.
Next Morning: Mix together the remaining flours and salt. Add the oil to the 'sponge' and gradually work in the dry ingredients to give a pliable dough. Knead thoroughly. Put into greased bowl, covered, to prove. Knock back and knead into 3 loaves, two large and one small, and put into greased loaf tins. Prove. Bake at 375°F, 190°C, Gas 5 for 20 minutes then reduce heat to 350°F, 180°C, Gas 4 till cooked, 45-55 minutes in total.

Gluten-Free Bread

4 oz (100 g) potato flour	1 oz (25 g) whole ground almonds
6 oz (175 g) chickpea flour	2 oz (50 g) soya bran
4 teaspoons carob powder	4 teaspoons vegetable oil (not corn oil)

4 teaspoons gluten-free baking powder 8 fl oz (225 ml) cold water
½ teaspoon seasalt

Oil a small loaf tin and dust with potato flour. Sieve together flours, carob, baking powder and salt; mix in almonds and bran. Add oil and water and beat well. Smooth into tin and bake at 350°F, 180°C, Gas 4, about ½ hour.

Cheese and Herb Rolls

To 1 lb (450 g) prepared bread dough, after first proving, use 4 oz (100 g) grated cheese, ½ teaspoon dry mustard powder, 2-4 cloves garlic, pressed, and 2-3 tablespoons finely chopped parsley. Mix these ingredients well together and work into the dough, kneading to produce even distribution. Divide into 6 or 8 and knead into rolls. Place on greased baking sheet, covered, to prove, and bake about 15 minutes at 400°F, 200°C, Gas 6.

Sweet Cinnamon Bread

To 1 lb (450 g) prepared bread dough, after first proving, use 4 oz (100 g) muscovado sugar and 1-2 teaspoons powdered cinnamon. Pat the dough out into a large flat disc and sprinkle over the sugar and cinnamon. Work it all together, kneading to produce even distribution in your small shaped loaf. Cover, prove, and bake in usual way.

Hot Cross Buns

6 fl oz (180 ml) hot water
1 teasoon honey
10 fl oz (300 ml) milk (or water)
1 tablespoon dried yeast
8 oz (225 g) plain 100%
  wholemeal flour
1¼ lb (550 g) extra wholemeal
  flour
Glaze: 1 tablespoon milk

4 oz (100 g) raw brown sugar
½ teaspoon ground cinnamon or
  mixed spice
6 oz (175 g) sultanas or currants
1 oz (25 g) chopped peel
2 eggs, beaten
4 oz (100 g) melted butter
½ teaspoon salty seasoning
1 teaspoon more honey

Dissolve the honey in the hot water and add the milk to produce a tepid fluid. Sprinkle on the dried yeast and leave 10 minutes to dissolve and fluff up. Put the 8 oz warmed flour into a large bowl and pour in the yeast fluid. Stir well to mix, then put in a warm place to 'set the sponge', ie become frothy and rise, about 20 minutes.

Mix thoroughly together the 20 oz (550 g) flour with the salt, sugar and spice and ensure there are no lumps in the sugar. Wash the sultanas or currants and drain. Add the peel. Stir the fruit into the flour. When the 'sponge' is ready, add to it the beaten egg and the cool melted butter and the mixed dry ingredients. Mix thoroughly, beating with the hand. Cover the basin with greased polythene and put in a warm place until 'proved' – risen until twice the size (about 1 hour). Grease and flour the baking trays. Lightly knead the dough on a floured board for one minute to knock it down. Divide into halves, then each portion into twelve. Roll each into round buns and arrange onto the oven trays. Mark each with a cross cut across the top. Cover with the greased polythene and put in a warm place to prove for about 30 minutes. Bake for about 15 minutes at 375-400°F, 190-200°C, Gas 5-6. Dissolve the honey in the milk for a glaze and paint on the buns when golden-brown and almost done. Cool on a rack, wrapped in a clean cloth.

Ann's Grain Free Bread
(also free from gluten, sugar, milk and eggs)

4 teaspoons special gluten-free baking powder	*3 teaspoons carob powder (optional)*
	½ oz (15 g) ground whole almonds
5½ oz (160 g) potato flour	*3 teaspoons vegetable oil*
5 oz (150 g) gram flour	*9 fl oz (275 ml) cold water*

Sieve together all dry ingredients, then add the water and oil and mix well together, beating with a wooden spoon. Oil a medium loaf tin and flour with potato flour. Put prepared mixture into tin and bake for about 1 hour until light brown. Turn out on wire rack to cool. Use as ordinary bread.

Wholemeal Scones

2 oz (50 g) raw sugar	*8 oz (225 g) S.R. 100% wholemeal*
2 oz (50 g) butter or vegetable margarine	*flour*
1½ oz (32 g) sultanas	*¼ teaspoon salty seasoning*
	¼ pint (150 ml) milk or water

Warm the milk and dissolve the salt and raw sugar. Remove from the heat. Add washed sultanas and leave to swell. Rub the fat into the flour until the mixture resembles fine breadcrumbs. Add the liquid and its sultanas and lightly work together, adding a little more milk if necessary to give a smooth soft dough. Knead on floured board till smooth and free from cracks. Roll to ½″ thick, cut into shapes and put on floured baking tray. Brush tops with milk. Bake at 375-400°F, 190-200°C, Gas 5-6 for about 20 minutes. Put in a clean teatowel on a wire rack and cover with the towel while cooling to prevent overcrispness.

Barleymeal Scones

10 oz (275 g) barley meal	*1¼ teaspoons baking powder*
⅛ teaspoon salty seasoning	*2 oz (50 g) butter*
1 egg	*¼ pint (150 ml) milk (approx)*

Sieve dry ingredients together to mix well and aerate. Rub butter into the barley flour until mixture resembles fine breadcrumbs. Beat the egg with half the milk, make a well in the centre of the barley mixture and add the egg to make a smooth soft dough, adding more of the remaining milk as necessary. Flour a board with barley meal and turn out the soft dough. Work the dough lightly with the hands until free from cracks, then transfer to a greased baking sheet and roll out to ½″ thick. Mark into squares by almost cutting through. Bake at 375-400°F, 190-200°C, Gas 5-6 for about 20-25 minutes, till lightly browned. Cover with clean cloth while cooling. Good served warm with butter.

Savoury Wholemeal Scones

8 oz (225 g) S.R. 100% wholemeal   *2 oz (50 g) butter or vegetable*
flour   *margarine*
¼ pint (150 ml) milk   *1 teaspoon Tastex*

Warm a little of the milk and dissolve the Tastex in it. Cool. Rub fat into the flour. Add all the milk quickly, mixing with a knife to form a soft dough without overhandling. Turn onto floured surface and pat into round shape, about ½″ thick and cut into scones or approximate squares or wedges. Put on floured baking tray and bake at 400°F, 200°C, Gas 6, for about 12-15 minutes. Cover with a dry cloth on rack while cooling. Serve warm with butter or Flora, and cheese and cress perhaps.

Potato Girdle Scones

8 oz (225 g) hot cooked potato   *potato flour or brown rice flour*
½ oz (12 g) butter   *paprika or cayenne*

Scrub potatoes well and slice in 2 or 3 pieces, boil and then remove skins. Drain and mash with the butter and correct seasoning.

Add sufficient flour to make a workable dough and for rolling out very thinly. Cut into scone shapes, prick well with a fork and cook on a hot girdle – or a large shallow frying pan, lightly greased, turning carefully. Serve hot with butter or vegetable margarine.

Spiced Walnut Scones

½ teaspoon cinnamon or mixed spice   *2 oz (50 g) butter or vegetable*
2 oz (50 g) raw brown sugar   *margarine*
2 tablespoons chopped walnuts   *milk to mix*
8 oz (225 g) S.R. 100% wholemeal   *1 egg, beaten*
flour   *(see Wholemeal Scones recipe p.121.)*

Mix the cinnamon, ½ the sugar and the nuts together. Make scones with half the sugar and roll out quickly. Sprinkle with the nut mixture, fold into three and roll quickly again. Cut or mark into scone shapes and bake at 375°F, 190°C, Gas 5 for about 15 minutes.

Rye Fruit Loaf

16 oz (450 g) washed sultanas
½ pint (300 ml) hot strained herb tea
2 teaspoons baking powder
little water

4 oz (100 g) raw brown sugar
10 oz (275 g) 100% rye flour
2 eggs
2 × 1 lb loaf tins

Put sultanas and raw sugar into a large bowl and pour over the hot tea. Stir to dissolve the sugar and leave several hours or overnight for the fruit to swell. Mix and sift together the rye flour and baking powder and retain the bran. Beat the eggs and add to the soaked fruit mixture. Stir well. Add the rye flour and stir together to mix thoroughly, adding a little water if necessary to give soft loaf mixture. Bake for 50-60 minutes at 350-375°F, 180-190°C, Gas 4-5, covering top after 30 minutes to prevent over-browning. Cool on rack, wrapped in a teatowel. Serve cold sliced with butter or margarine.

Molasses and Apple Loaf

6 oz (175 g) apples, thinly sliced
4 fl oz (125 ml) water
1 teaspoon cinnamon
¼ teaspoon powdered cloves
1 egg, beaten

12 oz (350 g) S.R. 100% wholemeal
    flour
4 oz (100 g) molasses sugar
3 oz (75 g) butter
¼ teaspoon powdered nutmeg

Gently cook the apples in water with the molasses sugar until soft. Cool and liquidise. Sift together the dry ingredients and rub in the butter. Add gradually to the apple mixture with the egg, stirring well to keep smooth. Pour into greased tin and bake at 350°F, 180°C, Gas 4 for about 30 minutes.

Keith's Yorkshire Pudding

4 oz (100 g) 100% wholemeal flour
2 eggs (not chilled)
¼ pint (150 ml) iced water

pinch salt
¼ pint (150 ml) cold milk
vegetable oil

Place half the flour, eggs, and milk (flour already sieved together with salt) into liquidiser. Blend to smooth paste. Add rest of flour, start to blend, adding water gradually so that a smooth mixture results. Leave to stand. Place tin in very hot oven (425°F, 210°C, Gas 7) with ¼ teaspoon oil in each compartment until oil is smoking. Give mixture a stir to disturb bubbles on top and add mixture to ¾-½" deep to each compartment. Cook for 20-25 minutes without opening oven door whilst cooking.
NOTE: Tin is for traditional 4" compartments and quantities for 4 persons as a starter or 6 persons as part of main course. To give a much lighter pudding, try 80% wheatmeal flour.

CHAPTER 14

Pastry

Wholemeal pastry-making is different from white pastry. Forget about keeping everything cool. Wholemeal pastry has not the elasticity of white and so cannot be stretched or rolled so very thinly. The wholegrain flour is heavier, of course, so there are fewer pastry variations. But, with a little practice, you will soon be making delicious short wholemeal pastry. Experiment to find the method which suits you best! (Butter makes better wholemeal pastry than margarine.)

Wholemeal Shortcrust Pastry

8 oz (225 g) wholemeal flour
1 egg, beaten (optional)
1-2 tablespoons water

4 oz (100 g) butter or vegetable
margarine or a mixture

Sift the flour, reserving the residual bran – keep back enough bran for rolling out and replace the rest with the measured flour in a large bowl. First cut in the fat with a knife and then rub it in with the fingertips until the mixture resembles fine breadcrumbs. Stir in the egg and enough water to bind, mixing lightly into a ball.

Place pastry on large sheet of greaseproof paper on working surface, sprinkled with bran. Roll into a long oblong, fold in three, turn clockwise and roll again into an oblong. Repeat the folding and turning and roll out again to required shape.

For lining a flan tin, or covering a pie, slide the pastry off the paper to avoid difficulty in handling this very short pastry.

Wholemeal 'Flaky' Pastry

8 oz (225 g) 100% wholemeal flour, plain
¼ teaspoon salty seasoning
2 tablespoons water, cool

3 oz (75 g) soft lard or butter
3 oz (75 g) soft butter or margarine
1 teaspoon lemon juice

Choose finely ground wholemeal flour and sift with the salt. Rub in the lard. Combine the lemon juice with the water and use just enough to blend into a workable dough. Cream the butter till light and fluffy. On a well floured surface, roll out the pastry into an oblong, then spread ⅓ of the butter over ⅔ of the pastry. Fold over the unspread third, and then the remaining third and turn to the right; repeat the process till all the butter has been incorporated into the pastry, keeping the board well floured to prevent sticking. For the final rolling use greaseproof sheet for transfer to flan tin or pie dish as the pastry is very short and brittle. Best for savoury dishes – too short for easy eating with fingers!

Rich Shortcrust Pastry

12 oz (350 g) S.R. 100% wholemeal flour   7½ oz (210 g) butter
2 eggs, beaten

Tip flour onto a large clean surface and shape into circle with a hollow in the centre. Using a pallette knife chop the butter into the flour until in small pieces. Tip the beaten eggs into the centre well and continue working with fingertips to incorporate all the butter and flour into a pastry dough, kneading lightly until even. Roll out lightly into an oblong shape and then fold into 3 and seal edges. Turn clockwise, and repeat the rolling and folding twice. Use as required. For two large flan tins, cut pastry into 2 pieces and roll out each to fit one tin. Bake blind.

Sweet Pastry

8 oz (225 g) 100% plain wholewheat flour   5 oz (150 g) butter or soft vegetable
2 oz (50 g) raw brown sugar   margarine
1 whole egg & 1 extra yolk

Mix together the flour and sugar and tip onto work surface, make a well in the centre and put in the egg and sliced butter. Using fingers, gradually work the fat and the egg into the flour until all is incorporated. Knead. Roll out once. Bake at 350-375°F, 180-190°C, Gas 4-5.

Rich Wholemeal Pastry

6 oz (175 g) butter or margarine   8 oz (225 g) 100% wholemeal flour

Cream the butter till light and fluffy. Gradually blend in the flour to form a soft dough. Roll out thinly on well floured greaseproof paper. A good short pastry with a good flavour, suitable for sweet or savoury use.

Quick & Easy Shortcrust Pastry

2 oz (50 g) soya flour   *½-¾ teaspoon salty seasoning*
2 oz (50 g) barley flour   *3 tablespoons water*
4 oz (100 g) 100% wholemeal flour   *6 tablespoons vegetable oil*

Sift flours and salt together – or use all wholewheat flour. Whisk water and oil together in a cup. Add liquid all at once to flours and stir lightly together to mix to a soft dough. Roll out between greaseproof paper sheets. Bake blind at 350°F, 180°C, Gas 4, or fill before baking.

Wholemeal Quiches

Make wholemeal pastry and roll out thinly on large sheet of greaseproof paper, to aid its transference to the sandwich tin. Ease into position without stretching and trim top, crimping the cut edge. Use filling of choice. Serve hot or cold.

For base filling:

A. A savoury egg and milk base: Use 3 eggs to 1 pint (600 ml) milk as required and season with Tamari, Worcester sauce, Tastex or Vegit, herbs and spices as required.

B. A thick bechamel sauce, seasoned appropriately.

C. Quark or cottage cheese blended with a little bechemel sauce.

The pastry case may be baked blind when using bases B or C with a filling ingredient which has already been cooked (e.g. asparagus) and then thoroughly heated through before serving.

When using base A, the pastry case may be filled with the desired grated cheese etc., the savoury egg and milk poured over and all baked immediately for 45-60 minutes at 350-375°F, 180-190°C, Gas 4-5, till golden.

Quiche Fillings

1. Salmon and tomato in savoury egg and milk base.
2. Cheddar or Lancashire cheese and tomato, with oregano or chives, in egg and milk base, seasoned with little mustard or cayenne.
3. Sardine and tomato, with tarragon, in egg and milk base.
4. Asparagus and cheese in savoury egg and milk, curd cheese or quark base.
5. Cooked chicken, mushroom and onion, in egg and milk base.
6. Tonabanga (soya sausages) or beef chipolatas and onions in egg and milk base.
7. Mushrooms and spring onions in curd cheese or quark base.
8. Baked beans and ham pieces (or soya sausages); stir a beaten egg into the beans.
9. Green pepper pieces with mushrooms, ham, onions and tomato in egg and milk base with oregano.
10. Prawns and cooked peas in egg and milk base.

Refrigerator Mincemeat
– without suet – can be used uncooked –
keeps in refrigerator for up to 6 months

1 lb (450 g) currants
½ lb (225 g) sultanas
2 oz (50 g) dried peel
1 lb (450 g) seedless raisins
1 lb (450 g) cooking apples, peeled
and cored

Mince these ingredients together coarsely.

½ lb (225 g) grapes, halved and
de-pipped or seedless grapes
1 lb (450 g) soft light brown sugar
4 tablespoons sherry or rum
2 oz (50 g) finely chopped almonds
2 lemons, zest and juice
2 teaspoons mixed spice

Add these to minced fruits and mix together well. Pack into sterilised jars, seal and refrigerate.

Mince Pies with Rich Wholemeal Pastry
– makes 24 small mince pies

See recipe for rich wholemeal pastry   *12 oz (350 g) prepared mincemeat*
2-3 cooking apples (6 oz 175 g)   *(see recipe above)*

Make the pastry. Put the prepared mincemeat in a basin. Peel the apples and coarsely grate into the mincemeat, mixing well. Roll out the pastry three times, folding into three and turning clockwise each time. Roll out very thinly and cut into circles for the pans. Put a teaspoon of mincemeat mixture in each, cover and seal with pastry. Glaze with egg white and sprinkle over very little brown sugar. Bake for 25-30 minutes at 375°F, 190°C, Gas 5.

Apple Pie with Pâte Sucrée

8 oz (225 g) 100% wholemeal flour   *2 eggs*
4 oz (100 g) butter   *2 oz (50 g) soft brown sugar*
apples, finely sliced   *honey sparingly to taste*

Pile the flour and sugar onto a clean working surface and make a well in the centre. Slice the firm butter into pieces and put into the centre, together with one whole egg and the second egg yolk (reserving the second white for glazing). Using a palette knife work the butter and eggs into the flour with a chopping action, adding a little cold water to produce a stiff dough. Knead lightly to finally mix the pastry. Roll out on greaseproof paper and transfer to pie dish. Trim. Prepare apples and arrange slices over the pastry base. Add honey sparingly to taste – some apples, e.g. Coxes, need no extra sweetening. Bake.

Ann's Jam or Fruit Tarts
(free from grains, gluten, sugar, milk and eggs)

2 oz (50 g) gram flour   *2½ tablespoons cold water*
2 oz (50 g) potato flour   *½ oz (15 g) soya flour*
1 oz (25 g) vegetable oil   *1 teaspoon gluten free baking powder*

Sieve together the flours and baking powder, add oil and cold water and mix well. Knead into ball and roll out pastry. Cut into rounds or line tart tins. Bake near top of oven for 15 minutes at 425°F, 220°C, Gas 7. Allow to cool slightly before removing from tins. Fill with sugar free jam, puréed or stewed apricots or apples. Eat same day as baked.

Ann's Date Tart
(free from grains, gluten, sugar, milk and eggs)

2 oz (50 g) vegetable oil	*2 oz (50 g) gram flour*
2 oz (50 g) potato flour	*3 oz (75 g) grated apple*

Mix ingredients well together, press into tin and cook at 375°F, 190°C, Gas 5 until just golden.
Meanwhile, cook together:

4 oz (100 g) chopped dates (hard)	*¼ pint (150 ml) water*
zest ½ lemon	

until soft and smooth. Cool slightly and spread over pastry base. Return to oven and cook a further 10-15 minutes.

Variations
1. Top pastry with stewed apple flavoured with cinnamon and sweetened with sultanas.
2. Use a mixture of date and apple.

CHAPTER 15

Biscuits

Melrose Biscuits

8 oz (225 g) butter or margarine
6 oz (175 g) Muscovado sugar
1 egg yolk
zest of 1 orange

10 oz (275 g) 100% wholemeal flour
1 cup cornflakes
1 egg white
pieces of dates or dried apricots for
  decoration

Cream together the butter and sugar till light and fluffy, and beat in the egg yolk. Mix in the orange rind, flour and cornflakes. Space out teaspoonsful of the mixture onto 3 greased baking sheets and flatten slightly. Lightly whisk the egg white and brush over the tops of the biscuits. Top with a piece of date or apricot. Bake at 350-375°F, 180-190°C, Gas 4-5 for about 20 minutes, when golden. Remove carefully to rack to cool, when they will become crisp.

Sultanates

4 oz (100 g) butter or margarine
6 oz (175 g) raw brown sugar
2 eggs
8 oz (225 g) S.R. 100% wholemeal flour
½ teaspoon powdered cinnamon

¼ teaspoon ground nutmeg
¼ teaspoon powdered cloves
10 oz (275 g) sultanas, washed
3 oz (75 g) chopped nuts

Cream together the butter and sugar till light and fluffy, and beat in the eggs. Sieve together the dry ingredients retaining the bran, and fold into the creamed mixture. Stir in the fruit and nuts. Drop teaspoonsful onto greased baking sheet or greased patty tins. Bake at 350-375°F, 180-190°C, Gas 4-5 for 10-20 minutes according to size.

Melting Moments

4 oz (100 g) wholemeal flour
2 oz (50 g) fine oatmeal
2 oz (50 g) riceflour

7 oz (200 g) butter – essential
3 oz (75 g) soft light brown sugar
½ teaspoon vanilla essence

Sift together the 3 flours. Cream together the butter and sugar till light and fluffy and beat in the vanilla. Fold in the flour. Put teaspoonsful onto greased baking trays. Bake 350-375°F, 180-190°C, Gas 4-5 for 12-15 minutes. Leave for 1 minute before carefully lifting off to cake rack to cool. When cold decorate with topping and a slither of glacé pineapple, if needed.

June's Afghans

9 oz (250 g) butter or margarine	9 oz (250 g) SR 100% wholemeal flour
4½ oz (135 g) raw Muscovado sugar	2 tablespoons carob powder
½ teaspoon vanilla essence	3 oz (75 g) cornflakes

Cream together the butter and sugar, and add vanilla. Sift together the flour and carob, retaining the bran. Fold in, with the cornflakes. Space teaspoonsful on to greased baking sheets. Bake at 350°F, 180°C, Gas 4 for about 10 minutes. Remove to wire rack after few minutes. Ice when cold.

Eve's Biscuits

6 oz (175 g) sunflower margarine	3 eggs
6 oz (175 g) raw Muscovado sugar	6 oz (175 g) SR wholemeal flour
3 oz (75 g) honey	3 oz (75 g) cornflakes

Cream together the margarine, sugar and honey till fluffy, and beat in the eggs. Fold in the flour and the cornflakes. Space teaspoonsful on greased baking sheets (they spread!). Bake at 350°F, 180°C, Gas 4 for about 15-20 minutes. Remove to wire rack while hot.

Austrian Chocolate Biscuits

4 oz (100 g) SR 100% wholemeal flour	2 oz (50 g) Muscovado sugar
1 oz (25 g) carob powder	¼ teaspoon vanilla essence
4 oz (100 g) butter or margarine	

Sift together the carob and flour, retaining the bran. Cream together the butter and sugar till light and fluffy and add vanilla. Fold in the dry ingredients. Roll teaspoonsful of the mixture into balls and space out on greased baking sheets. Flatten with wet fork. Bake 350°F, 180°C, Gas 4 about 12 minutes. Leave 1 minute before carefully lifting onto rack to cool. When cold, sandwich together in pairs with mocha butter filling.

Mocha Butter Filling

Simmer 1 oz (25 g) Carob in a little boiling water with 1 tablespoon Barleycup, to produce a thick paste. Cool. Cream 2 oz (50 g) butter with 4 oz (100 g) Muscovado sugar and beat in the mocha paste, adding a few drops of vanilla or rum if preferred.

Stewart's Shortbread

4 oz (100 g) brown rice flour	4 oz (100 g) pale Muscovado sugar
4 oz (100 g) 100% wholemeal flour	6 oz (175 g) butter – firm

Mix the flours together with the sugar and tip onto a clean work surface. Put the lump of butter in the centre and cover with flour. Using the hands, gradually knead the butter into the flour, till all is evenly incorporated. Divide into 3 and put into 3 flan tins, pushing and patting to obtain even depth (or roll out). Prick all over with a fork. Bake 300-325°F, 150-160°C, Gas 2-3 till just done but not coloured. Cut into pieces before quite cold.

Crisp Ginger Biscuits

4 oz (100 g) plain wholewheat flour
1 teaspoon ground ginger
¼ teaspoon Garam Masala
2 oz (50 g) butter or vegetable margarine

3 oz (75 g) raw brown sugar
2 teaspoons thin honey
1 tablespoon milk, approx.
½ teaspoon Bicarbonate of Soda

Sift the flour and spices together. Cream the butter and sugar and beat in the honey. Dissolve the bicarbonate of soda in the milk. Mix the creamed mixture into the flour, adding the milk to make into a soft pastry dough – add a little more milk if necessary. Roll out very thinly (⅛in-1/10in thick) and cut into small round biscuits. Place on 3 greased baking trays and bake 10-12 minutes at 300°F, 150°C, Gas 2 until golden. Cool slightly before gently lifting onto a wire rack as they crispen on cooling.

Foresight Four-Grain Biscuits

7 oz (200 g) butter
7 oz (200 g) raw Barbados sugar
7 oz (200 g) plain wholemeal flour
½ teaspoon bicarbonate of soda

5 oz (150 g) sugar free muesli base
(Browns or Prewetts)
2 oz (50 g) dessicated coconut

Cream butter and sugar together till light and fluffy. Sift flour and bicarbonate together and mix with the cereal muesli and coconut. Stir the dry ingredients into the creamed mixture. Roll into small balls and place on greased oven tray. Bake 20-25 minutes at 325-350°F, 160-180°C, Gas 3-4. Cool on wire rack (soft and flexible while hot).

Jonathan's Date Crackers

10 oz (275 g) stoned dates
¼ pint (150 ml) boiling water
finely grated rind of 1 lemon
7 oz (200 g) butter
7 oz (200 g) dark or soft brown sugar

8 oz (225 g) 100% wholemeal flour
½ teaspoon bicarbonate of soda
5 oz (150 g) rolled oats (not pre-cooked)
juice of ½ lemon

Mash together the chopped dates and the boiling water, heating if necessary. Add the lemon rind and juice, and mix well. Cool. Cream the butter and sugar together. Sift together the flour and soda bicarbonate, and mix in the oats. Add to the creamed mixture, blending until well mixed together. Spread half of the crumb mixture over base of tin and press down firmly (about ¼ in thick). Spread over the date pulp and then the remaining crumb mixture. Press down lightly. Bake for 35-45 minutes at 325°F, 160°C, Gas 3. Cut into squares while warm.

Oatmeal Digestive Biscuits

8 oz (225 g) fine oatmeal
¼ teaspoon bicarbonate of soda
¼ teaspoon salty seasoning

2 oz (50 g) raw Muscovado sugar
3 oz (75 g) butter or margarine
little egg

Mix the dry ingredients and rub in the butter. Add just sufficient beaten egg to produce a pastry dough. Roll out thinly and cut into circular biscuits. Bake at 350°F, 180°C, Gas 4 about 8-10 minutes.

Sarah's Oatcakes

10 oz (275 g) fine oatmeal
½ teaspoon sea salt

2 tablespoons oil
7 tablespoons water

Mix dry ingredients together in a large bowl and make a well in the centre. Whisk oil and water together in cup and pour onto oatmeal, combining to give a soft dough (add a little more water if needed). Sprinkle board with oatmeal and roll out very thinly. Cut circles for biscuits and place on greased oven trays. Bake 375-400°F, 190-200°C, Gas 5-6 about 20 minutes without browning. Lift off gently onto wire rack to cool. Serve with butter and cheese.

Rye Flapjacks

4 oz (100 g) butter or margarine
4 oz (100 g) raw brown sugar
4 oz (100 g) whole rye flour

1½ oz (35 g) dessicated coconut
½ teaspoon bicarbonate soda

Melt butter over gentle heat without boiling. Remove from heat and add sugar. Mix rye flour, coconut and soda bicarbonate. Mix dry ingredients into butter and sugar mixture, and stir well to mix thoroughly. Put into shallow tin, smoothing gently without pressing down firmly. Bake about 15 minutes at 375-400°F, 190-200°C, Gas 5-6 when it will still be soft. Cut immediately into fingers and leave in hot tin for 5 minutes to set. Carefully remove hot biscuits onto wire rack to cool.

Biscuits for Joy
(allergic to wheat, rye, corn and milk)

4 oz (100 g) brown rice flour
½ teaspoon bicarbonate of soda
2 oz (50 g) desiccated coconut

6 oz (175 g) rolled oats
7 oz (200 g) sunflower margarine
6 oz (175 g) raw brown sugar

Sift together the rice flour with soda bicarbonate, then mix in coconut and rolled oats. Cream the margarine and sugar until light and fluffy. Stir the dry ingredients into the creamed mixture until evenly incorporated. Roll into small balls and place on 2 greased baking sheets. Bake 15-20 minutes in a slow oven 300°F, 150°C, Gas 2. Allow to cool a little and crispen before lifting off onto a rack.

Oat Crunchy Squares

6 oz (175 g) butter or margarine
6 oz (175 g) raw brown sugar
½ teaspoon bicarbonate of soda

4 oz (100 g) fine oatmeal
6 oz (175 g) rolled oats
2 tins 6 × 6 in

Melt butter over gentle heat. Add sugar to melted butter and remove from heat. Mix soda bicarbonate with the oatmeal and rolled oats, and add to the butter and sugar. Mix together thoroughly. Smooth into baking tins. Bake 12-15 minutes at 375°F, 190°C, Gas 5 taking care not to burn. Cut into squares while still hot. Cool 10 minutes and then lift onto cake rack to crispen while cooling further.

'Regulators' – Spiced Bran Biscuits

8 oz (225 g) SR 100% wholemeal flour
½ teaspoon mixed spice
¼ teaspoon salty seasoning
4 oz (100 g) fine bran and wheatgerm
4 oz (100 g) raisins or sultanas
1 oz (25 g) chopped walnuts

4 oz (100 g) honey
4 oz (100 g) butter or margarine
2 oz (50 g) raw Muscovado sugar
½ teaspoon soda bicarbonate
¼ pint (150 ml) natural yoghurt or milk
2 eggs, well beaten

Sift together the flour, spice and salt, and mix in the bran. Wash the dried fruit and add to nuts. Weigh the saucepan empty and then add honey to right weight, add butter and sugar and melt together gently till well mixed. Cool. Dissolve soda bicarbonate in the yoghurt or milk. Whisk the beaten egg into the honey mixture. Stir in flour and yoghurt alternatively, then fruit and nuts, and mix well. Drop teaspoonsful of the mixture onto a greased baking sheet. Bake 375°F, 190°C, Gas 5 for about 10 minutes.

Sultana Bran Muffins

4 oz (100 g) plain 100% wholemeal flour
1 oz (25 g) dried milk powder
⅛ teaspoon salty seasoning
2½ teaspoons baking powder
4 oz (100 g) fine bran (soya or oat)

8 fl oz (250 ml) milk
4 tablespoons honey
1 egg
3 tablespoons sunflower or safflower oil
6 oz (175 g) sultanas

Mix and then sift together, the flour, milk powder, salt and baking powder into a large bowl. Lightly mix in the bran. Warm a little of the milk and dissolve the honey in it. Beat the egg and add the cold milk and the cool honey-milk. Add oil to the wet ingredients and whisk lightly. Wash the sultanas well and drain. Make a well in the centre of the dry ingredients, pour in the wet ingredients, add sultanas and stir to give a slack mixture. Grease and flour 24 patty tins or lay out paper cases on 2 baking sheets. Put spoonsful of muffin mixture into the tins or cases. Bake at 375-400°F, 190-200°C, Gas 5-6 for about 20 minutes.

Ann's Tea Biscuits
(free from gluten, grain, sugar, milk and eggs)

3 oz (75 g) chickpea (gram) flour
1 oz (25 g) potato flour
3 teaspoons gluten-free baking
  powder

1 oz (25 g) Tomor margarine or
  sunflower or soya oil
3 tablespoons water

Sieve together the dry ingredients. Rub in the margarine or whisk together the oil and water and add, mixing to knead. Divide into 6, roll into balls and flatten slightly on greased baking tray. Bake at 425°F, 220°C, Gas 7 about 15-20 minutes, until golden. Serve fresh, with spreading of choice.

Note to those sensitive to wheat – see page 144.

CHAPTER 16

Cakes

Butter Sponge for Gateaux
(has a delicious flavour)

6 oz (175 g) SR 100% wholemeal flour
6 oz (175 g) butter
6 oz (175 g) raw brown sugar

3 eggs, whipped to a froth
milk – approx 3 tablespoons

Grease 2 × 8½ in or 3 × 7 in sandwich tins and dust with flour. Sift the flour, retaining the bran. Cream butter and sugar till light and fluffy. Gradually beat in the egg, adding a little flour at the end. Fold in the flour alternately with the milk to give a soft dropping consistency. Smooth into tins. Bake 350-375°F, 180-190°C, Gas 4-5 for 20-25 minutes. Let sit for 5 minutes before turning onto wire rack to cool. Sandwich together with cream and honey or home-made jam, fresh strawberries or raspberries and cream, or a butter cream.

Orange Cake

This recipe is based on the weight of 3 of the 4 eggs in butter, sugar and wholemeal flour – say 7 oz (200g):

7 oz (200 g) butter or vegetable
margarine
7 oz (200 g) Muscovado sugar
zest of 1 orange

4 eggs
7 oz (200 g) S.R. 100% wholemeal
flour
orange juice

Grease and flour 2 × 8 in sandwich tins. Cream butter and sugar till light and fluffy and beat in the zest. Beat in the eggs singly, adding a little flour with the last two. Fold in the flour alternately with enough orange juice to produce a soft dropping consistency. Smooth into the prepared tins. Bake 350-375°F, 180-190°C, Gas 4-5 about 25-30 minutes. When cold, sandwich together with home-made marmalade or lemon cheese, or make into a gateau with orange buttercream filling and decorate with flaked almonds.

Orange Buttercream Filling

4 oz (100 g) butter
3-4 tablespoons honey, to taste
zest of 1 orange

2-4 oz (50-100 g) fine oatmeal or
wheatgerm or powdered milk
little orange juice

Cream butter and honey till light and fluffy, and add zest. Beat in the oatmeal or wheatgerm till smooth, with a little orange juice, to produce a light buttercream of desired sweetness and spreading consistency.

Healthy 'Chocolate' Cake

5 oz (150 g) SR 100% wholemeal flour	6 oz (175 g) raw brown sugar
1 oz (25 g) carob powder	3 large eggs
2 oz (50 g) ground almonds	3-5 tablespoons milk
6 oz (175 g) butter or margarine	

Sieve together the mixed flour, carob and almond, retaining the bran. Cream together the butter and sugar till light coloured and fluffy. Whip in the eggs, adding a little of the prepared dry ingredients with the last egg. Fold the dry ingredients into the creamed mixture, gradually adding enough milk to maintain a soft dropping consistency. Smooth the sponge mixture into prepared tins and bake for about 22-25 minutes at 350-375°F, 180-190°C, Gas 4-5. Cool on wire racks. When cold, ice with Mocha Cream Topping.

Mocha Cream Topping

2 oz (50 g) butter	2-4 teaspoons carob powder
4 oz (100 g) dark Muscovado sugar	1-2 teaspoons Barleycup or Pioneer
4-8 tablespoons powdered milk	dissolved in 1-2 tablespoons boiling water

Cream together the butter and sugar. Add the carob powder and cooled 'coffee' concentrate, and beat in. Beat in sufficient milk powder to thicken to spreading consistency.

Spiced Coffee Cake

8 oz (225 g) SR 100% wholemeal flour	8 oz (225 g) raw brown sugar
1 teaspoon mixed spice	3 large eggs
2 tablespoons Barleycup or Pioneer	milk or water to mix
6 oz (175 g) butter or margarine	almond paste or mocha butter cream

Sieve together the flour, spice and Barleycup, retaining the bran. Cream butter and sugar till light and fluffy. Gradually beat in the eggs. Fold in the flour alternately with the milk to give a soft dropping consistency. Smooth mixture into 3 prepared 7 in tins. Bake 350-375°F, 180-190°C, Gas 4-5 about 25 minutes. When cool sandwich together with almond paste, mocha cream or quick demarara icing.

Quick Demarara Icing

2 tablespoons demarara sugar	3 tablespoons hot water
carob or Pioneer or other flavouring	dried milk powder

Dissolve the demarara (and carob or Pioneer or other flavouring) in the hot water. Add sufficient powdered milk to give a good spreading consistency.

Spiced Sultana Cake

6 oz (175 g) SR 100% wholemeal flour	*zest of 1 lemon*
¼ teaspoon ground ginger	*3 eggs*
¼ teaspoon ground cinnamon	*1 teaspoon honey*
¼ teaspoon mixed spice	*3 tablespoons warm milk*
6 oz (175 g) butter or vegetable margarine	*1 cup washed sultanas*
6 oz (175 g) raw brown sugar	*1 oz (25 g) demarara sugar*

Sieve the flour and spices together, retaining the bran. Cream butter and sugar till light and fluffy, and add zest. Gradually beat in the eggs with a little of the flour. Dissolve the honey in the warm milk. Cool. Fold in the flour alternately with the sweet milk and sultanas, and mix well. Smooth into prepared 8 in cake tin and sprinkle top with the demarara sugar. Bake 350-375°F, 180-190°C, Gas 4-5 for 45-50 minutes.

Madeira Cake

5 oz (150 g) butter or margarine	*8 oz (225 g) SR 100% wholemeal flour*
5 oz (150 g) raw brown sugar	*little milk*
1 small lemon, zest and juice	*chopped dried orange peel*
3 eggs	

Cream together the butter and sugar till light and fluffy. Beat in the zest and eggs, adding a little flour with the last. Fold in the remaining flour alternately with the lemon juice and enough milk to produce a soft dropping consistency. Smooth into prepared 8 in tin. Bake 350-375°F, 180-190°C, Gas 4-5. After 30 minutes cooking, arrange orange peel across the top and continue baking till cooked – a further 30-45 minutes.

Tropicana Cake

8 oz (225 g) SR 100% wholemeal flour	*little milk*
4 oz (100 g) ground almonds	*4 oz (100 g) dried papaya pieces*
8 oz (225 g) butter or margarine	*2 oz (50 g) blanched almonds, chopped*
8 oz (225 g) raw Muscovado sugar	*1 oz (25 g) whole or split almonds*
zest of 1 lemon	

Mix together the flour and ground almonds. Cream butter and sugar till light and fluffy. Gradually beat in the zest and eggs, adding a little flour with the last. Fold in remaining flour, adding enough milk to give a soft dropping consistency. Mix in fruit and chopped nuts. Smooth into prepared tin and arrange whole nuts across the top. Bake in cool oven 300-325°F, 150-160°C, Gas 2-3 for about 1½ hours. Keeps well. May be iced with coconut topping, decorated with papaya pieces.

Coconut Topping

6 tablespoons butter   desiccated coconut
4 tablespoons honey

Cream butter and honey together till light and fluffy. Mix in sufficient
coconut to produce the desired consistency.

Upside Down Cake

For cake:
4 oz (100 g) butter or vegetable margarine   For 'Topping':
4 oz (100 g) raw brown sugar   2 tablespoons extra butter
1 teaspoon thin honey   demarara sugar
2 large eggs   blanched almonds, walnuts
4 oz (100 g) SR 100% wholemeal flour   large raisins, dates, fig slices or
little milk or orange juice   pineapple pieces as available.

Line the sides only of 7 in cake tin with greaseproof paper. Generously
spread the base of the tin with 'topping' butter, to approximate depth of
1/16 in (1 mm). Sprinkle over an even layer of demarara sugar. Arrange
nuts and fruit, pushing them down into the butter. Cream butter and
sugar till light and fluffy and gradually beat in the honey and eggs. Fold
in the flour, adding a little liquid if necessary to produce a soft dropping
consistency. Carefully smooth over the arranged base. Bake 350-375°F,
180-190°C, Gas 4-5 about 30-40 minutes. Turn upside-down while hot.
Ready to eat when cool.

Caraway Cake

8 oz (225 g) SR 100% wholemeal flour   8 oz (225 g) raw brown sugar
1 oz (25 g) soya flour   ½ teaspoon vanilla essence
¼ teaspoon mace   4 large eggs
2 tablespoons caraway seeds   little milk
8 oz (225 g) butter or margarine

Sift together the flours and spice, retaining the bran, and mix in the
seeds. Cream butter and sugar. Beat in the vanilla and eggs gradually,
adding a little flour at the end. Fold in flour alternately with sufficient
milk to produce a soft dropping consistency. Spoon into lined cake tin
and bake 350°F, 180°C, Gas 4 for about 40-50 minutes.

Jervis Fruit Cake

12 oz (350 g) sultanas   8 oz (225 g) soft butter or margarine
4 oz (100 g) chopped dried apricots   8 oz (225 g) dark Muscovado sugar
8 oz (225 g) raisins   5 eggs
10 oz (275 g) plain 100% wholemeal flour   juice of 1 orange
½ teaspoon mixed spice or allspice

Wash sultanas, raisins and apricots thoroughly, and allow to swell. Sift together the flour and spice, retaining the bran. Cream butter and sugar till light and fluffy and much paler in colour. Beat in the eggs singly, adding a little flour with the last. Fold the flour into the mixture, alternately with the washed fruit, adding sufficient orange juice to maintain a soft dropping consistency. Smooth the mixture into prepared tins and bake about 45-55 minutes at 350-375°F, 180-190°C, Gas 4-5. When cold, cut with a serrated knife.

Foresight Christmas Cake

4 oz (100 g) dried apricots, minced	*5 oz (150 g) raw brown sugar*
8 oz (225 g) sultanas	*3 large eggs*
6 oz (175 g) raisins	*10 oz (275 g) SR 100% wholemeal flour*
4 oz (100 g) cut mixed peel	*4 oz (100 g) split almonds*
1 can (15 oz) pineapple in natural juice	*2-4 tablespoons sherry (needed to*
7 oz (200 g) butter or *margarine*	*preserve the cake if not being eaten within 2 weeks)*

Wash the dried fruit well, drain it, then soak in the juice from the pineapple, and add to the chopped pineapple. Prepare a 9 in cake tin with several layers of lining greaseproof paper. Cream butter and sugar till light and fluffy. Beat in the eggs with a little of the flour. Fold in the flour and then the drained fruit to give a soft dropping consistency, and then spoon into the prepared tins. Bake for ½ hour at 325°F, 160°C, Gas 3 then arrange split almonds in a pattern on the top and return to the oven. Reduce the heat to 300°F, 150°C, Gas 2, after a further ¾ hour, and cover the top with several layers of greaseproof paper if necessary to prevent over-browning. Bake till done (1¾-2¼ hours in all). Cool. Invert cake and prick base with fine knitting needle. Pour over the sherry to moisten all the base. Replace greaseproof paper and wrap in greaseproof and then foil, store in a cool place. Decorate cake with wide red ribbon or a Christmas cake frill.

Rich Christmas or Wedding Cake

4 oz (100 g) currants	*1 teaspoon salt*
1 lb (450 g) raisins	*1½ teaspoon baking powder*
2 lb (900 g) sultanas	*1½ teaspoon mixed spice*
8 oz (225 g) cut peel	*½ teaspoon cinnamon*
8 oz (225 g) dried apricots	*1¼ lb (550 g) butter*
10 oz (275 g) tinned pineapple in own juice	*1¼ lb (550 g) raw Barbados sugar*
6 oz (175 g) chopped walnuts	*3 dessertspoons black treacle*
1½ lb (675 g) 100% wholemeal flour	*9 large eggs*
6 oz (175 g) ground almonds	*1 large lemon*
	little brandy

Line a 10-12 in tin with 3 layers of greaseproof and with a band of folded newspaper tied around the edge. Wash the fruit thoroughly and drain. Chop apricots and pineapple into small pieces, and mix in the prepared fruit. Pour over the pineapple juice from the tin of pineapple. Leave soaking overnight. Add walnuts.

Mix and sift together the flour, almonds, salt, baking powder and spice, throwing back the bran. Cream the butter, add the raw sugar and cream again till light and fluffy. Beat the black treacle into the mixture. Beat in the eggs singly, adding a little of the flour with the last two eggs. Strain the fruit from any surplus juice and coat in a third of the flour mixture. Wash the lemon well and grate the rind into the flour. Squeeze the juice. Fold dry ingredients into the creamed mixture, using lemon juice as necessary to maintain a soft dropping consistency. Stir in the fruit to distribute it evenly. Spoon the raw cake into the prepared tin and smooth out to leave a slight hollow in the centre. Set on baking tray covered with several layers of newspaper.

Bake for 1 hour at 325°F, 160°C, Gas 3, then cover top of cake with several layers of brown paper and bake for the next hour at 300°F, 150°C, Gas 2. Complete the baking at 275°F, 140°C, Gas 1, testing with fine skewer. Large deep cake will take about 5-6 hours.

Sprinkle a little brandy over the base of the cake. Wrap in greaseproof and then foil for storage to mature the flavour.

Eggless Fruit Cake
using sour cream, yoghurt or buttermilk

12 oz (350 g) S.R. 100% wholemeal flour
¼ teaspoon cinnamon
¼ teaspoon allspice
¼ teaspoon ground ginger
8 fl oz (250 ml) sour cream or yoghurt or buttermilk

1 tablespoon black treacle
8 oz (225 g) butter or vegetable margarine
8 oz (225 g) raw Muscovado sugar
½ teaspoon soda bicarbonate
1 lb (450 g) mixed dried fruit, washed

Sieve together the flour and spices, retaining the bran. Slightly warm the sour cream or alternative and dissolve the black treacle in it. Cream together the butter and sugar till light and fluffy. Fold in a little of the flour. Add the soda bicarbonate to the sour milk and mix till it froths. Fold into the mixture alternately with the remaining flour and the fruit. Bake 350-375°F, 180-190°C, Gas 4-5 for 1-1¼ hours.

Molasses Toffee Topping

1 tablespoon butter
2½ tablespoons molasses sugar

1 tablespoon orange juice

Gently heat all together and simmer, stirring, for five minutes. Pour over cake while hot.

Date and Walnut Cake with Fudge Topping

½ pint (300 ml) boiling water
8 oz (225 g) hard dates, chopped
1 teaspoon bicarbonate of soda
10 oz (275 g) plain 100% wholemeal flour
1 teaspoon baking powder

3 oz (75 g) butter or vegetable margarine
8 oz (225 g) raw brown sugar
2 eggs, beaten
½ teaspoon vanilla
3 oz (75 g) chopped walnuts

Pour the boiling water over the chopped dates and mash together with the soda bicarbonate. Leave to cool. Sieve together the flour and baking powder, retaining the bran. Rub the butter into the flour, add the sugar and mix. Add eggs, then other ingredients, and mix well. Smooth into prepared tin and bake 350-375°F, 180-190°C, Gas 4-5 about 40 minutes. Make Fudge or Molasses Toffee Topping, pour over, and decorate with walnuts.

Fudge Topping

2 tablespoons butter
2 tablespoons cream

5 tablespoons raw Muscavado sugar
walnuts for decoration

Heat butter, sugar and cream gently together and boil for one minute, stirring. Pour over cake while hot. Decorate with walnuts.

Marmalade cake

4 oz (100 g) marmalade
4 oz (100 g) black treacle
3 oz (75 g) butter or vegetable margarine
8 oz (225 g) raw Muscovado sugar
12 oz (350 g) plain 100% wholemeal flour

¼ teaspoon ground ginger
¼ teaspoon ground cinnamon
2 eggs, beaten
½ pint (300 ml) milk
2 teaspoons bicarbonate of soda

Weigh a large saucepan empty and then re-weigh as you add the marmalade, treacle, butter and sugar. Heat together gently, stirring, till dissolved. Cool. Sift together the flour and spices, retaining the bran. Stir the eggs into the mixture in the saucepan. Warm the milk to blood heat and add the soda bicarbonate, stirring well till dissolved. Add the milk mixture alternately with the flour, and mix well. Smooth into prepared cake tins. Bake 300-325°F, 150-160°C, Gas 2-3 for 50-60 minutes. When cold, top with a spread made from marmalade, curd cheese and honey, creamed together.

Jackie Applebee, of the Wholefood Cookery School in Leicester, has kindly contributed her recipe for:

Vegan Cake
– easily digestible fruit cake

apple cider vinegar
20 oz (525g) mixed dried fruits
2 oz (50g) mixed dried peel
1½ pts (900ml) boiling water
8 oz (225g) 100% wholemeal flour
1 tablespoon carob powder
1 tablespoon Barleycup
2 oz (50g) ground almonds

¼ teaspoon ginger or cinnamon
¼ teaspoon nutmeg or allspice
6 tablespoons soya flour*
2 fl oz (50ml) corn oil
¾ pt (450ml) Guinness* (measured
   below froth)
1-2 tablespoons brandy
* denotes raising agents

Wash dried fruits in acidulated water to remove sprays (use 1 tablespoon cider vinegar to one pint of hot water). Drain. Pour over the boiling water, just bring back to the boil, and skim off any scum from paraffin oil dressing. Leave to swell and cool. Line 8″ tin with greaseproof paper. Sift together the dry ingredients, retaining the bran, and work in the oil. Mix in the Guinness, drained fruit, and sufficient of the fruit water to produce a creamy pouring consistency. Pour into lined tin and leave standing overnight (about 12 hours) in a warm place, for fermentation to take place. Bake 300°F, 150°C, Gas 2 for 6-7 hours. When cold, prick base with needle and pour over brandy as a preservative. Store wrapped in greaseproof paper, in caketin.

Fruity Gingerbread

1 lb (450 g) 100% wholemeal flour
¼ teaspoon salty seasoning
2 teaspoons ground ginger
1 teaspoon ground cinnamon
2 teaspoons baking powder
8 oz (225g) vegetable margarine
8 oz (225g) vegetable margarine
8 oz (225g) raw muscovado sugar
  OR molasses sugar

4 oz (100 g) currants
14 oz (400 g) sultanas
4 oz (100 g) chopped glacé ginger
2 oz (50 g) chopped dried orange peel
8 oz (225g) black treacle or molasses
¼ pt (150ml) warm milk
¼ pt (150 ml) warm milk
1 teaspoon soda bicarbonate
3 eggs beaten

Sift together the flour, salt, spices, and baking powder, retaining the bran. Rub in the fat. Stir in the sugar and washed fruits. Dissolve treacle in milk, and stir in the soda. Pour the milk mixture and eggs into the dry ingredients and mix to a soft dough. Smooth into large square lined tin and bake 350°F, 180°C, Gas 4 about 1¼-1½ hours. Mature 3-4 days before cutting.

Banana Cake

5 oz (150 g) butter or margarine	*6 oz (175g) raw brown sugar*
3 eggs, beaten	*2 tablespoons natural yoghurt*
8 oz (225 g) SR 100% wholemeal flour	*10 oz (275 g) very ripe mashed banana*
1 teaspoon bicarbonate of soda	

Cream butter and sugar till light and fluffy. Beat in the egg, adding a little flour at the end. Dissolve the soda bicarbonate in the yoghurt and blend in with the banana. Fold the flour into the creamed mixture alternately with the banana. Pour into 3 greased and floured 6 in sandwich tins and bake at 325°F, 160°C, Gas 3 about 20-30 minutes; allow to cool a little before turning onto wire racks. Sandwich together with filling made from mashed ripe banana, lemon juice, honey and a little cream or yoghurt, and eat immediately.

Pearl's Carrot and Pineapple Cake
– gluten-free

2 cups chickpea flour	*1 cup crushed pineapple – drained*
2 tablespoons soya flour	*2 cups raw Muscovado sugar*
½ teaspoon sea salt	*1¼ cups vegetable oil – soya, corn or*
2 teaspoons cinnamon	*sunflower*
2 teaspoons soda bicarbonate	*1 cup desiccated coconut*
3 eggs	*1 cup chopped walnuts – optional*
2 cups grated raw carrot	

Sift together the flours, salt, cinnamon and bicarbonate of soda. Beat the eggs. Combine all the ingredients, mixing well. Pour into paper-lined cake tin, and bake at 350°F, 180°C, Gas 4, about 60-80 minutes.

Potato and Carrot Cake
– gluten-free

3 oz (75 g) chickpea (gram) flour	*1 cup grated raw potato*
¼ teaspoon fine sea salt	*1 teaspoon bicarbonate of soda*
1 teaspoon allspice	*4 oz (100 g) Muscovado sugar*
½ teaspoon cinnamon	*½ cup soya or sunflower oil*
½ teaspoon ground nutmeg	*6 oz (175 g) washed sultanas*
1 cup grated raw carrot	

Sift together the flour, salt and spices. Scrub the carrot and potato thoroughly, and grate without peeling. Mix the soda bicarbonate into the grated potato. Mix all ingredients together thoroughly and smooth into paper-lined tin. Bake 1-1½ hours, 350-375°F, 180-190°C, Gas 4-5.
N.B. Gluten-free cakes are best slightly undercooked, or they crumble uncontrollably.

Arrowroot Sponge
– gluten-free, low fat

2½ oz (65 g) arrowroot	pinch sea salt
2 teaspoons chickpea flour	3 eggs
1 teaspoon gluten-free baking powder	4 oz (100 g) soft brown sugar

Grease and flour 2 × 7 in sandwich tins. Sift together twice the arrowroot, baking powder, flour and salt. Whip eggs alone till thick. Gradually beat in the sugar. Fold in dry ingredients and smooth into tins immediately. Bake 350-375°F, 180-190°C, Gas 4-5, 8-10 minutes. Fill with ripe banana mashed with tofu and honey.

Ann's Fruit Cake
– Gluten, grain, sugar, milk and egg free.

3 oz (75 g) minced dried apricots	2 oz (50 g) soya flour
8 oz (225 g) sultanas	4 oz (100 g) potato flour
5 oz (150 g) raisins	3 oz (75 g) chickpea flour
12 fl oz (350 ml) pineapple juice	2 tablespoons gluten-free baking powder
3 tablespoons sunflower oil	2 teaspoons mixed spice
3 oz (75 g) grated carrot	2 teaspoons cinnamon
6 oz (175 g) grated sweet apple	4 oz (100 g) ground almonds (or nuts)

Wash dried fruit and soak in pineapple juice. Oil and flour 8 in tin, using potato flour. Add oil, grated carrot and apple quickly and stir to prevent oxidation. Sift together dry ingredients and mix well. Combine wet and dry ingredients and beat to mix well. Cook at 400°F, 200°C, Gas 6 about 1 hour till just done.

Rye and Barley Cake

5 oz (150 g) wholemeal rye flour	6 oz (175 g) butter or margarine
2 oz (50 g) wholemeal barley flour	6 oz (175 g) dark brown sugar
1 teaspoon baking powder	3 large eggs
1 oz (25 g) ground almonds	little milk or orange juice

Sift together the first 3 ingredients, then mix in the ground almonds. Cream butter and sugar till light and fluffy. Beat in the eggs, adding a little flour with the last. Fold in the flour, adding enough milk to give soft dropping consistency. Smooth into two prepared flan tins and bake at 350°F, 180°C, Gas 4 about 25 minutes.

Note to those sensitive to wheat
Most of the recipes can be made with wholemeal rye and barley flour in place of wholewheat flour. Barley flour is better in pastry than in bread. Oatmeal is good in biscuits; yellow maizemeal in breads. Experiment! Chickpea flour (gram or garbanzo flour) tastes good in recipes too. Potato flour is more refined and less recommended for extensive use.

CHAPTER 17

Desserts and Puddings

Blackberry and Apple

1 lb (450 g) cooking apples
2 oz (50 g) honey or muscovado sugar

¼ lb (100 g) blackberries

Peel, core and slice apples and stew gently with the blackberries in the minimum amount of water, adding honey when cooked but still hot. Stir in well. Serve hot or cold.

Apple and Orange Foam

1 lb (450 g) cooking apples
¼ pint (150 ml) orange juice
3 cloves
1 orange, peeled, sliced and cut into small pieces

2 tablespoons honey
½ lemon – zest and juice
¼ pint (150 ml) evaporated milk, chilled

Peel, core and slice the apples into orange juice and cook with cloves until the apples are pulpy. Remove cloves and then mash, sieve or liquidise and add honey, lemon juice and zest. Whip the evaporated milk in a large basin until light and fluffy. Stir in the apple mixture. Divide between four dessert bowls and decorate with pieces of fresh orange.

Apple Batter Pudding

4 oz (100 g) plain wholemeal flour
3 oz (75 g) raw brown sugar
milk to mix
1-1½ lb (450-675 g) cooking apples

1 tablespoon carob powder
2 oz (50 g) butter or vegetable margarine

Mix together the flour, sugar and carob powder and rub in the butter. Add milk to produce a thick batter consistency and beat well. Prepare the apple; chop into small pieces, stirring into the batter. Pour into a greased pie-dish and bake at 350°F, 180°C, Gas 4 for 50-60 minutes.

Baked Apples

4 ripe cooking apples
hard dates and/or sultanas

1 tablespoon brown sugar
2 tablespoons water

Wash apples thoroughly and remove cores with potato peeler. Stuff the cavities with dates and sultanas. Sprinkle over the sugar and add the water to the dish. Bake in moderate oven till soft – about one hour.

Apple Crumble in a Hurry

2 lb (900 g) cooking apples
2-4 tablespoons water
6 oz (175 g) raw brown sugar

4 oz (100 g) butter or vegetable oil
8 oz (225 g) wholemeal breadcrumbs
¼ teaspoon cinnamon

Prepare and finely slice the apples, and stew gently in covered saucepan with the water, cinnamon and 2 oz (50 g) of the sugar. Warm the oil and add the remaining sugar and breadcrumbs, heating right through. Put the hot stewed apple in a greased pie-dish and smooth the crumble over the top. Put under a hot grill for a few minutes to crisp the top.

Apple Crumble

2 lb (900 g) cooking apples
6 oz (175 g) raw brown sugar
¼ teaspoon cinnamon

4 oz (100 g) vegetable oil or butter
8 oz (225 g) wholemeal flour
2 tablespoons water

Peel, core and slice the apples thinly. Put into greased casserole with the water, cinnamon and 2 oz (50 g) of the sugar and mix the sugar through. Warm the oil and pour onto the remaining sugar and flour. Mix well and spread over the apples. Bake in moderate oven (350°F, 175°C, Gas 3-4) till apples are cooked and top is crisp: about ¾ hour.

Apple Sponge Pudding

1 lb (450 g) cooking apples
raw brown sugar to taste
4 oz (100 g) raw brown sugar
5 oz (150 g) 100% SR wholemeal flour
¼ teaspoon cinnamon

3 tablespoons orange juice or water
4 oz (100 g) butter or vegetable
   margarine
2 eggs

Peel, core and slice the apples and stew gently in the orange juice till soft. Add sugar to taste. Transfer to a greased casserole. Sift together the flour and spice. Cream together the butter and sugar and beat in the eggs with a little of the flour. Fold in the remaining flour and spread over the apple. Bake in moderate oven (350°F, 175°C, Gas 4) until sponge is firm to the touch; about ½ hour.

Apple Cracknel

1 lb (450 g) cooking apples
4 tablespoons orange juice
4 oz (100 g) butter or vegetable margarine

honey to taste
8 oz (225 g) cornmeal or oatmeal

Gently cook the sliced apples in the orange juice and add honey to taste. Pour into a greased pie-dish. Melt the butter and mix in the cornmeal. Sprinkle over the apple. Bake in moderate oven till crisp and golden.

Copenhagen Apple Layer Pudding

2½ lb (1125 g) cooking apples
1 lemon
3 oz (75 g) washed sultanas
3 cloves (optional)

1-2 tablespoons water (approx)
6 oz (175 g) digestive biscuits
3 oz (75 g) butter
6 oz (175 g) raw brown sugar

Finely peel, core and slice apples. Using potato peeler, finely peel off the yellow rind from the lemon in one long piece and add to the apples. Squeeze the juice and add to the apples. Add sultanas, cloves and sugar to the mixture and just sufficient water to avoid burning. Simmer until tender. Remove lid while cooking to allow evaporation. When cool, remove and discard lemon peel (and cloves if prefered). Crush biscuits. Melt butter and add crumbs, mixing well. About an hour before serving assemble the pudding in four layers, starting with apple and finishing with crumb mixture. Decorate and serve warm or chilled.

Surprise Apple Tart
Gluten free

1½ lb (675 g) steamed potatoes
2 oz (50 g) butter or vegetable margarine
3 tablespoons thin honey

1½ lb (675 g) cooking apples
½ teaspoon sea salt
brown rice flour as required

Steam the scrubbed potatoes in their skins and peel them while hot. Immediately mash them with some of the butter and the salt till smooth. Melt the remaining butter and add to the cooled potato on a work surface sprinkled with the rice flour and knead to produce a soft pliable pastry, not too dry. Roll out and divide for two tarts. Cover with sliced apples, drizzled with honey. Bake at 350°F, 180°C, Gas 4 till done.

Nut and Apple Pudding

1 lb (450 g) cooking apples
honey to taste
4 oz (100 g) raw brown sugar
4 oz (100 g) walnuts or cashew nuts, grated

2 tablespoons orange juice
3 oz (75 g) butter or margarine
1 egg
2 oz (50 g) rice bran or oatflakes

Peel, core and slice the apples and put in a casserole with the orange juice and a drizzle of honey to sweeten. Stir to mix. Cream the butter and sugar, beat in the egg, then whisk in the mixed nuts and oats until fully incorporated. Spread over the apples and bake in a moderate oven until apples are soft and top is nicely cooked; about one hour. (Gluten free when rice polishings are used.)

Fluffin

4 tablespoons barley flour   2 cups milk
grated nutmeg   honey

Mix the barley flour and milk together to a smooth paste. Bring to boil, stirring and simmer for five minutes. Add grated nutmeg and honey to taste.

Old English Frumenty

½ cup kibbled wheat   1 cup water
pinch mixed spice   2 tablespoons currants or sultanas
honey   cream

Soak the kibbled wheat in the water for 8-24 hours. Then simmer in the soaking water about three minutes, till tender, with the spices and dried fruit. Serve with cream and honey.
(See also Kruska recipes in Muesli chapter)

Summer Pudding

Mixture of soft fruits – preferably:

raspberries, strawberries,   wholemeal bread – thin slices
redcurrants, loganberries or   orange juice
blackcurrants   honey

Simmer ½ cup of loganberries or blackcurrants in a little orange juice till soft adding honey to taste. Line a pudding basin or casserole with the thin slices of bread. Add the raw soft fruits to the cooled stewed loganberries and mix together. Pour into the bread-lined bowl and cover with a plate. Refrigerate for twenty-four hours. Serve with R. A. Reddell's Cottage Cream, page 152.

Toasted Betty

4 slices wholemeal bread, toasted   2 cups raisins
zest of 1 orange   ½ cup chopped walnuts
juice of 2 oranges   2 teaspoons honey
2 large eggs, beaten   ½ pint (300 ml) milk
2 thin slices wholemeal bread, buttered   ¼ teaspoon grated nutmeg

Wash the raisins and soak them in the orange juice with the zest for 2-3 hours. Butter the toast, cut into dice and mix with the walnuts and raisins. Put in a well greased pie-dish and pour over the milk and egg mixture. Drizzle over the honey. Cover with the remaining pieces of bread, butter side uppermost. Grate nutmeg over the top. Sit the pie-dish in a baking dish of hot water and bake at 325°F, 160°C, Gas 3 for about 30-40 minutes, till set.

Warm Barley Pudding

1 cup barley kernels   *2 tablespoons honey*
2 cups cold water   *½ lb (225 g) dried apricots*
pinch of salty seasoning

Soak the washed apricots for 24 hours, then chop them. Bring to the boil and simmer for five minutes with the barley kernels. Stir in honey to taste.

Sweet Pancakes

2 oz (50 g) honey   *1 egg*
¼ pint (150 ml) natural yoghurt   *¼ pint (150 ml) milk*
1 oz (25 g) butter or vegetable margarine   *4 oz (100 g) 100% wholewheat flour*

Beat the egg and whisk in the yoghurt and the milk. Melt the butter and honey and stir together over gentle heat. Cool a little. Make a well in the flour and pour in the milk mixture and the melted butter and honey. Whisk the wet ingredients into the flour to form a smooth batter. Cook spoonfuls of the batter in a hot greased frying pan and serve with lemon juice and a drizzle of honey, or with 4 tablespoons natural yoghurt mixed with 4 tablespoons orange juice sweetened with honey to taste or with strawberry sauce, see page 151.

Cornmeal and Cinnamon Pudding

1 cup yellow cornmeal (maize meal)   *4 cups milk*
3 tablespoons molasses   *1 tablespoon butter or vegetable oil*
1 teaspoon cinnamon   *¼ teaspoon nutmeg*
½ cup raisins or sultanas   *1 egg, beaten*

Mix the cornmeal with sufficient of the cold milk to make a smooth paste, free from lumps. Heat the remaining milk and beat into the cornmeal. Bring to the boil, stirring constantly, and boil for 7 minutes. Add molasses, butter, spices, raisins and stir well together. Mix in the beaten egg. Pour into a greased casserole and stand in a baking tin of hot water. Bake at 275°F, 140°C, Gas 1 for ¾-1 hour.

Junket

1 pint (600 ml) raw milk   *½ teaspoon rennet*
1 tablespoon raw brown sugar

Warm the milk to blood heat and dissolve the sugar in it, then stir in the rennet and leave to set.

Jay's Fruit Soufflé

6 oz (175 g) hard dates   *3 oz (75 g) dried apricots*
2 ripe bananas   *grated rind of 2 lemons*
1 tablespoon arrowroot   *3 eggs*

Wash the dates and apricots, soak till softened, and either mince or chop finely. Mash the bananas and blend with fruit and arrowroot. Beat the egg yolks and add. Whisk the egg whites till stiff and fold in. Smooth into greased soufflé dish and bake in moderate oven ¾-1 hour, till just set. Serve hot or cold.

Baked Bananas

Ripe bananas   thin honey (optional)
cream or evaporated milk

Put the whole (unpeeled) bananas in a dry baking dish and bake in moderate oven for 20-25 minutes. The skins will go completely black when ready. Skin and serve with thin honey and cream or evaporated milk. (Really ripe bananas need no added sweetening.)

Banana Fluff

¼ pt (150 ml) natural yoghurt   2-3 sweet apples (Cox preferred)
¼ pt (150 ml) unsweetened pineapple   3-4 very ripe bananas
 juice   honey if necessary

Finely peel and core apples and chop into small slices. Blend in liquidiser with yoghurt and pineapple juice. Add peeled bananas and blend until smooth. Serve as soon as possible. This is one of Ruth's favourites!

Banana Ice Cream

juice of 1 lemon   1½ cups soft brown sugar or honey
orange juice   2 cups evaporated milk
2 cups mashed very ripe bananas

To the lemon juice, add sufficient orange juice to make up to 1 cup. Mash bananas, measure and add to juices. Add the sugar and milk. Mix in electric blender or whip thoroughly. Put to freeze. Re-whip before quite frozen to break up ice crystals. Freeze.

Orange Ice Cream

1 packet gelatin or agar agar   4 oz (100 g) honey or soft brown sugar
1 pint (600 ml) orange juice   ¼ pint (150 ml) double cream

Dissolve the gelatin in 3 tablespoons of the orange juice, heated over boiling water. Add the honey or sugar and remaining orange juice and beat to dissolve sugar. Cool. Whip in the cream. Put to freeze. Re-whip before quite frozen to break up ice crystals. Freeze.

'Strawberry' Sauce

4 oz (100 g) strawberries
1 ripe tomato
1 tablespoon honey or to taste

1 sweet eating apple
½ pint (300 ml) natural yoghurt

Choose a sweet flavoured tomato, scald for ½ minute in boiling water and remove skin. Peel and core the apple and chop. Hull the strawberries and add them all to the yoghurt and liquidise. Add honey to taste and mix well. Serve with pancakes, with home-made ice-cream or sponge pudding, or add to sliced ripe bananas as a dessert on its own.

Custard Sauce

1 pint (600 ml) milk
1 tablespoon honey

2 eggs

Beat egg. Add warmed milk and honey and cook gently in a double saucepan, stirring occasionally, until custard starts to thicken. Cover and keep hot in the double saucepan until needed for stewed fruit, crumble or sponge pudding.

Coconut Custard

4 oz (100 g) fresh wholemeal breadcrumbs or barley kernels
1 pint (600 ml) milk
3 eggs

1 tablespoon honey
2 oz (50 g) desiccated coconut

Warm the milk and dissolve the honey. Beat the eggs and add the warm milk and breadcrumbs or barley kernels and whisk together. Pour into casserole standing in a pan of hot water. Bake in cool oven 275-300°F, 140-150°C, Gas 1-2 till set. Sprinkle coconut over the top and serve hot or cold.

Christmas Custard

1 pint (600 ml) milk
1 tablespoon chopped hard dates
1 tablespoon currants
2 teaspoons honey

3 eggs, beaten

(or 3 tablespoons home-made mincemeat
in place of fruits and honey)

Warm the milk and beat in the eggs, fruits and honey. Pour into casserole and stand in baking tin of hot water. Bake in cool oven 275°F, 140°C, Gas 1 until set, about 1 hour.

Spanish Cream

1 pint (600 ml) milk	*2 eggs*
½ cup raw brown sugar	*2 dessertspoons gelatine or agar agar*
2 tablespoons hot water	*vanilla*

Dissolve the gelatine in hot water. Whisk together the egg yolks, sugar and vanilla. Scald the milk and whisk into the sugar mixture, over a gentle heat. Add dissolved gelatine and allow to curdle slightly. Remove from the heat. When cold, whisk egg whites stiff and fold in. Pour into serving dish. Refrigerate to set.

R. A. Reddell's Cottage Cream

3 tablespoons natural curd cheese	*2 tablespoons natural yoghurt*
1 teaspoon cold-pressed safflower oil	*2 teaspoons honey or to taste*
or All Blend Oil	

Whisk all the ingredients well together and use instead of cream with fruits and desserts.

Gran's Cream

natural yoghurt	*honey*
dried milk powder (optional)	

Mix well together the honey and yoghurt, adding the skimmed milk powder to thicken if necessary. Use proportions suited to the acidity of the yoghurt and to your personal preference.

Non-Dairy Topping

½ tin Plamil (soya milk)	*2 tablespoons apple juice concentrate*
2 tablespoons agar-agar	*little hot water*

Dissolve the agar-agar in the minimum amount of hot water. Cool. Combine with the other ingredients and chill. Whisk lightly before use.

Cashew Cream

5 oz (150 g) broken cashew nuts	*5 fl oz (150 ml) water*

Liquidise together to produce a creamy fluid. Strain through a sieve to remove any remaining lumps. Almonds or walnuts may similarly be used to produce a nut cream.

Pavlova

2 egg whites	*baking tray*
4 oz (100 g) soft brown sugar (pale)	*safflower or sunflower oil*
1 tablespoon cornflour or arrowroot	*strawberries or raspberries*
½ teaspoon apple cider vinegar	*runny honey*

For this recipe, a cake mixer used at high speed is advantageous. Having separated eggs carefully, ensure that no yolk leaks into the whites. Whisk whites until stiff and dry. Add sugar gradually, whisking until stiff again. Beat in the sprinkled cornflour. Beat into pale meringue mixture which holds its shape. Transfer to forcing bag. Cover tray with a piece of greaseproof paper with a 6″ or 7″ circle drawn on it. Lightly smear all over with oil (wipe off to avoid any surplus). Pipe circles of meringue from the pencil line inwards to form a meringue base. Build up an outer wall with the remaining meringue. Bake about 1-1½ hours at 225-250°F, 110-120°C, Gas ¼-½. Remove carefully from greased paper and invert to allow bottom to dry out as it cools. Fill with fresh strawberries or raspberries and serve with 'runny honey' and cream. Dissolve honey in warm apple juice to give a pouring consistency. Serve cold from a jug.

Milk Jelly with Gelozone

1 pint (600 ml) milk
1 teaspoon gelozone
2 tablespoons cold water

honey to taste
vanilla essence or grated nutmeg

Mix the cold water into the gelozone, stirring to make a smooth paste. It will thicken as it mixes. Then slowly stir in the cold milk, whisking to avoid lumps. Bring to the boil and simmer for 2 minutes, stirring continuously. Sweeten and flavour to taste. Leave to set.

Note Gelozone is made from caragheen moss and is a vegan alternative to gelatine. Used in greater concentration it is a valuable herbal remedy for digestive disturbances e.g. diarrhoea.

Compôte

½ lb (225 g) dried apricots or prunes

Wash the dried fruit well. Soak in ample water to cover for 24 hours. Can be served without cooking or simmered for 5-10 minutes with the soaking liquid. Should be sweet enough as it is – or add a little honey or raw brown sugar.

Cooked Pears and Peaches

While ripe peaches and pears are delicious eaten raw – and more nutritious also – sometimes they become 'sleepy' and unappetising. These fruits are improved by stewing gently in a little water sweetened with either honey or raw brown sugar.

Prune Swizz

½ lb (225 g) prunes
½ pint (300 ml) water
1 tablespoon gelatine or agar agar

1 tablespoon raw brown sugar
small tin evaporated milk, chilled
juice of 1 small lemon

Soak the prunes for 24 hours in the water and then simmer gently for 5 minutes or until really soft. Remove stones. Mash the prunes and stir in the juice and sugar. Dissolve the gelatine in 2 tablespoons hot water and then cool. Whip the chilled evaporated milk until doubled in volume. Stir gelatine into the prunes and then fold in the evaporated milk foam. Pour into individual dishes and refrigerate.

Gooseberry Fool

1 lb (450 g) dessert gooseberries   honey to taste
2 fl oz (50 ml) natural yoghurt

Choose ripe, sweet, soft gooseberries and liquidise them with the yoghurt, adding honey to taste.

Rhubarb Snow

1 lb (450 g) rhubarb   ¼ pint (150 ml) pineapple juice
2 tablespoons honey or to taste   1 packet gelatine or agar agar
8 tablespoons powdered milk (optional)

Wipe rhubarb and cut into short lengths. Simmer in pineapple juice till tender and add honey. Pour off half cup of the hot juice and sprinkle on it the powdered gelatine. Stir till dissolved. Add to the rhubarb and liquidise or beat together. Leave to cool to blood heat. Then whisk in the powdered milk gradually, so that lumps are not formed (or liquidise). Pour into serving dish to set.
Note: If fresh sweet cicely is available, lay several leaves across rhubarb during cooking, then remove. Rhubarb will now require little extra sweetening (see page 27.)

Strawberry 'Lollies'

½ lb (225 g) strawberries   honey to taste
½ pint (300 ml) natural yoghurt   1 tablespoon lecithin (granular)

Liquidise the strawberries with the yoghurt and lecithin, adding honey to taste. Freeze in lolly moulds. Other fruit may be substituted as available.

Patience Pudding

1 lb (450 g) sweet ripe grapes   6 oz (175 g) digestive biscuits
½ pint (300 ml) double cream

Halve the grapes, removing pips and skin and catching the spilt juice (here patience is required!). Whip cream until stiff, incorporating the caught grape juice. Crush the biscuits to fine crumbs. Into a deep souffle dish arrange layers of digestive crumbs, cream and grapes to the top, finishing with grapes. Refrigerate until ready to serve.

Blackcurrant Pudding

4oz (100g) fresh wholemeal
  breadcrumbs
1 pt (600 ml) milk
honey to taste

2-6 oz (50-175 g) blackcurrants
  (as available)
2 large or 3 small eggs
¼ teaspoon cinnamon

Soak the breadcrumbs in half the cold milk. Wash the blackcurrants and put into a greased dish. Warm the remaining milk to dissolve the honey. Beat the eggs and add to the milk and crumbs, then add the honey milk and cinnamon and beat again. Pour over the fruit. Stand the pie-dish in a baking dish of hot water and bake at 325°F, 160°C, Gas 3 until just set – about 45 minutes. Variations: Use blackberries or redcurrants instead of blackcurrants.

Gooseberry Pudding

1 lb (450 g) green gooseberries
4 oz (100 g) soft wholemeal breadcrumbs

honey to taste
2 eggs, well beaten

Gently stew the gooseberries in the minimum amount of water till soft and pulpy. Mash well and add honey to taste and the breadcrumbs. Cool, then whisk in the eggs. Pour into a greased pie-dish and bake 30-40 minutes at 300-325°F, 150-160°C, Gas 2-3.
Note: If fresh sweet cicely is available, lay several leaves across gooseberries during cooking, then remove. Gooseberries will now require less sweetening. (See page 27.)

Layered Marrow Pudding

1½ lb (675 g) marrow (young)
2 tablespoons sweet molasses
2 oz (50 g) raw brown sugar
1 oz (25 g) butter or oil

8 oz (225 g) soft wholemeal breadcrumbs
zest and juice of ½ lemon
2 tablespoons water

Choose a deep casserole and grease it well. Wash the marrow well and slice thinly (as for stewed apples) and sprinkle with the lemon juice and zest. Stir to distribute. Mix the sugar with the breadcrumbs and put into the dish. Cover with a marrow layer and drizzle over some molasses. Repeat layers, ending with breadcrumbs and dot with the remaining butter. Add the water and bake in a moderate oven until done – when marrow is soft and the top is crisp – about 1 hour.

Fruit Fluff

2 oz (50 g) apricots (soaked overnight)
1 lemon – zest and juice
1 cup orange juice
chopped nuts

4 oz (100 g) raisins (soaked 1-2 hours)
8 good-flavoured apples
plain yoghurt or cream

Wash and slice apples, retaining skins and liquidise with 1 cup orange juice and the lemon juice. Add the soaked dried fruit and sufficient of the soaking liquid to process all into a purée. Mix with yoghurt and nuts to taste and eat soon, while full of vitamins.

Foresight Fruit Salad
(party quantities)

1 lb (450 g) Victoria plums (fresh or frozen raw)
½ pt (300 ml) pineapple juice (unsweetened)
3 tablespoons honey (or to taste)
2 cups raspberries (fresh or frozen)
2 oranges

½ lb (225 g) grapes, halved and de-pipped
2 lb (900 g) ripe pears, raw, peeled and diced or ripe melon, cut into balls
2-3 ripe bananas
2 passion fruit (granadillos)

Simmer the plums in the pineapple juice with the honey till tender. Cool and remove the stones and skin. Cut into pieces. Peel the oranges, slice them and add. Stir in pears or melon. Stir in the flesh and pips of the passion fruit. Add raspberries and sliced bananas. Mix well together and check – add a little more honey or pineapple juice as necessary. Delectable!

Winter Vitality Fruit Salad

4 oz (100 g) dried apricots
4 oz (100 g) hard figs
2 oz (50 g) sunflower seeds
2 oz (50 g) sultanas

4 oz (100 g) hard dates, de-stoned
2 oz (50 g) dried peaches
2 oz (50 g) raisins
1 pint (600 ml) pineapple juice (unsweetened)

Wash the dried fruit. Soak the apricots, dates, figs and peaches and sunflower seeds for 8-24 hours. Wash and soak raisins and sultanas for 1-2 hours, in pineapple juice. Cut up the soaked fruit into convenient sized pieces and add to pineapple juice. Serve with tofu, unsweetened baked custard or quark.

Fresh Fruit Salad

juice and rind of 1 lemon
4 pears
6 oz (175 g) grapes, washed

2 ripe bananas
2 oranges (un-dyed)
2 oz (50 g) cashew, almond or walnuts

Peel the bananas and pears and slice into lemon juice to prevent oxidation. Toss and add to other fruit. Add grated peel from orange and lemon, then add cut orange flesh. Halve and de-pip the grapes and mix with the nuts. Add and mix all well together. Served with more nuts, yoghurt (or quark) and wheatgrem, this will make a meal in itself.

Eager Fruit Salad

12-16 dried prunes	2 oranges
2-3 really ripe bananas	¼-½ cup natural yoghurt

Wash and soak prunes for 24 hours. Remove stones and cut into quarters. Slice the bananas into the prune juice. Peel the oranges and cut the flesh into small pieces and add to the mixture. Mix in the natural yoghurt to taste.

R. A. Reddell's Ideal Fruit Salad

2 teaspoons fresh lemon juice	2 teaspoons honey
2 tablespoons water	2-3 soaked dried apricots
2-3 soaked prunes	1 tablespoon raw wheatgerm

Mixed nuts: cashews, almonds, sunflower seeds as available
3-4 fresh fruits, organically grown when possible, chosen from: ripe peaches, pears, grapes, strawberries, raspberries, bananas, pineapple (choose fruits with a variety of colours to delight the eye!)

Mix together the honey, lemon juice and water. Stone the prunes and quarter them, and cut up the apricots, adding them to the lemon water. Add the larger fruits, slicing them into the mixture. Add the washed grapes whole. Arrange decoratively and serve with the wheatgerm and nuts and R. A. Reddell's Cottage Cream.

Party Apricot Dessert

12 oz (350 g) dried apricots	1½ cups water
½ cup sweet white wine	1″ cinnamon stick
1-2 tablespoons honey	1 teaspoon lemon juice
1 tablespoon Kirsch	flaked almonds for decoration

Wash the apricots well the night before. Put them to soak in the water and wine, covered. When well swollen, add lemon juice, honey, cinnamon and a little more wine if necessary. Simmer gently about 5 minutes, till tender. Remove cinnamon and add the kirsch. Transfer to serving dish and decorate with flaked almonds.

Banana Cheesecake

2 teaspoons gelatine or agar agar	4 oz (100 g) curd cheese
3 tablespoons hot water	1 tablespoon honey
1 lemon	¼ pt (150 ml) double cream
3 very ripe bananas	
Crust: 3 oz (75g) butter	8 oz (225g) muesli base (cereals
3 tablespoons honey	only)

Sprinkle the gelatine on the hot water and stir till dissolved (stand cup in bowl of boiling water if necessary). Put to cool. Squeeze juice from ½ lemon and put in large bowl. Mash the two ripest bananas into it. Whisk in the curd cheese and honey and the cool gelatine. Whip cream and fold into the mixture. Oil loose-bottomed cake tin and ladle in the almost setting mixture. Refrigerate to set. *Crust:* Meanwhile melt the butter, stir in the honey to blend, then stir in the muesli base till well mixed. Cool. When just hand hot, spread carefully over the top of the cheesecake, smoothing level and gently pressing down. Refrigerate to harden. When ready to serve, squeeze remaining ½ lemon and slice third banana into the juice, stirring to ensure every slice is coated. Put large flat serving dish over the cake tin, invert and press out. Decorate with the banana slices.

Pineapple Cheesecake

1 lb (450 g) curd cheese or *quark*
1 lb (450 g) tin pineaple pieces in
  natural juice
¾ cup pineapple juice (from above)
2 eggs, separated
1 large caketin with removeable base
Crust: 3 oz (75 g) butter
8 oz (225 g) digestive biscuits

1 lemon
1 oz (25 g) gelatine (2 envelopes)
8 oz (225 g) soft brown sugar or
  honey
¼ pt (150 ml) double cream

2 tablespoons soft brown sugar or
  honey

Method using liquidiser: Put into blender the cheese, lemon zest and juice, and most of the partly drained pineapple, reserving some for decoration. Sprinkle gelatine on top of heated cup of pineapple juice, standing in pot of boiling water. Stir till dissolved fully. Add hot gelatine solution and sugar to blender and liquidise. Blend in egg yolks. Leave to cool. Add cream to mixture and beat in quickly. Whisk egg whites until stiff, then fold into cheesecake mixture. Oil inside of tin, blotting off any excess. Ladle in the mixture and refrigerate until set. *Crust:* Gently melt the butter with the sugar. Crush the biscuits into fine crumbs. Mix in well. When nearly cool, spread gently over the cheesecake, smoothing till level and press down lightly. Refrigerate. Just before serving, invert onto flat serving plate. Decorate with pineapple pieces.

CHAPTER 18

Sweet Nibbles

Why Cut Down on Chocolates?

What is wrong with chocolate? Most of us will admit that, while we realise chocolates are not really good for us, we still enjoy indulging in them! We prefer to forget its association with acne, migraine, obesity, tooth decay, diabetes and coronary disease.

Cocoa and chocolate both contain caffeine and theobromine; drug-like chemicals which upset your digestion, make your heart beat faster and make you 'nervy'. Breast-feeding mothers are well advised to avoid cocoa and chocolates totally, as the caffeine and theobromine reaching baby through the breast milk may produce diarrhoea, constipation, eczema and/or irritability.

Chocolate is one of the most common sources of allergy. It can be a causative factor in headaches, migraine, depression, confused mental states, hyperactivity and anxiety neuroses. While it is commonly believed that milk chocolate drinks are a good source of calcium, the oxalic acid present in cocoa makes the calcium unabsorbable by the body.

Carob as a Superior Alternative

Carob (the 'locust bean' or 'St John's Bread' are the alternative names for the pods of the carob tree) has much to commend it, both in flavour and in nutritional value. Carob powder is prepared from grinding the roasted pulp of the carob bean pod. It is high in protein and in vitamins A, B1, B2 and niacin and D; and in minerals, calcium, magnesium, potassium, iron, manganese, chromium, copper and nickel. It also has a high pectin content, giving it herbal properties for regulating digestion and protecting against diarrhoea. So it has logical claims to its other name, 'the tree of life'.

Carob contains no caffeine or theobromine, no oxalic acid nor other harmful substances. It has none of the allergenic properties of cocoa and chocolate. It contains more natural fibre and more natural sugars, so it requires less added sweetening. Yet because it contains less fat, it is considerably lower in calories than cocoa. Add to all these advantages the pleasant chocolate-like flavour of carob powder and you will realise the great advantage of using it instead of cocoa.

Mosaic Squares

10 oz (250 g) digestive biscuits
2 oz (50 g) broken walnuts
4 oz (100 g) butter

4 oz (100 g) honey or Muscovado sugar
2 oz (50 g) carob powder
2 eggs

Break biscuits into small pieces. Chop the walnuts roughly and add. Melt the butter in a fairly large saucepan, add honey and carob powder, stirring until boiling. Remove from heat. Whip the eggs and add to hot mixture. Stir well and mix in biscuits and nuts. Press firmly into a greased 7 in square tin and refrigerate to set. Cut into squares.

Carob Balls

1½ oz (35 g) butter
4 oz (100 g) carob bar
1 tablespoon honey

few drops oil of peppermint
7 oz (200 g) stale wholemeal cake
    crumbs

Melt the butter and carob bar on low heat with the honey and stir till well blended. Remove from heat and stir in peppermint oil, and cake crumbs. Roll into balls and store in refrigerator.

Fruit Balls

2 oz (50 g) dried figs or hard dates
2 oz (50 g) dried apricots
2 oz (50 g) raisins or sultanas

3 tablespoons sunflower margarine
little carob powder

Wash and dry the fruit. Chop finely or mince and mix well. Cream the margarine and mix all together. Add sufficient carob powder to enable rolling into balls. Rolling in carob powder will correct any stickiness.

Fruit and Nut Fudge

1 lb (450 g) raw brown sugar
3 tablespoons butter
4 tablespoons evaporated milk

4 oz (100 g) sultanas
2 oz (50 g) chopped nuts

Boil the sugar, butter and milk together until thickened. Remove from heat and beat thoroughly till paler in colour, adding the fruit and nuts. Press into greased tray while still hot and mark into squares.

Bubbles

4 oz (100 g) butter
2 teaspoons honey
6 oz (175 g) raw Muscovado sugar

pinch salty seasoning
4 cups rice crispies

Gently melt butter with honey, sugar and salt, stirring. Boil gently for 5 minutes, then stir in rice crispies and mix well. Press into a greased tin, and cut in squares when cool.

Treacle Candy

1 cup black treacle   *2 teaspoons butter* or *oil*
½ cup cold water   *little potato flour or alternative*

Put treacle and water in thick based saucepan over low heat to dissolve slowly. Bring to brisk boil and boil until a little dropped in cold water forms a soft ball. Generously butter or oil a tin and pour in the candy, leaving to cool considerably. When cool enough to handle, flour the hands and work the candy into a ball. Stretch, tease and knead the candy until it becomes paler in colour. Twist into long pieces.

Sweet Millet Balls

4 oz (100 g) butter or *margarine*   *3 oz (75 g) rolled oats*
4 oz (100 g) raw brown sugar   *1 oz (25 g) flaked millet*
2 oz (50 g) coconut   *flaked millet for coating*

Cream the butter and sugar and beat till light and creamy. Combine and mix the dry ingredients and stir into creamed mixture till evenly blended. Roll teaspoonsful of the biscuit mixture into balls and coat with millet. Refrigerate.

Fridge Sweets

4 oz (100 g) butter or *vegetable margarine*   *2 oz (50 g) rolled oats*
4 oz (100 g) clear honey   *2 oz (50 g) wheatgerm*
2 oz (50 g) desiccated coconut

Cream the butter, add honey and continue beating till light and creamy. Mix dry ingredients together and stir into the creamed mixture until evenly blended. Press into shallow dish and refrigerate. Cut into squares and store in fridge.

Other Healthy Nibbles
Dried Fruits: raisins, sultanas, apricots, peaches, nectarines, prunes and bananas.
Nuts: cashews, walnuts, cobnuts, peanuts, brazilnuts, tigernuts, almonds, dried broadbeans and sweet chestnuts.
Fresh Fruits: especially washed grapes, apples, plums, clementines, etc.

CHAPTER 19

Milk Recipes

Cow's milk was intended by Nature to be the complete food of the young calf. Pasturisation enables us to obtain 'safe, fresh milk' but the nutritional value is lessened. **Bulgarian yoghurt** made from raw goat's milk is, therefore, the most easily digested and nutritious milk product, after breast milk.

For this you need the real Bulgarian culture but no special equipment. The culture resembles cooked white rice or cauliflower florets, and is a living bacterial 'plant'. The bacterial strain is much stronger than with other yoghurts, so there is no need to scald milk before use. Raw goat's or cow's milk (if obtainable – make sure it is TB tested) can be used to produce a yoghurt of the finest nutritional value.

Pour tepid milk onto the culture in a non-metal container, stirring once (using a wooden or plastic spoon), and leave in a warm room to set. This yoghurt is quite thin – like the whisked sub-cultured yoghurt or very thin cream. At this stage the yoghurt is separated from the culture by straining it through a nylon sieve without pressing the culture. The culture should then be rinsed in cold to tepid water and replaced in more milk to grow and carry on the process, whilst the made yoghurt can be refrigerated until needed.

This Bulgarian yoghurt is especially valuable in re-establishing the natural lactobacilli acidophilus bulgaricus flora in the colon when these have been destroyed by antibiotics. Bulgarian yoghurt is the best form of pre-digested milk, i.e. can be a useful food in cases where milk is not well tolerated. The taste is much stronger and more sour than bought yoghurts – an acquired taste.

Home-Made Yoghurt from Sub-Culturing

There are many gadgets on the market for making yoghurt, but a simple way is to use a wide-necked thermos jar. Buy a small pot of natural living yoghurt and eat all but one tablespoon of it. Heat 1 pint or 1 litre of milk to boiling point, with a 'milk saver' in the large pan, and simmer for 5 minutes to destroy all the bacteria naturally present. Cool to 105°F (blood heat), add the tablespoon of yoghurt and whisk well together. Pour into warmed thermos jar, close the lid and leave it in a warm place until set, when the yoghurt is ready. This natural yoghurt is not stabilised and will separate into curds and whey as you use it. So whisk it all well to produce evenly distributed curds in the yoghurt – quite a thin creamy consistency.

Enton Hall Way to Serve Yoghurt
Try your home-made yoghurt stirred with thin raw honey and raw wheatgerm for an easily digested, most nutritious dessert. At Enton Hall it is served this way in the re-education of the digestive tract after fasting.

Fruit Yoghurt
Sweeten the natural yoghurt with a little thin honey and/or pineapple juice and add chopped raw fruit as available: sliced ripe banana, red or black currants, chopped sweet apples, chopped ripe pears, dried apricots (which have been soaked for 24 hours, then chopped), strawberries, raspberries, dessert gooseberries chopped, or chopped plums or greengages.

Quark and Soft Curd Cheese
Quark is made from yoghurt, curd cheese from sour milk. Make your home-made yoghurt with skimmed milk (or skim the cream off the bottle) and hang it in a cloth – or speed the process by covering a plastic colander with a clean tea towel, (standing it in a large bowl) and tipping in the yoghurt or soured milk. Keep a plastic spatula in the colander and give it a stir several times a day, to facilitate faster draining of the whey.

As pasturised milk does not naturally sour, add a tablespoon of fresh natural cottage cheese to milk at blood heat and incubate in a warmed large-necked thermos jar until set like junket. Then proceed as before to produce soft curd cheese. The whey can be used as a substitute for buttermilk in some recipes, or in scones in place of some of the milk. Any surplus milk available can be converted into quark or curd cheese and frozen ready for making cheesecake, cheese dips or cake frostings.

Quark with Fresh Herbs

4 oz (100 g) quark or curd cheese	*2 teaspoons chopped parsley*
(made from 1 pt yoghurt or milk)	*2 teaspoons chopped tarragon*
salty seasoning	*2 teaspoons chopped dill*
paprika	*1 small clove garlic*

Mash the pressed garlic into the cheese and add fresh chopped herbs and mix well. Season to taste. Refrigerate. Make several hours before needed for the herb flavours to extend through the quark.

Curd Cheese or Quark with Dried Herbs

4 oz (100 g) curd cheese made from 1 pint soured milk	
1 teaspoon dried chervil	*1 teaspoon dried thyme*
herb salt	*freshly ground black pepper*
pinch cayenne pepper	

Mix ingredients.
Variation: Coat cheese with crushed sesame seeds and thyme, mixed.

Crunch Dip

8 oz (225 g) curd cheese or quark
1 tablespoon lemon juice
1 tablespoon mayonnaise
3 tablespoons crunchy peanut butter

4 tablespoons natural yoghurt
1 teaspoon Worcester sauce or tamari
1 tablespoon onions and gherkins,
   finely chopped, lacto fermented
   (Eden brand)

Mix the ingredients well and serve with **crudités** of small pieces of raw carrot, cauliflower, celery, cucumber, radishes and spring onions.

Cucumber Dip

½ cucumber, peeled and grated into:
1 teaspoon lemon juice
2 tablespoons chopped chives

4 oz (100 g) curd cheese or quark
½ teaspoon garam masala

Liquidise the last 4 ingredients, then add the cucumber. Dunk **crudités** into the mixture: cucumber sticks, raw cauliflower florets, carrot sticks, baby courgettes slices, celery sticks; young French beans (steamed for 2-3 minutes then cooled); cubes of sharp dessert or cooking apples dipped in lemon juice and put on toothpicks.

Curry Dip

½ cup natural yoghurt
½ teaspoon curry powder
¼ teaspoon paprika

½ cup of home-made mayonnaise
½ teaspoon powdered ginger
few drops Tabasco sauce

Mix well together all the ingredients, preferably 2 hours before serving, for flavours to blend right through.

Crabmeat Party Dip

8 oz (225 g) curd cheese or quark
1 ½ tablespoons lemon juice
flaked crabmeat

4 tablespoons plain yoghurt
1 tablespoon home-made mayonnaise

Mix all together and serve with crudités.

Ruth's Savoury Yoghurt

Traditionally in Eastern Europe, yoghurt is served as a savoury dish. My favourite quick yoghurt snack meal is made from:
   Chopped spring onions
   Grated raw carrot
   Any beansprouts (mung, alfalfa, etc.)
   All in a bowl of Bulgarian yoghurt.

Curd Cheese Icing

8 oz (225 g) curd cheese   *ground almonds* or *fine oatmeal*
¼ cup honey   or *powdered milk, as required*

Cream honey and cheese together, adding chosen dry ingredients to give required flavour and consistency. Or use home-made or Whole Earth marmalade or jam in place of the honey. Can be used on wholemeal sponge cakes and biscuits.

See other mock cream recipes in Puddings chapter.

CHAPTER 20

Health Drinks

What should we drink?

The human body needs pure water and oxygen as well as nutrients for the health of every cell. While the answer to our question could easily be 'pure water', it is not the answer which would appeal to most people, accustomed to drinking lots of tea and coffee! We need to know the facts before leading our young children into unhelpful habits.

What is wrong with tea, coffee and cola drinks?

A cup of tea contains caffeine and tannin, as well as many other substances. A cup of coffee has twice as much caffeine as the tea, and the soft cola drinks are also likely to be high in caffeine. These chemicals, caffeine and tannin, are comparable to drugs. Caffeine affects the brain by stimulating the central nervous system, producing an emergency 'alert' as stored blood-sugar is released into the bloodstream. This gives us the 'lift' we enjoy from our favourite 'cuppa'. But this false stimulation of the adrenal glands brings the compensating reaction of the pancreas, producing more insulin to rebalance the swinging blood-sugar levels. The same sequence is produced by eating refined sugar – and many people take sugar in, or eat sweet biscuits with their coffee and tea, so worsening the reaction.

Repeated cups of coffee and tea 'to buck you up' put a continued strain on the adrenals and the pancreas and could lead to nervous troubles, possibly to caffeine addiction and frequent headaches.

Caffeine stimulates the stomach to churn faster and encourages the body to excrete extra water as urine (acting as a diuretic). The acceleration of the digestion relieves an over-burdened stomach after an excessively large meal – hence the popularity of the after-dinner cup of coffee. The diuretic effect tends to flush away many needed water-soluble vitamins, to the body's loss.

The acidity of tea and coffee may also upset the digestion.

But you still want to drink tea, so . . . . . . drink weak tea with lemon or milk and you will be binding the tannin in it, and getting less caffeine by choosing to drink it weak. Some teas have more tannin and caffeine in them than others (e.g. Matté tea). Try a variety of China teas – they vary in flavour. Rooibosch Eleven O'Clock Tea tastes similar to Indian tea and has the advantage of being tannin free, and almost caffeine free. Make in the usual way.

Heath and Heather's English Style Herb Tea is a herbal tea similar to traditional tea and can be served with milk or lemon juice.

Japanese twig tea is also tannin free and almost caffeine free, with a mild, pleasant flavour, not requiring milk, lemon or sweetening. The twigs should be simmered for 10-20 minutes, and may be re-used many times until the flavour disappears. This alkaline drink aids digestion and is high in calcium.

Camomile, Rose Hip, Mint and Frutee are other herbal teas to try. There are also many blends of herbs available for refreshing drinks, to which you might like to add a little lemon, orange, lime, grape or pineapple juice. Herb teas take longer to infuse than the usual 'quick brew' Indian tea, and deserve to be made in a china teapot free from tannin stains. Use a cosy to keep the pot hot while the herbal tea infuses (5-10 minutes).

For coffee substitutes, see Alternatives, page 16.

THIRST QUENCHERS
Fresh Chlorophyll Delight (for 1)

1 cup fresh orange juice   *1 sweet ripe apple*
Handful green leaves e.g.
2-3 small spinach leaves   *4-5 small dandelion leaves*
2 sprigs parsley   *2 sprigs mint*
6-8 chives

(This selection of green leaves is available in my garden, compost grown, so I can pick them immediately before use. Otherwise use mustard and cress, parsley, watercress, spring onion tops, etc., as available.)

Wash the leaves and apple. Finely slice the apple into the orange juice in the liquidiser. Remove woody stems and roughly chop the longer leaves. Liquidise in the blender till beautifully green. Strain through nylon sieve and drink immediately. (Dry residue can go into the stock pot.)

Homemade Lemonade

6 lemons (or 4 lemons and 2 limes)   6-8 oz (175-225 g) raw muscovado
2 pints (1200 ml) water   sugar

Scrub and dry the lemons. Finely grate the rind of three into half pint (300 ml) of the water. Squeeze the juice from all the lemons and add to the water with rind. Boil the remaining 1½ pints (900 ml) water and pour over the remaining six lemon skin halves and the sugar. Simmer for five minutes then leave to cool. Combine the two when cold; remove lemon skins and store in clean bottles in the refrigerator. Serve diluted 50:50 with water.

Citrus Sparkle

2 oranges   2 lemons
1 grapefruit   water
honey

Peel and quarter the fruits, removing the pips. Blend together in liquidiser. Dilute with equal volume of water and drink. Add a little honey only if necessary.

Barley Water

½ cup pot barley   2 lemons
2 oranges   2 pints (1200 ml) water
honey to taste

Bring barley to boil in the water and simmer, almost covered, for two hours. Meanwhile scrub fruit skins, squeeze juice. Strain off the hot barley water on to the fruit skins and leave to cool. Remove skins and add juice and honey to taste.

Juliana's Drink*

1 teaspoon tamari soy sauce   ½ teaspoon apple cider vinegar**
1 cup boiling water

Pour the boiling water onto the other ingredients – vary proportions to taste.

Shoyu Reviver

1 teaspoon shoyu   1 cup hot Japanese twig tea

Add the shoyu or tamari to the freshly made twig tea. Excellent when suffering from a tension headache.

Bedtime Drink

2 teaspoons apple cider vinegar**   2 teaspoons honey
1 glass hot or cold water

This acid drink can aid relaxation and help balance the alkaline salad and vegetable meals.

Slimmer's Drink I*

2 teaspoons apple cider vinegar**   1 glass water

Slimmer's Drink II*

juice of ½ lemon   1 glass hot or cold water

*Not to be taken more than twice a day.
**NB Apple cider vinegar is a health food containing malic acid, the acid nearest to that produced by the body. It helps regulate the intestines, dissolve mineral wastes (i.e. in cases of rheumatism and arthritis) and aids digestion and sleep. Small amounts only.

Chilled Orange Refresher

2 teaspoons China tea
juice of 1 lemon
juice of 2 oranges
ice cubes

1 pint boiling water
1 orange sliced thinly
honey to taste
fresh borage or apple mint

Make the China tea and leave to infuse. Strain and cool. Add other ingredients and serve.

Pineapple Velvet

¼ glass natural yoghurt
½ glass pure pineapple juice

¼ glass pure orange juice

Whisk together, or vary proportions to suit your taste.

Mixed Fruit Cup

2 cups orange juice
1 cup pineapple juice
fresh mint springs

½ cup lemon juice
2 cups water or rejuvelac

Mix together and preferably leave standing for an hour before serving.

Rejuvelac

This enzyme-rich 'water' is made by soaking well-washed bio-dynamically produced whole wheat, brown rice or pot barley in pure cold water for 8-12 hours. The grains can then be used for sprouting (see chapter 7) and the strained water is 'rejuvelac'. This should be drunk soon after preparation, without heating – which would kill the enzymes. It still tastes primarily of water but is a worthwhile substitute when milk cannot be tolerated.

MEALS IN A GLASS

Not advised for prolonged meal replacement, but for occasional use.

Tiger's Milk (for 2-3)

½ pint (300 ml) milk
1 oz (25 g) dried milk powder
1 raw ripe apple, pear or banana
few drops vanilla essence

1 teaspoon cold-pressed safflower or
sunflower or All Blend Oil
1-2 teaspoons brewers yeast powder

Put the milk in the liquidiser and drop into it the peeled, chopped fruit. Liquidise. Add the other ingredients and blend again. Drink very slowly.

Strawberry Shake (for 2)

½ cup fresh strawberries
1 egg yolk
1 teaspoon honey

1 cup natural orange juice
3 tablespoons natural yoghurt

Blend all together in a liquidiser. Sip slowly.

Slimline Lunch

1 cup tomato juice
2 teaspoons chopped chives
½ teaspoon cold-pressed safflower,
   sunflower or All Blend Oil

2 oz (50 g) cottage or curd cheese
2 teaspoons fine bran (oat, soya or
   wheat bran)
little shoyu, tamari or Worcester
   sauce

Blend all together in a liquidiser. Sip slowly.

Fruit Salad Shake

1 cup orange juice
1 ripe pear
1 tablespoon ground sweet almonds

1 small ripe banana
1 small sharp ripe apple
1 tablespoon washed raisins

Thoroughly wash pear and apple skins and slice into the orange juice in
the blender. Add sliced banana, ground almonds and raisins. Liquidise
till well blended and sip slowly – remember this is a real meal which
deserves to be savoured.

Instant Nourishment (for 2)

½ cup natural yoghurt
½ cup orange juice
1 teaspoon cold-pressed safflower,
   sunflower or All Blend Oil
½ teaspoon lecithin granules
½ cup alfalfa sprouts (or other
   sprouted seeds, beans or grains)

2 teaspoons honey
2 sweet eating apples
1-3 teaspoons brewers yeast powder
4 tablespoons raw wheat or oat germ
little extra orange juice
2 tablespoons sunflower seeds or
   broken nuts

Put the yoghurt, orange juice, oil, lecithin and honey into the blender
and liquidise together. Add the alfalfa sprouts and liquidise. Wash the
apple well, slice thinly into the liquidiser and blend again. Mix together
the brewers yeast and wheatgerm in a bowl and pour on the blended
mixture, using the extra orange juice to rinse out all the contents. Stir
well to incorporate.

Divide between two cereal bowls and sprinkle over the nuts or
sunflower seeds. Eat immediately, chewing well. This pick-me-up
complete meal is high in protein, vitamins E, F, C and B complex, trace
minerals and enzymes. It is palatable and quickly prepared – good for
enhancing the quality of breast milk of a lactating mother.

Fruit Foam

juice of 2 lemons   *1½ cups natural orange juice*
½ cup natural yoghurt   *3 ripe bananas*
1 sweet apple

Thoroughly wash the apple skin. Put wet ingredients into blender and add sliced apple and banana. Liquidise. Sip slowly.

Carob Protein Drink (for 1)

1 cup milk   *1½ teaspoons carob powder*
1 raw egg yolk   *1 teaspoon honey*
½ teaspoon cold-pressed All Blend Oil 1 tablespoon raw wheatgerm

Mix all together till well blended, preferably in liquidiser, and drink very slowly.

Mock Chocolate Milk Shake (for 2)

¾ pint (425 ml) cold milk   *1 tablespoon carob powder*
honey to taste   *little block carob*
¼ teaspoon cold-pressed safflower or All Blend Oil

Liquidise together the powdered carob with the milk and oil, adding honey to taste. Serve immediately, decorated with a little grated carob.

Hot Mock Chocolate Drink (for 2)

¾ pint (425 ml) warm milk   *1 tablespoon carob powder*
2 teaspoons honey or raw brown sugar

Blend together the warm milk, carob and honey. Heat till almost boiling and serve.

Banana Special (for 2)

1½ cups water or rejuvelac   *1 teaspoon clear honey*
½ cup ground or broken almonds   *1 very ripe banana*

Use liquidiser to whip all ingredients together. Sip slowly.

Protein Drink Without Milk

2 tablespoons sunflower seeds   *1 cup water*
2 teaspoons honey   *½-2 teaspoons spirulina powder*
2 teaspoons wheatgerm

Soak the sunflower seeds in the cold water for 8-12 hours to start sprouting. Add honey, wheatgerm, spirulina powder and liquidise. Sip slowly.

Vitamin Cocktail I

½ cup natural pineapple juice   1 small carrot, grated or 2 tablespoons
½ teaspoon brewers yeast powder   Biotta carrot juice
1 teaspoon wheatgerm   1 teaspoon lemon juice
½ teaspoon cold-pressed safflower or All Blend Oil

Liquidise all together and drink immediately, sipping slowly.

Vitamin Cocktail II

1 tablespoon fresh lemon juice   1 cup water or rejuvelac
1 carrot   2 tablespoons raw wheatgerm
2 tablespoons sesame seeds   2 tablespoons chopped hard dates

Scrub the carrot and grate it into a basin containing the lemon water. Transfer to blender and add all other ingredients. If possible, leave to soak 15-30 minutes before liquidising. Sip slowly!

Salad Cocktail

1 cup tomato juice   1 tablespoon chopped watercress*
1 teaspoon chopped parsley   2 tablespoons chopped celery
2 tablespoons grated carrot   ½ teaspoon brewers yeast powder
1 teaspoon lemon juice   ¼ teaspoon kelp powder

Blend. Sip slowly.
*See page 34.

Energy Cocktail

1 cup milk   ½ teaspoon cold-pressed safflower or
1 teaspoon brewer's yeast powder   All Blend Oil
Juice of 1 lemon   2 teaspoons molasses
honey to taste   2 tablespoons raw wheat germ

Blend together the milk, oil, lemon juice, yeast powder and wheatgerm. Add the molasses and blend in. Taste and add honey if necessary. Drink slowly.

Instant Nourishment for Nursing Mothers

1 free range egg yolk   2 teaspoons cold-pressed safflower,
2 tablespoons protein powder   sunflower or All Blend Oil
1 tablespoon lecithin granules   ½ pt (300 ml) milk or rejuvelac
1 large ripe banana   ¼ pt (150 ml) orange juice

In the blender put the egg yolk, protein powder, lecithin and the oil. Blend briefly. Then add milk, sliced banana and orange juice and liquidise together. Savour slowly – this is really a meal!

Drinks for Babies (First see chapter 22 on infant feeding)

1. FRESH GRAPE JUICE — Choose large ripe grapes, black or white. Skin, halve and de-pip them. Put into a strong clean finely woven cloth (old handkerchief is ideal) and twist and squeeze to extract the juice. Dilute.

2. FRESH MELON JUICE — Choose a really ripe melon. Press the melon flesh through a fine nylon sieve. Do not mix with any other fruit as melon digests better when separated from other fruits. Dilute.

3. FRESH STRAWBERRY JUICE — Cut washed, organically grown strawberries into several pieces and squeeze through a finely woven cloth. Dilute.

4. FRESH CARROT. JUICE — Scrub the carrots, grate them finely, then squeeze through a fine cloth. Dilute.

5. CASHEW MILK — Soak 4 tablespoons broken cashew nuts in 8 tablespoons water for one to two hours. Add ½ teaspoon honey and blend till smooth.

6. ALMOND MILK — Liquidise together:
    4 tablespoons freshly ground or finely chopped almonds
    8 tablespoons cold water
    ½ teaspoon honey
OR pound the almonds in a pestle and mortar before liquidising with the honey and water. Strain through fine cloth before serving. A most nutritious liquid food.

7. SESAME MILK — Soak 4 tablespoons washed sesame seeds in ¾ cup of water for eight to twelve hours in a cool place. Liquidise till well broken up. Strain through fine cloth before serving.

8. SUNFLOWER SEED MILK — Make as for sesame seed milk.

CHAPTER 21

Packed Lunch and Picnic Suggestions

Muesli in a jar
Soup in a vacuum flask or jar
Slice of wholemeal quiche
Slice of wholemeal pizza
Wholemeal sandwiches
Wholemeal scones
Filled wholemeal rolls
Special meal in a drink, chilled in a vacuum flask
Salads in a closed pot
Unsalted nuts and raisins
Cheese, apples and celery
Wholemeal patties
Ripe bananas and nuts
Stuffed baked potatoes
Home-made beefburger, celery and watercress
Beanburger, celery and tomato
Nut cutlets, cos lettuce and tomato
Pot of ratatouille, cheese and watercress
Avocado with cottage cheese and walnuts
Home-made fish cakes with cucumber and carrot sticks
Jar of natural yoghurt, honey and wheatgerm
Natural yoghurt, sunflower seeds, chopped red pepper and mung
  beansprouts.
Natural yoghurt, banana and pear
Dip with crudités (raw vegetables e.g. asparagus, radish, spring onions,
  cauliflower florets, strips of cucumber, celery, red and green
  pepper).
Herb butters† and special breads.†

Suggestions for fillings for your 100% wholemeal bread sandwiches or rolls:

1. Tastex and mung beansprouts† (chop the beansprouts into ¼-½ inch lengths to make the sandwich easier to manage!
2. White Cheddar cheese, home-made mayonnaise†, alfalfa sprouts.
3. Mashed sardine and chopped watercress.
4. Tastex and chopped walnuts with few alfalfa sprouts† or lettuce.
5. Grated carrot with coconut and sultanas.

6. Watercress, orange slices, chicory and chopped walnuts.
7. Cold scrambled egg with a little horseradish sauce.
8. Softly boiled egg mashed with lots of fresh chopped chives or parsley.
9. Cottage cheese, lentilsprouts† (cut shorter) and natural peanut butter.
10. Tastex, sliced tomato and parsley.
11. Avocado pear and grapefruit slices with alfalfa sprouts†.
12. Sliced cheese with grated carrot and pinch summer savory.
13. Cottage cheese with Tastex and either chopped watercress, sliced tomato, cut beansprouts†, finely sliced celery, mustard and cress, sliced cucumber, alfalfa sprouts† or any combination.
14. Tartex paste with chopped celery, lettuce or alfalfa sprouts†.
15. Cottage cheese mixed with cooked chicken, Tastex or Worcester sauce and cut beansprouts†.
16. Cold lamb, sliced marinated beetroot and finely chopped mint.
17. Cold chicken with home-made mayonnaise†, shredded lettuce, chopped beansprouts†, mustard and cress, or cucumber and tomato.
18. Quark† with chopped nuts (and drizzle of honey if desired).
19. Quark† with sultanas and chopped nuts.
20. Hard boiled egg slices with home-made mayonnaise† and sliced olives.
21. Hard boiled egg slices with home-made mayonnaise† and salad ingredients.
22. Cottage cheese or quark† mixed with a little blue cheese, with chopped watercress, sliced cucumber, or cut beansprouts†.
23. Sliced cold beef with grated carrot and chopped parsley.
24. Sliced cold pork with little mayonnaise† and thin slices of apple.
25. Sliced cold pork with mashed banana and alfalfa sprouts†.
26. Sliced cold pork with cooked stoned prunes and crisp lettuce.
27. Home-made mayonnaise† with cut beansprouts†, chopped raw pear and finely sliced red pepper.
28. Finely chopped raw cabbage with walnuts and raisins in home-made mayonnaise†.
29. Houmous† with sprouted alfalfa†, chopped celery or cut beansprouts†.
30. Home-made liver paté* with cucumber slices or alfalfa sprouts.
31. Peanut butter and sultanas.
32. Peanut butter, home-made mayonnaise†, sliced tomato and alfalfa sprouts†.
33. Tuna fish mixed with home-made mayonnaise†, cut beansprouts† or celery.
34. Home-made mayonnaise† with chopped walnuts, celery, apple and grated carrots.

35. Chopped hard dates, softened with a little boiling water, with a squeeze of lemon juice and chopped fresh mint.
36. Mashed banana with a trickle of honey and chopped nuts.
37. Chopped hard dates, softened with a little orange or pineapple juice, with chopped nuts.
38. Soyabean sandwich spread* with sliced tomato.
39. Potted rabbit† with chopped beansprouts or tomato slices.
40. Home-made 'jam'* with sliced apple or banana.
41. Cold meat slices with home-made chutney*.
42. Cheese slices with home-made chutney*, and alfalfa sprouts†.
43. Cashew nut paté*.
44. Sesame paste* with lettuce, sprouted seeds or roasted buckwheat.
45. Grated carrot with home-made mayonnaise†, chopped raisins and nuts.
46. Mashed tuna fish with finely sliced onion and tomato.
47. Cottage cheese or quark† creamed with home-made mayonnaise†, with finely chopped tart apples, celery and parsley.
48. Mix together cottage cheese or quark† with home-made mayonnaise†, with slivers of cold chicken and shredded lettuce.
49. Tofu mixed with flaked millet and a little Tastex and chopped parsley.
50. Tofu mixed with pear and apple spread and desiccated coconut.

Finally: Try to balance your packed meal. Does it contain wholegrain starch, protein and raw saladstuff and/or a raw fruit? Check that there is at least one ingredient high in vitamin C. Make it varied and appetising, giving plenty so that the eater is well satisfied. Dried fruits or home-made biscuits can add satisfaction for the sweet tooth.

*Recipes follow.
†See index for recipes or instructions.

Cashew Nut Paté

4 oz (100 g) cooked potato
4 oz (100 g) grated cashew nuts
1 teaspoon Tastex
2 teaspoons vegetable margarine
1 tiny onion, crushed in garlic press

1 egg, beaten
1 tablespoon tomato paste
1 teaspoon chopped fresh mint
1 tablespoon chopped fresh parsley

Steam potatoes in their skins before skinning and mashing them with the margarine and Tastex. Cool. Add all other ingredients and beat well together. Press into small bowl or terrine. Needs no cooking.

Chicken Liver Paté

1½ lb (675 g) chicken livers
6 oz (150 g) onion, sliced
1 tablespoon sunflower or soya oil

1 slice wholemeal bread
2 tablespoons parsley, finely chopped
salty seasoning and paprika

Sauté the onion and then the chicken liver in the oil, until tender. Mince them and the wholemeal bread. Blend in chopped parsley and seasoning to taste. Press into bowl or terrine, needs no further cooking. Eat within two days, with salad.

Sugar-Free Chutney

Bought chutneys contain refined sugar. Here is a recipe for a good chutney containing no sugar or honey.

4 lb (1.8 Kg) prepared cooking apples	1 lb (450 g) onions
2 cloves garlic	1 lemon
1 lb (450 g) sultanas	1 tablespoon ground allspice
½ lb (225 g) prunes	1 teaspoon cinnamon
1 teaspoon mustard seed	1 tablespoon whole cloves
1½ pints (900 ml) cider vinegar	

The day before soak the prunes in the vinegar. Remove the stones and chop the prune flesh. Into a large preserving pan (not aluminium) put the vinegar, prunes, lemon juice, sultanas, crushed garlic and spices. Finely chop the onion and add. Windfall apples may be used for this recipe, using only the perfect parts of the apples, cut small, and add immediately to the vinegar. Bring to the boil and simmer, uncovered until sufficiently thick, stirring more frequently as the water evaporates. Pot into hot sterilised jars and seal immediately.

Raspberry Jam (with less sugar)

4 lb (1.8 Kg) raspberries	2 lb (900 g) Guyanan demerara sugar
1 teaspoon fine sea salt	

Gently heat raspberries in preserving pan and bring to the boil. Boil until soft and pulpy. Stir in the salt and sugar. Boil for a further 10 minutes and test for a set. Pour into heated jars and seal immediately. Redcurrants can be used in place of raspberries. With other fruits longer boiling will be necessary.

Freezer 'Jam'

While this is not strictly a jam, it is my favourite, as no sugar is needed and the lovely fresh flavour of the raw fruit is retained. This is the recipe I use:

2 lb (1 Kg) raspberries	1½ tablespoons brown riceflour or ground rice
1 cup water	honey to taste

Mix the brown rice flour to smooth cream with a little of the water, add to the rest of the water and bring to the boil, stirring. Simmer gently for about four minutes, until thickened and cooked. Cool. Mash the fruit with honey to taste and beat in the rice when it is just warm. Pot into small clean containers, allowing head-space. Freeze. Once thawed, the freezer jam should be stored in the refrigerator, and consumed within three days, hence the need to choose small containers.

Apricot 'Marmalade'

4 oz (100 g) dried apricots   2 oz (50 g) sultanas
½ pint (300 ml) orange or apple juice   honey to taste

Wash the fruit well. Soak overnight in the fruit juice. Bring to boil and simmer till soft. Liquidise with just sufficient of the juice to produce a thick purée. Mix in honey to taste. Pot and store in refrigerator.

Soyabean Sandwich Spread

3 tablespoons cooked soya beans   3 tablespoons crunchy peanut butter
1 tablespoon chopped fresh chives or   1 tablespoon chopped parsley
1 tablespoon chopped spring onions   little Tastex

Mix everything together until well blended. This is a high protein filling.

Sesame Paste

Blend together 2 teaspoons each of tahini and lemon juice with one teaspoon of tamari with a fork to produce a tasty protein spread.

CHAPTER 22

Infant Feeding from Birth to 18 Months

By Mrs Belinda Barnes, Chairman of Foresight Charity, the Association for the Promotion of Preconceptual Care.

Hopefully, mums who have been on the Foresight programme will approach childbirth in rude health and enjoy a natural birth. So from the start the Foresight mum will be able to provide drug-free colostrum (the first breast-milk) to an enthusiastically sucking baby. If neither partner is sedated, the baby will become hungry every few hours or even more often and start searching around for the breast. Hopefully he will be kept close beside his mum, so that he can feed on demand, making for contentment for both.

Colostrum is an important first food which contains exactly what the baby needs to cleanse the digestive tract and start the digestive system working smoothly. No other species is denied this vital start – and no other species has 'feeding difficulties' and constant screaming from their young! When the colostrum is laced with anaesthetic, however, the value is more dubious – another reason for making every possible effort to achieve a natural birth.

Gradually, after three or four days of frequent suckling, the colostrum changes to whole breast milk. During the first few months, there should be no arbitrary feeding times – just let the baby feed on demand.

If he is still feeding at 2-3 hourly intervals by three months, it may be that the breast milk is slightly lacking in quantity or in quality. The best way to ensure a steady supply of top quality breast milk is for mum to take 2 Foresight vitamins, 2 Foresight minerals and 2 Foresight Iron Formula daily and include raw polyunsaturated fats in a wholesome diet. That is, use sunflower seed oil or safflower oil in salad dressings and include such foods as fresh raw nuts, nut butter, milk shakes, seeds, avocados and cooked oily fish in her wholefood diet.

A nursing mother should try to live as 'hassle-free' a life as possible. A contented mum makes for a contented baby.

Let your mother or the neighbours do everything they offer to do – do not underestimate how much they love doing it! In many primitive cultures, mums with new babies are looked after by female helpers for up to 40 days and nights. It is a deep-seated primitive driving-force to want to help new mothers, so you will be pleasing them by accepting their help, instead of claiming that you are 'all right' while you become more and more tired!

At first, the baby will need a night feed. His tiny tummy will not hold enough to last till morning. Leaving him to cry will not teach him that it is night and he should sleep longer! Far from having this effect, the terror of feeling abandoned and left to starve alone in the dark may stay with him all his life, leaving him with a fear of the dark and nightmares. If he is fed whenever he cries – as every other species (rabbits, horses, pigs, kittens, etc.) can take for granted – as his tummy grows bigger and he takes more milk at each feed, gradually he will be able to do longer and longer stints. After about two months the night gap gets to about eight hours and things begin to look up! By now breastfeeding should be well established and he will probably be gaining 6-10 oz per week.

Despite pressures not to weigh babies for fear of worrying mum, I think recording successful weight gains each week is a great morale booster. The usefulness of the warning sign of no weight gain, is also worth consideration. If the weight gain is poor then mum knows she needs to look more closely to her diet and increase her intake of fresh natural foods, the B vitamins and polyunsaturated fats. Maybe he should be wakened for more frequent feeding. See the chapter on Health Drinks and the 'meal in a glass' recipes.

Some babies are upset by cow's milk in the mother's diet, in which case all bovine products – milk, cream, butter, cheese and yoghurt should be avoided while breast-feeding.

Starting Mixed Feeding

Start from a position of strength, i.e. with the fully breast-fed baby thriving and sleeping well. If the baby is grizzling on a cow's milk, sugar and water formula, or an inadequate supply of breast-milk, both mum and the baby may be tempted to rush the transition to solids, resulting in an upset stomach and the possible start of allergies. There is no need to add fruit juice drinks and cod-liver oil (for vitamins C, A and D) as supplements to the very young baby totally breast fed by a mother who is eating an ideal diet. This consists of natural wholefoods with plenty of fresh fruits, salads, some cold-pressed sunflower oil or safflower oil as salad dressings every day and taking 2 Foresight Vitamins, 2 Foresight Minerals and Foresight Iron Formula to ensure no trace mineral deficiencies. Her breast milk will contain all the nutrients baby needs in the most easily digested, natural form. It is important that breast feeding is correctly managed and going well, before introducing any other factors. Ideally start somewhere between 16 and 24 weeks (probably around 16 lbs in weight), with little tiny tastes of fresh fruit juice or strained fruit diluted with a little cooled, boiled water. Pear, grapes, ripe bananas, tomato and stewed unsulphured prunes, raisins and apples are good 'first tastes'. Put half a teaspoon of the puréed fruit into an egg cup and mix with a teaspoon of boiled water, given in tiny sips from a teaspoon. Sit him up on your lap and feed him carefully so that he does not feel in danger of drowning!

First tastes, (of one new food only in one day) are best given around 10 am so that should it disagree with him, the complaints will be over by bedtime! When the fruit tastes are happily introduced, half a teaspoon of sieved vegetable can be given after the lunchtime feed and later bone broth. At this stage, always give the full breastfeed first and give his tiny tastes afterwards.

Gradually increase the morning helpings of pulped fruit and after 20-24 weeks you can add the first carbohydrate feed – a little baby rice or other gluten-free baby cereal mixed with boiled water at first and later with a few teaspoons of cow's milk. Cow's milk is more likely to produce an allergic reaction when a) either parent has allergies, or b) cow's milk has been introduced in hospital during the first few days of baby's life. Allergy may cause nappy rash, other skin rash (e.g. eczema), runny nose, catarrh or asthma. Crying may indicate it has produced colic or headpains – never ignore crying. There are suitable soya milk alternatives if he proves allergic to cow's milk or he may be able to tolerate goat's milk. (see Alternatives)

Remember to start with the smallest amount and increase very gradually. Baby's stomach has to learn how to digest each new food, so never give more than one new food each day. Then if baby grizzles, gets a nappy or other rash, has a runny nose or diarrhoea, you know which food to suspect and can remove it from his diet. Right at the start – if a food upsets him, **leave it out.** Six months later he **may** be able to take it – but notice again if it upsets him and cut it out. This is the way to avoid developing allergies.

If many dietary restrictions have to be continued after the cessation of breast feeding, seek professional advice from a Foresight Clinician, or a qualified dietician or nutritionist who fully understands allergy problems. Refer to Allergy chapter to see how other pre-disposing factors (e.g. chlorinated tap water, North Sea gas and cigarette smoke) can pre-dispose to food sensitivities.

From 22 weeks half a teaspoon of soft boiled egg yolk can be added to the cereal, twice and then three times a week. This can be gradually increased until he is taking the whole yolk. His lunch can be extended to include bone broth with strained vegetables gradually increased and thickened up with cereal, potato, or pulses put through a fine sieve or liquidised. After a few weeks, brains, herring roes, sieved soft fish and meat (e.g. plaice, liver and chicken) can be introduced, in tiny amounts at first, keeping the consistency smooth so that he encounters no 'chokey' lumps which frighten him and so make him react by spitting them out.

Postpone starting solids later in the day until about 30 weeks. Two meals incorporating solids require quite a lot of digesting. Also if he goes down at 6.30 pm on a very full stomach he may not need his 10 pm guzzle. But mum's breasts need this late evening feed-time in order to go through the next eight hours in comfort! So it is a good idea to try to keep to the five feeds in 24 hours as long as possible.

Around 30 weeks, when he is awake more in the afternoons, he can be introduced to rusks while sitting on your lap. Never leave him alone with a rusk in case he chokes. The ideal rusk can be grasped in his hand and the business end sucked and chewed on, so that it gradually dissolves, but does not break off. Rusks can be made by soaking fingers of wholemeal bread in meat stock and drying out in a very cool oven. Rye bread is excellent for protecting new teeth. Little helpings of fruit – pulped pear, mashed ripe banana or stewed apple, etc., can be given at this time with egg custard, or milk and cereal, if this suits him. Later little sandwiches can be introduced, with honey, Harmony natural peanut butter or mashed banana – and after one year old, thinly scraped Tastex or Marmite. The salt in these yeast extracts is a stress on the kidneys of too young a baby.

If he is not milk-allergic, a little finely grated cheese can be added to baby's diet at about one year of age; and once he has cut his molars cress, tomato, cucumber, grated apple and carrot can all take a turn. Chopped salad sandwiches make a good tea, and when he is old enough to chew, 'cheese parcels' – tiny cubes of white cheese wrapped in a small piece of lettuce.

If baby is still breast fed at bedtime (approx 6.30 pm) he can have a drink of diluted fresh fruit juice at teatime (at about 4-4.30 pm).

At around 30 weeks, wheat, rye, barley and oat cereals (containing gluten) can be cautiously introduced – again a very little at a time – at breakfast. Gradually these can be extended to a little baby muesli, Weetabix, wheatgerm, etc. (i.e. natural, unsugared, wholegrain cereals). By 9-10 months he will probably have a commanding position from the high chair, and be demanding little tastes of whatever everyone else is eating – so the value of setting a good example cannot be too highly stressed! Pinhead oatmeal, brown rice, and millet porridge make excellent breakfasts too.

Foods for baby to enjoy from about 12 months include natural wholegrain cereals (muesli should be soaked overnight), porridge (with cow's milk, goat's milk or nut milk), egg, mild white low fat cheeses, pounded fish, meat, all offal (liver, kidney, brain, heart, tongue, sweetbreads) and poultry, mixed whole grain breads and toast, Ryvita, unsugared rusks, oatcakes, vegetable soups, and all fresh vegetables and fruits. Sieve, pulp or grate the food until his teeth are through for chewing.

It is as well to avoid giving puddings too soon. Refined sugar is not a good item to add to any diet and avoiding the development of a 'sweet tooth' will greatly benefit his health and his teeth for the rest of his life. Later: egg custards, boiled or baked and sweetened with a little honey and perhaps a little molasses, wholegrain semolina, brown rice pudding, sago, tapioca, cornmeal (polenta), barley kernels and honey, Gelozone milk jelly, stewed prunes or apricots, or baked eating apples stuffed with dates or sultanas, or stewed fruit sweetened with a little honey or raw Muscovado sugar, can be given as a second course. Sponges and crumbles can be made with wholegrain flours, etc.

Keep a small supply of Milupa, Gerber, Heinz or Johanus ready prepared savoury baby foods on hand for the odd emergency and use them occasionally without being consumed with guilt!

Protect your baby from pollution

If you live in a soft water area, it would be as well to use a water filter to remove toxic metals such as lead, cadmium and copper, which may leach off from the plumbing, or use bottled spring water.

When taken shopping, babies in low push-chairs and toddlers on foot tend to be at exhaust pipe level, and so are likely to inhale more lead from exhaust fumes. A carrying sling and an old fashioned high pram keep the baby a little further from the source of the fumes.

Use stainless steel or enamel saucepans to avoid aluminium toxicity (see "Keeping the goodness in our foods", page 13).

If you live in a city and the baby has a consistantly poor appetite, it is a good idea to get him out for a day in the country or at the seaside as often as possible. Never try to force him to eat, but ask yourself 'Why has he a poor appetite?'. In city children, the answer is very often the high level of lead in the air, and it may be well to get in touch with our organisation, Foresight, for specific advice and possibly hair analysis. Leaking gas, or stuffy smoke-filled rooms can also inhibit appetite – open the windows, even in a town. Just follow your baby's lead, notice what he is ready for, what he enjoys, and what seems to suit him and do not bother too much about what the books say! You know him, we do not!

Remember though that with your first baby you will perhaps feel a great need to prove you are an adequate mother, and this can be quite hard on both the baby and mum! Everything about his feeding and progress may develop into a matter of great concern to you both. But with the second baby you will be more relaxed; and with number three you will forget to weigh him, fail to write down his milestones, not pay a lot of concern to what he says, does or eats at each meal – and he will still be a cheerful, bouncing fellow at the end of the day!

CHAPTER 23

Allergies, Hyperactivity and Metal Toxicity

It is common practice for seed wheat to be dipped in mercury to ensure that no mould spoils the seed or rodents eat it before it is sown. These poisoned seeds are then usually grown in soil that is unbalanced by years of chemical fertilisation. The plants are fed with the principal chemical nutrients to stimulate fast growth, with the result that the other essential trace minerals (zinc, chromium, manganese, etc.) are not taken up from the soil. The wheat is then chemically sprayed to inhibit further growth of the stem – heavy ears of grain too readily blow over and spoil when supported by long stems. After harvesting, the wheat is usually heavily processed to produce white bread, with many nutrients removed (see page 199) and chemical anti-staling agents added.

Is it surprising that more and more people are showing sensitivities to wheat? You can understand why we keep stressing the value of growing food organically – without poisons, unbalanced fertilizers, chemical pesticides and herbicides!

Human beings have evolved over hundreds of thousands of years, during which time all foods were entirely natural and wholesome. Our bodies and metabolism have developed to flourish on these natural whole foods. The situation has dramatically altered in such a short space of time – about three generations – 'the blinking of an eye' in comparison with the aeons before. Now food is chemically grown, heavily processed and fractionalised (divided up, with parts removed) and then stabilized. Our bodies have not had time to develop the means to assimilate these modern flavour-enhanced foods with their long shelf life. Nature gives us living, balanced foods. Even to-day's salads, fruits and brassicas may be sprayed with poisonous insecticides.

From the 1950's to the 1970's the chemical barrage has steadily increased; but recently enlightened farmers are becoming more aware of the nutrient losses and health hazards thus caused.

Edison said: 'The doctor of the future will give no medicine but will interest his patients in the care of the human frame, in diet, and in the causes and prevention of disease'.

When enough housewives keep asking for pesticide-free, organically grown produce, the demand will become so great that the supply will increase, and farming policies will be changed. Women have achieved much through such bodies as the Women's Institute – let us speak out for the health of our children and our nation, now!

Cooking for people with suspected allergies
When you encounter a friend with symptoms of allergy (skin problems, breathing problems, headaches, digestive disorders, etc.) show sympathy and understanding. He could easily be made very ill by being given even a very little of any food to which he is sensitized.

Everyone is a unique individual. Sensitivities vary in different people, even those exhibiting similar symptoms. 'Gluten-sensitive' people cannot tolerate any food containing gluten i.e. wheat, barley, oats, rye or buckwheat. Others may be very allergic to wheat, barley and rye, and yet able to tolerate oats or buckwheat. Remember grains are constituents of many drinks as well as cereals, flours, breads, cakes, biscuits, gravy, and sauces.

To give you an idea of the complexity of the problem of avoiding 5 foods commonly found to trigger allergic type reactions, here are 5 lists:

Foods which may contain wheat:
Bread (even if sold as cornbread or ryebread), biscuits, buns, batter, cereals, wheatgerm, bran, muesli, cornflour, ryeflour, white flour, wholemeal flour, gluten flour, kibbled wheat, cakes, pastries, puddings, pancakes, dumplings, gravy, sauces, spaghetti and macaroni, etc., ice-cream cones, chocolates, sausages, stuffings, mustard, stews, meat or fish coated in flour or breadcrumbs before cooking, stock cubes, some salad dressings, beer, whisky, malted milk, Vitaquel margarine (contains wheatgerm oil).

Foods which may contain milk:
Biscuits, cakes, bread, prepared food mixes, pancakes, puddings, custards, ice-cream, sauces, soups, boiled salad dressings, scrambled eggs, cream, butter, cheese, buttermilk, whey (in nearly all margarine except Tomor), yoghurt, soufflées, au-gratin dishes (with a cheese sauce), quiches, mashed potato, chocolates, toffees, chocolate drinks, foods cooked in batter. 'Added protein' can mean added powdered milk (e.g. in sausages).

Substances which may contain corn (maize):
Adhesives on envelopes, stamps, etc., toothpaste, cough syrup, medicinal tablets (e.g. aspirin), baking mixes, baking powder, bleached flours, corn-on-the-cob, cornflour, gelatin, desserts, popcorn, cornflakes, starch, corn oil, frying oil, sweets, frosted icing, glucose products, instant coffee, instant tea, creamed vegetables, creamed soups, some sausage meat, salad dressings, gravy, margarine, jams, jellies, cakes, biscuits, puddings, ice-cream, sauces, custards, soya bean milk, chewing gum.

Foods, etc., which may contain refined sugar:
Sweets, chocolates, candyfloss, icings, jam, jellies, ice-cream,

puddings, tinned fruit, stewed fruit, glacé fruit, some fruit juices, cakes, biscuits, pastries, some breads, buns, fruit squash, beers, wines, fruit punches, some drugs and medications, cough syrup, toothpaste, pickles, chutneys, salad dressing, mayonnaise, tomato ketchup, sweet and sour sauce, barbeque sauce, tinned carrots, tinned peas, cooked beetroot, corned beef, fruit yoghurt, many breakfast cereals including some mueslis and some made with bran, hot chocolate powder, Ovaltine, malted milk, milk shakes, cordials.

Foods which may contain yeast organisms:
Breads, fungi, mushrooms, canned fruit juice (as rotting fruit may have been used), vinegar, and all salad dressings, etc., made with vinegar; and vitamin-enriched foods containing brewers yeast.

Check the small print on everything you buy. Watch out for chemical additives too. See 'Eating and Allergy' by Dr. Robert Eagle, and 'Not All in the Mind' and 'Chemical Victims' by Dr. Richard Mackarness for more information on this subject.

Other Pre-Disposing Factors
The contraceptive pill, the IUD, coil, North Sea gas, cavity wall insulation, tobacco smoke, traffic exhaust, moth-proofed carpets, chemicals used to destroy woodworm, etc., damp mould, aerosol sprays as well as fresh paint, glue and varnish can all pre-dispose the body to allergy.

Dr. Jean Munro has found many children allergic to tap water – fluoride, chlorine, lead or copper may be the cause. Bottled water or good water filters are the answer here. It is wise to keep a few bottles of spring water in reserve to use when tap water looks brown and smells strongly of chlorine.

Simple Home Detection Work
Dr. Vicki Rippere suggests that a 3-4 week careful food and reaction diary be kept, listing every food, drink and snack, noticed exposure to inhalants and allergic symptoms. When bad reactions occur, a check through the log for the previous 24 hours may gradually indicate the likely culprit.

This detailed food and drink list (e.g. 4 pm 2 cups tea with sugar and milk, 3 digestive biscuits – wheat flour, fat, oil, antioxidant, oatmeal, cornflour, milk, glucose, salt, soya, malt, emulsifiers, flavouring, egg, colour) may also reveal a dependency on the items occurring most frequently. What she terms the 'fearful five' – tea, sugar, cow's milk, coffee, wheat – recur as 'top favourites' in many of her patients. Dr. Rippere then puts them on a diet excluding these 'most frequent' foods and often the allergic symptoms disappear, only to recur on their 'testing' reintroduction – proof of the body's sensitivity to them. Read her book, "The Allergy Problem".

Stone-Age or Cave-Man Diet

Food sensitivities can affect physical, mental and emotional health, being one possible cause of hyperactivity, unsocial behaviour, depression, catarrh, wheeziness, headaches, fatigue, 'jumpy legs', colic, eczema, asthma, migraine, etc.

One way to ensure balanced eating while removing all most likely allergens is to return to the diet of our stone-age ancestors. The cave-man diet includes fresh free-range meats, offal, poultry, fish, organic local vegetables, fruits and nuts, with pure spring water or suitable herb tea to drink – all in the unadulterated form of pre-civilization days. All sugars, flours, sweets, grains, milk, butter, margarine, eggs, cheese, citrus and dried fruits are eliminated. Removed also are tea, coffee, alcohol and all processed or refined foods, drinks – and cigarettes.

Ideally, when needed to help a child, the cave-man diet is followed for two weeks by all the family together, thus saving many complications. All can benefit from it and make it a detection game as each 'new' food is subsequently introduced, one at a time. The reactions, if any, should be recorded for each individual on a Food/Reaction Diary Chart.

Foresight's booklet 'Guidelines for Future Parents' gives directions for a 'Rotation Diet for the Detection of Allergy' and 'Suggestions for starting a milk-free, gluten-free and egg-free diet'. There are some suitable recipes given here under the appropriate sections, and many other recipes can be adapted to exclude unwanted ingredients. We recommend the specialised recipe books by Rita Greer, Louise Templeton and Hilda Cherry Hills (see Recommended Books page 205), to help you further with these problems.

Louise Templeton's Recommended Diet

Miss Templeton, S.R.D., finds that the total removal of meat, wheat and dairy produce from the diet, and the inclusion of other wholegrains, pulses, vegetables, sea vegetables, nuts and seeds very often 'works wonders' in overcoming food sensitivities. Then return gradually to a wider wholefood diet, for at least six months before embarking on a pregnancy.

Foresight recommends that Cemac (B12) should be taken daily when avoiding animal protein foods.

The Cleansing Diet

During thirty years association with Enton Hall Health Hydro, the authors have seen thousands of patients find renewed good health and vitality from undertaking fasting and cleansing diets based on fresh organically grown fruit and vegetables, under professional supervision. These are age-old methods of 'spring-cleaning' the body of waste products accumulated over the years, but are not recommended for self-administration, nor for less than six months before pregnancy.

To understand the 'how and why' of this natural cleansing process, read 'Health Secrets from Europe' by Dr Paavo Airola, 'My Healing Secrets' by Boris R. Chaitow, 'Natural Remedies for Common Ailments' by Constance Mellor or 'The Grape Cure' by Basil Shackleton.

Foresight does not however, advocate using these cleansing diets less than six months prior to embarking on pregnancy, nor without the consent and supervision of your Foresight Clinician.

For those planning a pregnancy, see Foresight's 'Guidelines for Future Parents' and Margaret Brady's 'Having A Baby Easily'.

Recommended Food Combinations for Specially Sensitive Digestions – (The Hay Diet)

Where wholefoods produce 'allergic' digestive disturbances, it may possibly be found that it is the wrong combining of foods which is the true culprit. Compatible food combinations are achieved by:

1. Removing raw and dried fruits from any meal containing raw salads and vegetables.
2. Combining starchy foods (potatoes and wholegrains) with fats, green vegetables, root vegetables, sweet fruits and honey in one meal.
3. Predominantly protein foods (meat, fish, cheese, eggs and nuts) should be combined with green vegetables and salads. Acid fruits, (citrus, rhubarb, sour plums, etc.), may be included at this meal.

Incompatible food combinations: starches and proteins; and starches and acid fruits. It is possible that those can set up internal fermentation, which may produce ill-health in some 'sensitive' or 'allergic' people. See 'Good Foods that Go Together' by Esther L Smith for recipes based on these principles.

Heavy Metal Poisoning

Hyperactivity and allergic reactions can be caused by metal toxicities, as heavy metals such as lead inhibit the production of digestive enzymes. These rejuvenation programmes break the habit pattern of constantly repeated devitalised foods and drinks, and may help lessen the sensitivity to previously allergenic foods. These should be reintroduced in small quantities gradually, and increased cautiously if less sensitivity is demonstrated. In some cases a food may be tolerated once every 4-5 days, but not more frequently, but in many cases it may be better to eliminate the allergen from the diet permanently. – Small amounts of heavy metals may actually be eliminated by use of the cleansing diet or alternately with Miss Templeton's Recommended Diet on your Foresight Clinicians advice, or a diet including the following detoxifying factors.

Nutritional Detoxification of Toxic Metals

Exposure to toxic metals in heavily industrialised and heavy traffic areas, and in some occupations, is unavoidable. These foods give some degree of natural protection and can be used to help loosen these toxins which otherwise tend to accumulate in the body.

1. Sea vegetables are useful as they can gently loosen toxic minerals and encourage their elimination from the body by normal excretion. (See page 65).
2. Pulses are valuable cleansing foods.
3. Garlic, long famed as a prime blood purifier and natural antiseptic, has deep cleansing properties also.
4. The pectin from apples is especially effective for heavy metal removal – cook the apples gently with the pips (as the pips contain pectin) and then sieve to remove pips.
5. Vitamin C is a well known detoxifier.
6. The fibre contained in wholegrains is a protective agent.
7. Vitamin E helps prevent heavy metal toxicity, but needs to be supplemented cautiously.

The Feingold Diet to Combat Hyperactivity

Sometimes hyperactivity is caused not by toxic metal poisoning, nor by allergy to the foods themselves, but by intolerance to the chemical additives in foods and drinks.

Refined sugar can also increase hyperactivity.

The most troublesome chemicals come under the heading of artificial colourings, flavouring and anti-oxidants. So read the listed ingredients and avoid products with these additives. See *recommended books on hyperactivity* (page 206) to learn more about this vast problem.

Orange squash, jellies, and brightly coloured sweets are all suspect 'baddies' likely to contain chemical colourings, flavourings *and* refined sugar. Most packeted 'instant foods' (soups, cake and pudding mixes), most tinned and glacé cherries, tinned peas and strawberries, and margarines contain chemical colouring or flavouring or anti-oxidants – to name a few. Many savoury foods contain monosodium glutamate.

Home cooking, using fresh wholefoods, is the safe way to avoid unwanted ingredients.

Rebuild Total Health the Foresight Way

While allergic parents may produce children with even greater allergic tendencies – Foresight shows the way out of this downward spiral of diminishing health and vitality. As you see from this chapter, there are wholefood diets which can rebuild health when we choose to become responsible for our own and our family's well-being. Start by assessing the situation. Examine your eating and drinking habits. Track down and eliminate as many pollutant sources as you can. Check the ingredients in the foods you buy. Re-examine your general life-style to see if improvements can be made (e.g. putting the gas boiler outside the house to avoid inhalation of gas fumes). Read widely to increase your understanding of the problem and its solution (see Recommended books). Search out sources of organic produce, free range eggs, unsprayed fresh garden produce, – Foresight can help its UK members locate these.

You may be fortunate in having an enlightened doctor who understands the wholistic nutritional approach of this book, and who will help you. Otherwise Foresight doctors, qualified nutritionists and naturopaths could help you achieve better health when you need professional guidance.

CHAPTER 24

The Problem of Overweight

Extremes of both over-weight and under-weight are signs of wrong nutrition, and, with obesity, are directly related to ill-health, loss of vitality and premature ageing.

If your Doctor has told you that you need to lose weight, choose a method which will help you to reduce your weight and improve your general health at the same time. Crash diets are not the long term answer. Weight quickly lost is usually soon regained. As our 'normal' Western diets tend to be short of the nutrients our bodies need, a reducing diet may increase our deficiencies. This can bring greater risk to the new baby conceived by a parent who has previously been slimming. Hence the need for constructive suggestions for over-weight future parents.

Stress, food, ecology and genetic traits all contribute to make you the shape you are. Here we will concentrate on the dietary factor.

Calorie-cutting is not the whole answer

Most slimming diets explain how you must cut down your calories. A glance at the section on Fats and Carbohydrates (page 196) soon reveals how inadvisable it is to include high fat foods (full fat cheeses and other dairy products, fatty meat, sausages, oily food, fried foods, etc.), alcohol, refined sugar and white flour products in *any* diet. Furthermore, all of these foods are calorie laden and have no place in a healthy weight-reducing diet.

The basis of *our* successful weight-reducing diet is whole foods – wholegrain cereals, plenty of raw and cooked vegetables, fresh and dried fruits and a balanced amount of proteins, in three meals a day. Wholefoods are high in natural dietary fibre; they are satisfying, nutritious, keep the digestive tract working more efficiently and do not linger in the intestines.

With the replacement of refined starches and sugar by wholegrains, pulses, vegetables and fruits, there will be no rebound hunger (that is the craving for more food soon after a full meal). Take the time to chew your food thoroughly. Mastication mixes saliva with the food and helps you feel satisfied as it aids the digestion.

Whole fruits which require chewing are advised in preference to drinking them as juices. You are unlikely to eat seven oranges at one time, but might easily drink half a litre of orange juice when really thirsty! The best low calorie thirst quencher is pure water.

Lose weight slowly but steadily, and you will gain good health at the same time. You will simply be avoiding food that your body is better without anyway. Cutting down on salt intake is another important factor – salt encourages waterlogging of the tissues, often referred to as fluid retention.

By eating moderate amounts of protein (see pages 93 and 195), the metabolism is not so stressed and the diet is not expensive. Daily exercise is strongly recommended – not that it will 'burn up' the calories faster, but fresh air and exercise enhance all health-building regimes.

Some people will lose weight much faster than others. We are all different. Perseverance is what matters. Too rigid a regime that leaves you feeling hungry will tempt you to 'go off the rails'. If you genuinely keep to this reducing diet and do not lose any weight, it may be that you have a sensitivity to wheat and should seek professional help (see allergy chapter).

Suggested reducing Breakfasts (for 1)
1. Fresh fruit muesli.
2. Porridge made with 1 oz oats, water and a pinch of Biosalt or sea salt (eaten with molasses if preferred sweet) and little milk. Apples.
3. One large slice of wholemeal bread (or toast, cooled), little soft oil and butter spread. Half a grapefruit or orange.
4. 2 oz dried apricots or prunes, soaked and stewed without sugar with 5 oz natural yoghurt.
5. Slimmers muesli with skimmed milk or unsweetened apple juice.
6. Special nourishment in a glass – see chapter on drinks – to drink slowly.

Lunch or Supper daily
Fresh salad made from several of the following raw ingredients: watercress*, celery, parsley*, cucumber, beansprouts*, tomato*, lettuce, carrot, cauliflower*, shredded cabbage*, spring onions*, French beans, artichokes, beetroot, apples. Be sure to include a good serving of the vegetables marked* as these are good sources of vitamin C.

With your salad eat either two slices of wholemeal bread or a wholemeal roll, or 2 tablespoons cooked brown rice, millet, etc, or baked jacket potato and either 3 oz cottage cheese or hard boiled egg or 2-3 oz lean meat or lentil paté. Choose a salad dressing based on natural yoghurt or a slimmers dressing if required. 1 teaspoon of cold pressed safflower or sunflower oil which provides the essential polyunsaturated oils can be included either in the dressing or on the bread or potato, etc.

Instead of the salad, a good thick vegetable soup made with many vegetables and either some fish, meat or a combination of pulses and grains to provide balanced protein (see page 195).

Another alternative would be a nourishing 'meal in a glass' – see drinks chapter – and sip it very slowly, 'chewing' each mouthful to mix it well with saliva. This mastication aids digestion and appetite satisfaction. 'Fluid meals' should only be an occasional or temporary substitute for 'solid' whole foods.

Cooked Meals

Many of our cooked dishes are marked for their immediate suitability for slimmers, as well as being good for all the family. Most others are readily adaptable, bearing these points in mind.

If you like to have a starter, choose a small salad made of fresh green salad-stuffs or clear or all vegetable soup, or raw unsweetened fruits such as grapefruit or melon, or unsweetened fruit juice or tomato juice.

For the main course, your choice of protein dish, with several conservatively cooked vegetables – at least one green vegetable and one steamed root vegetable. For the protein dish, choose non-oily fish dishes, oven baked, lean cuts of meat casseroled with vegetables (and any excess fat blotted off with kitchen paper before serving), lean slices from roast and braised joints, chicken with the skin removed, mixed grain and pulses (all with only a little added oil, if used at all). Avoid rich sauces and gravies. Avoid adding sugar, spirits or too much salt (see chapter 5 on Flavour). Choose fresh fruit for dessert – or a piece of fresh celery, or small bowl of seasonal salad.

Suggestions for Packed Lunches for Slimmers

1. For slimmer's sandwiches – make the special slimmers' wholemeal bread with added bran, alternately with rye and mixed grain breads and use these for sandwiches – they are very filling!
2. Choose one of the special nourishing drinks and take it chilled in a vacuum flask.
3. Take a vacuum flask of hot home-made puréed soup or broth containing vegetables. Several fresh fruits and a few walnuts, almonds, sunflower seeds or hazelnuts.
4. A mixed salad in a sealed container – eaten with a fork or spoon, whichever is easier, with protein of choice, or sprouted or cooked wholegrains.
5. Fresh fruit muesli (in the right-sized container, so that no air is left in to cause oxidation) with sunflower seeds.

Nibbles

Cut out the old pattern of nibbles between meals: biscuits, salted nuts and crisps are very high in calories and can upset an otherwise well-balanced diet. Instead nibble celery, cucumber, raw carrots, peas, cauliflower, apples and pears. If you are consistently hungry between meals, eat a little more at mealtimes, chewing it longer. The natural high fibre content of wholefoods will help satisfy the appetite and aid the slimming efforts.

To begin with, a little hunger is a good sign indicating that you are eating less than usual!

The less sugar and sugary foods you eat, the more sensitive will your taste become to the natural sweetness found in fresh and dried fruits and many vegetables.

Use the minimum amount of butter or polyunsaturated vegetable margarine. Better still, cream together butter and cold-pressed vegetable oil for an additive-free spread and use sparingly. Or use an alternative spread (e.g. carrot purée, bean paté or houmous).

Change over gradually to this new dietary plan high in salads and wholegrain cereals, to allow your digestion to adjust to the greater bulk of health-building wholefoods.

Monitor your weight
Since we are all different in metabolism, build and energy needs, it is not possible to specify quantities for individual diets. Weigh yourself once a week and eat to maintain a gradual, steady weight loss.

Two kitchen aids for lessening fat intake:
1. A 'Romertopf' or 'clay baker' casserole for producing tasty roasts of meat without any added fat. The juices extracted during cooking can be strained and then put into
2. A 'saucière' or 'gravy-separator', enabling the meat stock to be poured off from the bottom without the fat.

CHAPTER 25

Nutrition

Proteins

Western man consumes 50% more protein than his body needs. Eating too much protein is not only costly and wasteful, but puts an unnecessary strain on the liver and kidneys; and it can lead to a tendency to rheumatism, arthritis and other health problems.

Protein requirements vary according to the number of body cells which are being built or repaired, so those needing more than the recommended minimum protein intake are:

1. Expectant mothers.
2. Nursing mothers.
3. Babies need more protein in relation to their body weight, as they are growing fast.
4. Children also need more protein at times when they are growing fast.
5. Convalescents need extra protein for the repair of broken bones, burnt tissue, or after undergoing surgery, for wound healing.

Combining foods to give better value protein

By combining selective groups of protein foods lacking in different amino acids, better value protein can be obtained. The complementary protein groups are:

1. Animal protein (milk, yoghurt, cheese, eggs, meat, fish, poultry or dried milk powder) with wholegrain cereal or vegetable protein.
2. Wholegrain cereal protein (wheat, bread, pasta, wheatgerm, flour, rice, corn, barley, oats, etc.) with animal or pulse protein.
3. Pulse protein (peas, beans, lentils, soya beans or soya products, peanuts) with wholegrain cereal, nut or seed protein.
4. Nut and seed protein (brazil nuts, almonds, sunflower seeds, sesame seeds, pumpkin seeds, etc.) with pulse or animal proteins.

Bread and beans, eaten together, give a better resultant protein than meat! So does bread and cheese. Similarly most traditional pairs of foods – fish and chips, roast beef and Yorkshire pudding, rice pudding, macaroni cheese, spaghetti Bolognaise, Cornish pasties – all give better value protein by their combinations of complementary protein groups.

No meat is actually necessary in a health-promoting diet. In fact recent research has shown how athletes perform better on diets containing lower amounts of protein (especially animal protein) as then there is less escess to be excreted as urea.

The best sources of dietary protein are:
1. 'Free range' eggs.
2. Fresh fish from unpolluted water.
3. Cooked dried beans with wholegrains, or sprouted beans and grains.
4. Wholemeal bread with cheese.
5. Wholegrain cereals with nuts and milk or yoghurt – muesli.
6. Lean dark meats of 'free range' wild animals – rabbit, pigeon, venison, pheasant, etc. (free from any danger of drug residue).
7. Organ meats – heart, brains, sweetbreads, tongues – which contain less cholesterol than muscle meats. Liver and kidneys are also very high in nutritive value, but as organs of purification may contain contaminants also.
8. Soya beans, which have the advantage of containing lecithin, the natural emulsifier and controller of cholesterol, and very little saturated fat.
9. Butcher's meat: lamb is more naturally produced than beef, veal or pork. Choose 'free range' fresh poultry whenever possible.

Fats and Oils
Fats and carbohydrates are the energy fuel foods. While proteins, starches and sugars all supply energy at the rate of 4 kcal/gm., fats and oils supply energy at the rate of 9 kcal/gm. – i.e. more than twice as fattening! (The other commodity in the energy table is alcohol, supplying 7kcal/gm.)

Oils are fats which are liquid at room temperature, sometimes due to a higher content of polyunsaturates.

The only animals which are fat in the wild are those exposed to icy temperatures and those ready for hibernation. This fat provides a food store and insulation against the cold. If we eat a lot of fat, we need to work very vigorously to burn it up. Many people consume as much as 40% of their calorific intake in fat, which is excessive.

Some fat in the diet (around 3-5%) is essential for health, for the absorption of vitamins A, D and E and to provide vitamin F (the essential fatty acids, which are found in polyunsaturated fats). The Hyper-Active Children's Support Group has researched the lack of essential fatty acids as a possible cause of hyperactivity, and found a correlation in many cases. Read *"Super Nutrition for Healthy Hearts"* by Richard Passwater to learn why we need balanced low amounts of both animals and vegetable fats for good health.

The butter or margarine controversy remains. Butter can be the natural product which has been consumed for hundreds of years (but avoid those butters containing colourings). Margarine is produced by a chemical process to make the oil solid at room temperature. The best margarines are the soft polyunsaturated vegetable margarines, low in cholesterol, and free from artificial chemicals (read the label to check).

Vitaquell and Alfonal's Safflower and Sunflower are good. Butter has a unique flavour, but is high in cholesterol.

A GOOD COMPROMISE SPREAD for use on bread or potatoes can be made by creaming together 50% fresh butter (uncoloured) with 50% cold pressed vegetable oil.

COLD-PRESSED VEGETABLE OILS, high in vitamin F, are best used sparingly in salad dressings, special nutritional drinks or cream substitutes where they are not spoilt by heating. Store them in a cold place. Rancid fats and oils are toxic and should be thrown away. For cooking, use the cheaper vegetable oils which have a longer shelf life.

POLYUNSATURATES. The best source of valuable polyunsaturated oils is found in wholegrain cereals, seeds, fish, avocado, fresh raw nuts, sunflower and safflower oil. (See also under vitamin F).

HIDDEN FAT is present in many foods – e.g. nearly all cheeses, eggs, fish, meats (even lean meat!), pastry, cakes, biscuits, ice-cream – and even more in potato crisps and roasted peanuts!

Carbohydrates

Starches and sugars, together called carbohydrates, need B vitamins for their metabolism into energy. Nature adequately provides these B vitamins in whole carbohydrate foods, but refining processes seriously deplete them.

It has been shown that there is a direct connection between the consumption of refined carbohydrates and many diseases prevalent today. This 'saccharine disease' includes gastric and duodenal ulcers, diabetes and hypoglycaemia, dental decay, diverticulosis, haemorrhoids, varicose veins, coronary heart disease, appendicitis, obesity and cancer of the colon.

Our bodies evolved to extract glucose slowly from complex carbohydrates – i.e. natural cereals, vegetables, pulses, fruits and nuts. Man had lived for thousands of years before refined sugar was ever produced. For the body's fuel, the purest, most highly refined carbohydrates – i.e. white sugar (sucrose) and dietary glucose – are far from ideal. It is comparable with putting petrol into a wood-burning stove!

Consider: a whole yard of succulent sugar-cane would take about half an hour to chew, leaving you well satisfied from a good snack containing many vitamins and minerals, good natural energising carbohydrate with a little protein and fat, and lots of fibre. This yard of sugar-cane, in processing, is stripped of all its nutrients, leaving only pure sucrose – one white sugar lump. Truly a junk food which contains nothing other than energy!

How sugar (sucrose) affects us

In ordinary people, the excessive consumption of refined sugar leads to demands for extra insulin to process the extra blood-sugar arriving in the bloodstream. Repeated high sugar intake overstimulates the pancreas and the adrenals, as they strive to maintain the blood-sugar concentration within healthy limits. When the adrenals become stressed, the pancreas may become over-stimulated and produce too much insulin. This produces a dramatic drop in the blood-sugar level, and rebound hunger brings a craving for more sugar as the energy level flags. So a dependence on sugar can be established with the widely swinging 'highs and lows' on the way to hypoglycaemia. Or the pancreas may become exhausted, fail to produce sufficient insulin to keep the balance, and lead the way to diabetes.

In the long run, eating sugar and sweets makes people tired rather than energetic, as it depletes the body's supply of the B vitamins needed to convert it into energy.

When we give our children sweets 'as a treat' or 'to keep them quiet', we pave the way for them to become irritable, unco-operative, troubled with spots and rashes, colds, catarrh – and even become hyperactive or slow learners!

Which is the best sugar to use?
1. First and best are the naturally occurring fruit sugars found in *sun dried and fresh sun-ripened fruits* – grapes, pears, peaches, apples, bananas (very ripe), etc; raisins, sultanas, dates, figs, prunes, and apricots.
2. *Honey* – best unpasteurised, see page 201. It is sweeter than sugar and contains many vitamins, minerals and enzymes – use in moderation.
3. *'Raw cane sugars'* are sucrose, but as a result of less processing, still contain some nutrients. They are produced in Barbados, Mauritius and the Demarara area of Guyana – look for the country of origin on the pack.

In order of preference, these are:
   i *Molasses sugar* – sticky, granular, almost black, with a strong molasses flavour – the least refined of all the sugars we can buy.
   ii *Muscovado sugar* – soft, sticky, granular and dark brown, containing a little less molasses.
   iii *Light Muscovado sugar* is paler and more refined.
   iv *Demarara sugar* – naturally crystallised sugar with a golden colour.
   All other sugars, (also sucrose), are highly refined and usually white. Where they are brown, they have been coloured.

Fructose or Fruit sugar as we purchase it, is as highly refined as ordinary white sugar, denuded of all its nutrients. Its advantages are that it is one and a half times as sweet as sucrose, and is more slowly metabolised.

Starch
'Give us our daily bread'.
The staff of life around the world is the locally grown cereal or starch crop. We have bread made from wheat; the Scots have oatmeal porridge; the Red Indians, maize; the Africans, yams; the Irish, potatoes; the Asians, rice. Barley, millet, buckwheat and rye also make their appearance.

As Nature provides it, the cereals other than maize are balanced whole foods, containing the complex carbohydrates which the body needs for the slow, steady production of blood-sugar for energy (like wood for the wood-burning stove!). Protein, roughage, vitamins, minerals and even essential fatty acids all naturally occur to produce a good balanced sustaining whole starch food.

Where there is a history of allergy, bio-dynamically grown whole grains, sprouted or cooked whole – or flaked and used as in the muesli and kruska recipes – may be better tolerated than bread or flour made from the same grains. Locally grown 'soft' organic wheat contains less gluten than the hard Canadian wheat, and so is less likely to produce a gluten sensitivity.

While a cave-man diet (see chapter on allergies) excludes all cereal grains, bread is a traditional food which has been happily consumed by man for thousands of years. It is a good food when made from the whole of the grain as God provided and Nature intended, grown on organically fertilised soil (and free from fungicide sprays). This is why this book advocates the use of 100% wholemeal flour – made from the whole grain including the outer bran covering, the growing point or germ, and the starchy centre.

Comparison with white bread
In the production of white flour, a tremendous nutrient loss occurs. Dr. Henry Schroeder, M.D. working on trace mineral metabolism, points out that white flour (as opposed to whole wheat flour) contains only '23% of the thiamine (B1); 20% of the riboflavin (B2); 19% of the nicotinamide; 29% of the pyridoxine (B6); 50% of the pantothenic acid; 33% of the folic acid; and 14% of the vitamin E.' He further points out that of the trace elements there is only '13% of the chromium; 9% of the manganese; 19% of the iron; 13% of the cobalt; 10-30% of the copper; 17% of the zinc; 50% of the molybdenum and 17% of the magnesium.'

White bread, by law, has four nutrients added back into it – calcium from powdered chalk, iron and two B vitamins, thiamine and niacin. This is still a poor cousin of our wartime National loaf, which helped many people improve their health despite food shortages. It was made from 85% wheatmeal flour instead of the 72% white flour of ordinary white bread. How poorly white flour and white bread compare with 100% wholemeal!

CHAPTER 26

Concentrated
Nutrient Sources

These good foods and nutrient concentrates may be used to enhance a good wholefood diet when necessary. We advise the use of the foods more regularly than the more concentrated nutrients, as over-consumption of one nutrient can create an increased need for others in order to maintain a good balance.

ALFALFA SPROUTS. These are easy to grow (see chapter 7), and particularly rich in vitamin K and nearly every vitamin and mineral. Valuable as a living food full of enzymes and amino acids – as are the other sprouted seeds, beansprouts, etc.

BONE MEAL (prepared for human use). This powder is a very good source of calcium, phosphorus, manganese, copper, nickel and fluoride – all essential for building strong teeth and bones, and is a useful supplement for those allergic to milk. It can be contaminated by traces of lead, so choose carefully.

BREWERS YEAST POWDER. This is an excellent source of the B complex vitamins, containing 17 vitamins, 16 amino acids and 14 minerals and one of the best sources of RNA (a nucleic acid that helps the body's immune system). Because brewers yeast has a high phosphorus to calcium ratio, it is advisable to mix it with powdered milk. Another high protein food, but one to use in small amounts as more and more people are becoming allergic to yeast through overdosage with it.

COLD-PRESSED SAFFLOWER, SUNFLOWER AND 'ALL BLEND' OILS are rich sources of essential fatty acids, found in these polyunsaturated oils (see 'fats and oils' and 'vitamin F') Use sparingly. Needs vitamin E.

CRUDE BLACK MOLASSES is the first extraction of sugar from sugar-cane. It contains the B complex vitamins: biotin, folic acid, inositol, pantothenic acid, B_1, and B_2, as well as vitamin E, and is rich in potassium, iron, copper, magnesium, phosphorus and calcium.

DESICCATED LIVER. This vacuum dried beef liver is prepared at low temperature, so most of the nutrients are conserved. It is rich in vitamins of the B complex, A, C and D, calcium, copper, iron and phosphorus.

GOAT'S MILK, yoghurt and cheese. Goat's milk, hygenically produced, is a palatable alternative to cow's milk, being more easily digested and found to be more suitable for some people suffering from eczema and other allergies.

HONEY. While all honey is organic, nectar from flowers unsprayed by insecticides and pesticides, gathered by healthy bees (winter-fed on honey and not on sugar) is much the best, so I buy unpasteurised honey from a hot sunny country. Honey contains natural sugars which are slowly released into the bloodstream, and is predigested by the bees. Containing traces of many minerals and vitamins, honey is a digestive aid, a wholesome source of energy and sweetness, and being bactericidal, is useful as a first-aid application to burns and cuts. Use in moderation.

KELP AND DULSE are powdered seaweeds and one of the best sources of iodine. They are also rich in calcium, magnesium, vitamins D, E and K and the B complex. Being salty in taste, it is a nutritious salt substitute – but use sparingly; like brewers yeast, it has an unusual flavour!

LIVE NATURAL YOGHURT (preferably Bulgarian). This is the best way to take milk, as the protein is pre-digested. At its best made from raw milk – preferably goat's milk. It is useful for re-introducing the beneficial bowel bacteria after the use of antibiotics – or use Miso.

MISO is a naturally fermented soya purée, containing lactic acid. Useful in stocks and soups.

SEAWEEDS OR SEA VEGETABLES – fresh dried, are even better than kelp and dulse. They are a balanced source of minerals and vitamins, including B_{12}, and may be powdered after crisping in a slow oven. While protective and curative in cases of heavy metal exposure, they are gentle on the kidneys, so are good natural chelators. Worth acquiring a taste for! (see page 65).

SPIRULINA. The powder made from this alga is a valuable food supplement. Spirulina contains perfect protein (comparable with egg, but without the disadvantage of the cholesterol), is a rich source of vitamin B_{12}, and is high in iron. It is also a valuable source of gamma-linolenic acid (an essential fatty acid).

WHEATGERM (best when raw and unstabilised). Wheatgerm contains the B vitamins: folic acid, niacin, pantothenic acid, B_1, B_2 and B_6; also vitamin E, phosphorus, iron, magnesium, selenium and zinc. It is high in protein and is a wonderful food for those who can tolerate wheat.

Rich Food Sources of Minerals and Vitamins

In nutrition, trace elements are even more important than vitamins, because it is generally believed that they cannot be synthesised by living matter as can vitamins. The minerals in foods depend on the soil from which they originated. As with vitamins, many minerals are lost in processing and food preparation, and may be thrown away with the peelings or the cooking water!

CALCIUM: Milk, yoghurt, cheese (both cow's milk and goat's milk), soya milk; turnip tops, broccoli, mustard and cress, cabbage, sea kale, sea vegetables, watercress; shellfish, especially cockles, shrimps, whitebait, sprats and sardines; blackstrap molasses; soya beans, haricot beans; sesame seeds, dates and figs; powdered milk, bonemeal*, dolomite*; raw muesli cereal grains when soaked overnight (see 'muesli').

CHROMIUM: Brewers yeast; molasses; corn oil, whole-grain cereals; black pepper, beetroot, mushrooms; liver, beef; beer.

COBALT: Offal – heart, liver, kidneys, sweetbreads, brains; chicken, turkey; seafoods – especially oysters; milk; green leafy vegetables; nuts; wholegrains.

COPPER: Lambs liver, calves liver, organ meats; seafoods; soyabeans, nuts, raisins, mushrooms, molasses; bonemeal*. (N.B. an excess is toxic)

FLUORIDE: Tea; fish and seafoods; cheese and meats; bonemeal*; whole rye grains and rye bread; fluoridated water and fluoridated toothpaste. (N.B. an excess of fluoride is toxic)

IODINE: Carageen moss, Gelozone, onions, garlic, watercress, carrots, potato skins, seafood, pears, pineapple, sea vegetables, kelp* and dulse*.

IRON: Organ meats – especially liver, lean meat, desiccated liver*, spirulina*, eggs, shellfish, fish, poultry; dried fruits – prunes, raisins, currants, apricots; pumpkin seeds; blackstrap molasses; leafy dark green vegetables – watercress, parsley, spinach; onions, garlic, raw cereal muesli grains when soaked overnight; iron cooking pots. (N.B. an excess of iron is toxic.)

MAGNESIUM: Milk, nuts; seafood; wholegrains, wheatgerm, wholegrain cereals; crude black molasses; dark green leafy vegetables; dolomite*.

MANGANESE: Wholegrains – wheat bran, corn germ, rice bran, oat bran, oats, brown rice; walnuts, chestnuts, almonds; spices – cloves, cardamon, ginger; parsley, onions, watercress, spinach, lettuce, green beans, carrots, lima beans, dandelion leaves; egg yolks; apricots, pineapple.

POTASSIUM: Lean meats; wholegrains – especially rye and maize; sesame seeds, millet, sunflower seeds, linseed; pulses – lentils, beans, peas; corn oil, safflower oil; walnuts, peanuts; spinach, sorrel; honey, molasses; Banbu, pioneer and Postum coffee substitutes; molasses and muscovado sugars; Ruthmol and Trufree salt replacers; vegetables.

SELENIUM: Herring, tuna; wheatgerm, wheatbran, wholegrains; broccoli; brewers yeast*; garlic; liver; eggs.

SILICA: Onions, garlic, chives, leeks, parsley; brown rice, pot barley, maize; kelp*; molasses; Pioneer coffee, equisetum herb tea (horsetail); figs, hard dates, prunes; lentils, beans; carob, caraway seeds.

SODIUM: Seafood, meat; salt – seasalt, Biosalt, herbsalts; baking powder, bicarbonate of soda; processed foods; milk, milk products; sea vegetables, kelp*.

VANADIUM: Fish; fats and vegetable oils; black pepper; olives.

ZINC: Seafoods, all shellfish – especially oysters, herrings; pork, liver, beef liver, lamb, beef; wheat bran, wheatgerm, whole oatmeal, maize, plain 100% wholemeal flour, whole rye flour, brown rice; peas, carrots, beetroot, cabbage; prunes, sultanas, raisins, currants; egg, egg yolk, milk; whole nuts, peanut butter.

VITAMN A (oil soluble): Liver, eggs, herrings, mackerel, crab, butter, cheese; yellow and dark green fruits and vegetables – apricots, peaches, prunes, watermelon, corn, cornmeal, carrots, pumpkin, silver beet, cress, watercress, spinach, kale, broccoli, parsley, kombu and nori (sea vegetables); cod liver oil*, dessicated liver*, halibut liver oil*. (N.B. an excess is toxic).

THE B COMPLEX are water soluble and heat sensitive:

VITAMIN B1 (THIAMINE): Rice polishings (rice bran), raw wheat germ, whole millet, barley, wheatbran, wholewheat, buckwheat, soya, brown rice; heart, brains, liver, pork, venison; Brazil nuts, sunflower seeds, mackerel, crab; chick peas, split peas, soya bean granules, black beans; brewers yeast*.

VITAMIN B2 (RIBOFLAVIN) – also light sensitive: Beef heart, kidney, liver, brains, chicken liver, meat, venison; dried milk, yoghurt, milk; almonds, hazelnuts, whole millet, wholewheat pasta, wheatgerm, soya flour, cheese.

VITAMIN B5 (PANTOTHENIC ACID): Organ meats – liver, heart, kidney, brains; egg yolk, dried milk; wholegrains – buckwheat, wheat bran, wheatgerm; sesame seeds, sunflower seeds, cashew nuts, peanuts, soya beans, dried peas; brewers yeast*.

VITAMIN B6 (PYRIDOXINE): Organ meats – beef liver, chicken liver; goose, mackeral, cod, crab, herring, trout, beef, chicken, lamb, rabbit; pot barley, wheatbran, buckwheat, brown rice, wheatgerm, soya.

VITAMIN B12 (CYANOCOBALAMINE): Organ meats – liver, kidney, heart; meat, mackerel, sardines; free range eggs; Miso, Shoyu; Spirulina*; sea vegetables.

BIOTIN: Organ meats – beef heart, kidney, liver, brains, tongue, lamb's liver; sweetbreads; peanuts, soya, brown rice; almonds, egg yolk, dried milk; crab, mackerel; banana; brewers yeast*. (N.B. Biotin is destroyed by the avidin in raw egg white: overcome this by immersing egg in very hot tap water (around 150°F) for 10 minutes.

CHOLINE: Soya beans, peanuts, fish, beef liver, egg yolks,
*Denotes the supplemental form.

wheatgerm; lecithin granules* and brewers yeast*.

FOLIC ACID: Green leafy vegetables – spinach, silver beet, beetroot tops, kale, broccoli, endive, asparagas, turnips, potatoes (just beneath the skin); liver and kidney; almonds, pumpkin seeds, chick peas, fenugreek seed, wheat bran, wheatgerm, soya flour; brewers yeast*.

INOSITOL: Beef brains and heart; wholegrains – bulgar wheat, wheatgerm, wholewheat, brown rice; nuts, citrus fruits, molasses; brewers yeast*, lecithin granules*.

NIACIN (NICOTINAMIDE): Organ meats – beef heart, chicken liver, lamb liver, rabbit, dark turkey meat; halibut, mackerel, trout, herring, cod, haddock; rice polishings; wheat bran, wholewheat, wheatgerm, pot barley, brown rice.

P.A.B.A. (PARA-AMINIBENZOIC ACID): Liver, eggs, molasses, wheatgerm, yoghurt; green leafy vegetables; brewers yeast*.

PANGAMIC ACID: Apricot kernels, pumpkin seeds, sesame seeds; organ meats; salmon; egg yolks; wholegrains, brown rice, wheatgerm, rice polishings; brewers yeast*.

VITAMIN C (water soluble, heat, light and oxygen sensitive): Rosehips, blackcurrants, citrus fruits, gooseberries, strawberries, parsley, raw cauliflower, sprouted alfalfa, other sprouted beans and grains, broccoli, Brussel sprouts, cabbage, spring greens, kale, kohl rabi, green pepper; Acerola cherries*.

VITAMIN D (oil soluble): Oily fish – sardines, cod, tuna, herrings, mackerel; milk, cheese, butter, egg yolks, enriched margarine; desiccated liver*, cod liver oil*, halibut liver oil*. (N.B. the action of sunlight on the skin enables man to synthesise his own Vitamin D)

VITAMIN E (oil soluble): Cold-pressed vegetable oils – safflower oil, wheatgerm oil, corn oil, soya oil; peanuts; wholegrains – wholewheat, wheatgerm, brown rice, oats; green leafy vegetables – spinach, broccoli, cabbage; molasses; avocado; kelp*, dulse*; cottonseed oil*.

VITAMIN F (essential fatty acids – oil): Sunflower seeds, walnuts, sesame seeds; cold-pressed vegetable oils – sunflower seed oil, safflower oil, wheatgerm oil, soya oil; avocado; spirulina*, evening primrose*.

VITAMIN K (oil soluble): Green leafy vegetables – spinach, cabbage, cauliflower, peas, carrots, tomatoes, potatoes, alfalfa sprouts; pork liver, lean meat; egg yolk, yoghurt, wheatgerm, soya beans; molasses; kelp.

VITAMIN P (BIOFLAVONOIDS – water soluble): Citrus fruit pith, skin and pulp; buckwheat; green peppers; apricots, cherries, grapes, blackcurrants, tomatoes, broccoli.

Remember that many minerals and vitamins are lost in food processing and preparation – see 'keeping the goodness in our foods' page 13 and how nutrients relate to the soil, page 10.

Recommended Books

The wholistic approach to health: 1. physical, 2. mental, 3. spiritual and
4. emotional:
Here's Health magazines.
A Way of Living – How to achieve natural health by Michael Wheatley
(Unwin).
1. *Rebuilding Health* by Ebba Waerland (James Clarke & Co., U.K.)
   Everybody's Guide to Nature Cure by Harry Benjamin, N.D.
   (Thorsons)
   Natural Remedies for Common Ailments by Constance Mellor
   (Granada)
   My Healing Secrets by Boris R. Chaitow (Health Science Press)
   Health Secrets from Europe by Paavo O Airola (Arco U.S.A.)
   The Grape Cure by Basil Shackleton (Thorsons)
2. *Getting Well Again* by O Carl Simonton, Stephanie
   Matthews-Simonton and James L. Creighton (Bantam Books
   U.S.A.)
   A Guide to Confident Living by Norman Vincent Peale (Cedar
   Books)
3. *Your Healing Is Within You* by Canon Jim Glennon (Hodder &
   Stoughton)
   The Prayer that Heals by Francis MacNutt (Hodder & Stoughton)
   Inspiring Messages for Daily Living by Norman Vincent Peale
   (Cedar Books)
4. *Handbook of the Bach Flower Remedies* by Philip M Chancellor
   (Daniel)
   Stay Alive All Your Life by Norman Vincent Peale (Cedar Books)

Diet and Special Recipes:
Eating for Health Science of Life Press
Diet for a Small Planet by Frances Moore Lappé (Ballantine Books,
   U.S.A.)
Food Combining for Health by Doris Grant and Jean Joyce (Thorsons)
Good Foods that Go Together by Esther L. Smith (Thorsons)
Rita Greer's Extraorinary Kitchen Notebook (Rita Greer)
Good Food, Grain-Free, Milk-Free by Hilda Cherry Hills (Roberts
   Publications)
Cook Yourself a Favour by Louise Templeton (Johnson Green)
Nutrition and Health:
Nutrition and Health by Sir Robert McCarrison (McCarrison Society
   Publication, London)

The Saccharine Disease by T. L. Cleave (John Wright & Sons, Bristol)
Nutrition and Physical Degeneration by Weston Price, M.D. (Price-Pottinger, U.S.A.)
Nutrition Against Disease by Dr. Roger J. Williams (Bantam Books U.S.A.)
Nutritional Science and Health Education by Dr. C. Curtis Shears (Nutrition Science Research Institute)
Mental and Elemental Nutrients by Carl C. Pfeiffer Ph.D., M.D. (Keats and Publishing Inc., U.S.A.)
Zinc and Other Micro-Nutrients by Carl C. Pfeiffer Ph.D., M.D. (Keats Publishing Inc., U.S.A.)
Nutrition Almanac Nutrition Search Inc. (McGraw Hill Book Co., U.S.A.)
The Trace Elements and Man by Henry A. Schroeder, M.D. (Devin-Adair).
Ortho-Molecular Nutrition by Abram Hoffer, Ph.D., M.D. and Morton Walker, D.P.M. (Keats Publishing Inc.)
Super-Nutrition for Healthy Hearts by Richard Passwater, Ph.D. (Jove Publications, U.S.A.)
Body, Mind and Sugar by E. M. Abrahamson, M.D. and A. W. Pezet (Pyramid Books, New York)
Hypoglycemia: A Better Approach by Dr. Paavo Airola (Health Plus, Arizona, U.S.A. 1977)
Hyperactivity:
The Hyperactive Child by Belinda Barnes (Thorsons)
Why Your Child Is Hyperactive by Dr. Ben Feingold (Random House, New York)
Can Your Child Read? Is He Hyperactive? by William G. Crook, M.D. (Pedicenter Press, U.S.A.)

Allergies:
Eating and Allergy by Robert Eagle (Futura Publications)
An Alternative Approach to Allergies by Theron G. Randolph, M.D. and Ralph W. Moss, Ph.D. (Lippincott and Cromwell, U.S.A.)
The Allergy Problem by Vicki Rippere (Thorsons)
Not All In the Mind by Dr. Richard Mackarness (Pan)
Chemical Victims by Dr. Richard Mackarness (Pan)
Food Allergy by Rita Greer and Robert Woodward, B Pharm., Ph.D. (Roberts Publications, London)

Babies:
Having a Baby Easily by Margaret Brady, M.Sc. (Thorsons)
Breast is Best by A. and P. Stanway (Pan 1980)
Let's Have Healthy Children by Adelle Davis (Unwin)

PreConceptual Care:
Guidelines for Future Parents (Foresight publication*)

Supplementary Chapters to Guidelines for Future Parents (Foresight publication*)

Environmental Factors and Foetal Health by Prof. J. Dickerson (Foresight publication*)

The Next Generation – avoiding damage before birth in the 1980s (Foresight publication*)

Running a Foresight Clinic (Foresight Publications* available from Foresight, The Old Vicarage, Witley, Godalming, Surrey, GU8 5PN)

International Journal of Environmental Studies, Vol. 17 No 1 the Foresight Symposium of March 1980, (Gordon and Breach, London and U.S.A.)

Gardening:

Organic Gardening by Lawrence D. Hills (Henry Doubleday Research Assn.)

Fertility Without Fertilisers by Lawrence D. Hills (Henry Doubleday Research Assn.)

The Bug Book (Harmless insect controls) by H. & J. Philbrick (Garden Way Publishing, Vermont, 1974)

Note:

Neither Foresight, Mrs. Belinda Barnes, the authors nor any members of their families derive any financial benefit from the sales of any product mentioned in this book. Brand names are given solely to help readers.

208

Oatcakes 132
Oat crunchy squares 133
Oat kruska 109
Oatmeal 15, 144
Oatmeal digestive biscuits 132
Obesity 9, 159, **191**, 197
Offal **89**, 202
Oils **196**, 203, 204
Old English frumenty 148
Omelette 51
Omitting breakfast 25
Onions 34, 59, 202
Onions, spring 34
Orange buttercream filling 135
Orange cake 135
Orange ice-cream 150
Orange refresher 196
Orange squash 189
Oregano 26, 27
Original Bircher Benner Muesli 105
Organically grown food 11, 49, 184, 187, 190, 199
Organ meats 89, 196, 202, 203, 204
Oven baked fish steaks 78
Oven temperatures 17
Overweight **191**
Oxalic acid 159

P

PABA 204
Packed lunches **174**
Packet cereals 109
Pancakes 149
Pancreas 166, 198
Pangamic acid 204
Pantothenic acid 203
Paprika 28
Parsley 26, 27, 34, 202, 203, 204
Parsnips 16, 59
Party apricot dessert 157
Passwater, Dr. Richard 196, 206
Pasta 16
Pasteurised milk 162
Pastry **124**
Pastry, flaky 124
Pastry, quick and easy shortcrust 125
Pastry, rich shortcrust 125
Pastry, rich wholemeal 125
Pastry, shortcrust 124
Pastry, sweet 125
Pate sucré 127
Paté 176
Patience pudding 154
Pavlova 152
Peaches 153

Pears 153, 202
Pear and grape salad 39
Pearl's carrot and pineapple cake 143
Pearl Reddell's dried muesli 106
Peas 29, 34, 59, 62, 63, 203
Pease pudding 65
Pea soup 73
Pectin 159, 189
Pepper, black 28
Peppermint 27
Pepper, red and green 34
Peptic ulcer 9
Persian nut savoury 96
Pesticides 10, 184
Physical health 205
Physical workload 19
Phytic acid 103
Picnic suggestions **174**
Pigeon 196
Pill, the 6, 8, 10
Pineapple cheesecake 158
Pineapple velvet 169
Pioneer 16, 202
Pizza, aubergine 96
Pizza base 112
Pizza variations 97
Plaice, grilled whole 77
Plamil 16
Planning a pregnancy 188
Pollution 6, 183, 190
Pollutants 10
Polyunsaturates 19, 179, 196, 197, 200
Pommes Dauphinoise 59
Poor appetite 183
Porridge 16, 107
Porridge, potato 108
Pork 30, 196
Post-natal depression 8
Potassium 202
Potassium broth 31
Potassium deficiency 16
Potassium and silicon broth 72
Potatoes 16, 29, 59, 199, 202, 204
Potato and carrot cake 143
Potatoes, baked in jackets 60
Potato eggs 60
Potato flour 15, 144
Potato girdle scones 122
Potato porridge 108
Potatoes with sardines 61
Potatoes with smoked cods roe 60
Pot roast brisket 80
Pot roast of beef 80
Potted rabbit 88
Poultry 29, **83**, 196, 202, 204